The
digital lexicon
networked business and
technology from A-Z

Keith Haviland and Nigel Barnes

Addison-Wesley

an imprint of Pearson Education

Boston • San Francisco • New York • Toronto • Montreal • London • Munich
Paris • Madrid • Capetown • Sydney • Tokyo • Singapore • Mexico City

PEARSON EDUCATION LIMITED

Head Office:
Edinburgh Gate
Harlow CM20 2JE
Tel: +44 (0)1279 623623
Fax: +44 (0)1279 431059

London Office:
128 Long Acre
London WC2E 9AN
Tel: +44 (0)20 7447 2000
Fax: +44 (0)20 7240 5771

www.it-minds.com
www.aw.com/cseng/

First published in Great Britain in 2002

The rights of Keith Haviland and Nigel Barnes to be identified
as authors of this work have been asserted by them in accordance
with the Copyright, Designs and Patents Act 1988.

ISBN 0 201 78473 4

British Library Cataloguing in Publication Data
A CIP catalogue record for this book can be obtained from the British Library.

10 9 8 7 6 5 4 3 2 1

Designed by Claire Brodmann Book Designs, Lichfield, Staffs
Typeset by Land & Unwin, Bugbrooke, Northamptonshire
Printed and bound in Great Britain by Biddles Ltd, Guildford

The Publishers' policy is to use paper manufactured from sustainable forests.

To Jackie, Sam and Imogen
Sally and Madeline

Contents

About the authors

Keith Haviland is a partner in Accenture Ltd. Among other responsibilities, he co-founded and leads its London Solution Centre, now a major 800-seat development center which undertakes complex development projects for Accenture including much e-commerce work. He is the lead author of *UNIX Systems Programming*, a successful guide to this major operating system first published in 1987, which according to Amazon has been hot in Albany, New York. His specialist areas include UNIX, technical architecture, e-commerce solutions and technology, and software solution delivery excellence at all scales. Most importantly, Keith has four energetic children who all clearly belong to the digital era.

Nigel Barnes is a partner in Acccenture Ltd. and one of the co-founders of its London Solution Centre where he specializes in large and complex systems-building engagements. He has developed component-based architectures using a variety of middleware and web-based technologies for clients in utilities, government, and financial services.

Nigel's first contact with TCP/IP and the internet came in 1987 as a student at the University of York, when he was fortunate enough to be introduced to some of the technologies that would shape to his subsequent career.

Born in Penzance, Cornwall, he now lives in Richmond, Surrey with his wife Sally and their marvellous daughter Madeline.

Introduction

Objectives

This book aims to serve a simple purpose: provide an easy-to-use description of some of the fundamental terms in e-commerce, and the world of the internet and other areas such as mobile computing. Unlike a simple glossary or dictionary, we wanted some of the key descriptions (like *internet* or *world wide web*) to be substantial enough to give a good, initial briefing. As a result, the book is structured alphabetically, like a glossary, but with a mixture of short entries and longer articles. And, in addition, we cover not only concepts, but some important personalities, companies, products and websites.

So, why write another book on e-commerce, or provide an extended glossary, when many are available on the web itself? When bright people talk about internet and e-commerce opportunities and ideas, there's a natural drive to focus on conceptual business models, or the coming Next Big Thing. Such a desire for insight is commendable. However, although the virtual space of the internet is vast and complicated, some of the fundamentals are simple. Our aim is that this book can give people a rapid start in understanding these fundamentals. We also cover both technology and business terms, and were surprised, when we looked at what's available online, by how few glossaries try to do this.

Our target audience consists of business or IT professionals and anyone with an interest in what goes on behind your favorite websites and e-businesses.

In terms of more specific objectives:

➡ We cover fundamental technology terms ranging from platform technologies (e.g. *UNIX*, *Linux*, *Oracle*) through relevant networking technologies and terms (*TCP/IP* and *HTTP*), languages and tools (*HTML*, *Java*) to the big concepts themselves (*internet*, *world wide web*). And clearly we will list commonly used technical jargon. We will not focus entirely on what is commonly understood as the internet, but also cover *mobile computing* and *digital television*, among other subjects. Understanding some of the technical aspects of the internet and similar platforms helps understand why e-commerce has exploded over the past decade, and why some types of business model have become successful, or even possible.

➡ We describe a range of e-business terms. This includes terms related to types of web business (*portal*, *e-tailer*, *B2B*) and terms related to the construction of new e-businesses (*funding*, *IPO*, *brand*).

➡ We have included a small number of important websites and associated companies and organizations. Our goal here is to provide a good list of paradigm sites that are striking because of scale, originality of business model, or significance in the development of e-commerce. This list does not aim for completeness.

➡ We have included a small number of products and product suppliers (*Cisco*, *Sun*, *Microsoft*) that provide much of the technology and business infrastructure of the web. The list is intended to focus on the major players, but it is obviously generated from our own experiences, and again we certainly do not claim it is exhaustive.

➡ We cover globally understood terms (which admittedly originate mostly from the USA). However, because of our own origins we do also list some UK and European entries (eg. *Lastminute.com*).

It is important to note that we are not trying to do any of the following:

➡ Produce a guide to using the web, or its content.

➡ Produce a general IT glossary. We don't cover terms like mouse or SNA. However, there are a few general terms (like *operating system* and *mainframe*) where we do have something special to say, and these entries usually focus on internet and e-commerce matters related to the general terms. We do cover some basic terms which are simply unavoidable, such as *button*, *bit* or *byte*.

➡ Cover all the hottest slang from Silicon Valley – although we do cover some that has bubbled up into the mass media. (Free feel to look up *Silicon Valley* of course!)

Using this book

We hope that this book can be used in a number of ways:

➡ As a reference when you need to know what a term means, or have read about a particular company, major website, or well-known industry figure.

➡ As something to read end-to-end to gain a general understanding of e-commerce, internet technologies and related matters.

If you are interested in fundamental concepts then the following table shows the larger articles in the text:

Internet and technology articles	
//	IP
.aero	IP address
.com	Java
ARPANET	Linux
DNS	Meta-tag
Domain name	Modem
e-mail	OSI
Interactive television	Registration
Internet	Security
Internetworking	

Web articles	
Browser	World wide web
HTML	XML
Measurement	
Search engines	

Mobile articles	
Mobile	
Mobile internet access	
WAP	
WML	

Business articles

Advertising	e-money
Aggregation	Exchange
Amazon	Intel
Auctions	Microsoft
B2B	Oracle
B2C	Sun
Bubble	Venture capital
CISCO	Viral marketing

Culture

Abbreviation
Community
Open source
Text
Usenet

Are there any prerequisites? We have tried to write for an intelligent lay person who has used the internet on a few occasions. Some of the technology entries are a little dry – by the nature of the subject matter – but we have attempted to make descriptions as straightforward as possible.

Conventions

We have used the following simple conventions.

➡ Each term is introduced as:

Term (classifications)
Descriptive text.

➡ Classifications – of which there could be several for each term – are:

Business term	A phrase or word relating to e-commerce businesses, or the creation of e-commerce businesses.
Company name	A commercial organization supporting or undertaking e-commerce.
e-mail term	Covers terms used in e-mail.

Internet term	A term related to the internet as a network, rather than the world wide web which is one of the services available on the internet.
Mobile term	A term related to mobile computing, mobile telephony or "mobile commerce."
Organization	A non-commercial organization.
Product name	Typically covers technical, mainly software, products used in building websites or similar.
Security term	Covers terms related to computer and internet security.
Slang	Self-explanatory – although some technical terms started off life as slang, and the boundary isn't always clear.
Technical term	Term related to computer technology.
Website	Denotes an actual website you can access. Most often websites will be listed under company names (e.g. Amazon), and we don't include the www part of standard website names.
Web term	A term specific to the world wide web rather than the more general concept of the internet.

➡ Names are listed by surname.

➡ References in the text to other entries are shown as **_bold italic_**. References to specific websites are in bold font, as follows: **www.amazon.com**. Programming language fragments (they are very few in number) are shown in `Courier`. These are intended for those with an interest in this sort of thing – they aren't essential to the text.

Tone and style

The cultural range of the internet and e-commerce worlds is vast (and arguably, this is one of the key reasons for their success and influence). As a result, some topics generate a lot of emotional heat. (Is spamming an evil? Is software something to share without cost?) When we stumble over such an issue, we try our best to be neutral. However, in one area we make no apologies. We are natural skeptics, but in writing what follows, we continuously found ourselves engaged and excited by the possibilities opened up by the current generation of technologies. Even given the recent roller-coaster ride in the New Economy, the mood of much of this text is decidedly optimistic.

Thanks and acknowledgments

Thanks are due to: Kris Wadia for supplying some of the text related to advertising and branding concepts; Alice Haviland for insights into (her) Generation Text; Tonya Hughes and Lucy Rutherford-Warren for helping with production; Simon Daniel, Azad Ootam, and Mark Patrick for their suggestions on entries.

Standard terms

// (web term)

This symbol neatly provides a way of introducing more fundamental concepts.

Consider:

http://www.eBay.com

This is a **URL** or Universal Resource Locator which is an easy, mnemonic way of representing a destination on the **world wide web**.

A URL can be decomposed as:

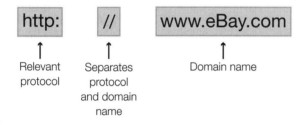

So the // symbol is a simple syntatical connection that separates the name of a **protocol** from a **domain name.** Let's explore these terms.

A protocol is a standard way of exchanging data across a **network**. In the case of a URL, there are two common choices. http: stands for Hypertext Transmission Protocol and means the destination is a website. FTP: stands for File Transfer Protocol and signifies an application with which you can exchange files.

The domain name is a reference to a location on the internet and translates ultimately into a numeric **IP address**. This numeric value is used by the underlying network software on the internet. Domain names are a slightly older concept than URLs, related to the internet. URLs are an extension for the web, which is in essence a service that sits on top on the internet.

Browsers – the normal user interface to the web – normally require just domain names, and so the terms URL and domain names are often used interchangeably, although slightly inexactly.

.aero (internet term)

A new *top-level domain* for the internet announced by the Internet Corporation for Assigned Names and Numbers (*ICANN*) in November 2000, which allows aviation websites to be grouped. This is one of seven selected alternatives to the more familar, original top-level domain names such as *.com* and *.net*. The full list of new, proposed top-level domain names is:

➡ .aero   aviation sites

➡ .biz   businesses

➡ .coop   cooperatives

➡ .info   general information

➡ .museum   museums

➡ .name   personal names

➡ .pro   professionals

At the time of writing, the process of formalization is not complete and these top-level domains are not formally active. The process has been controversial to say the least, and many popular suggestions were turned down, including *.kids* for child sites, *.geo* for sites related to places, .nom as a popular alternative to .name, and .xxx or .sex as a way of ring-fencing adult content. Many observers dislike the complex *ICANN* process, think it is weighted towards commercial interests, or think that many more top-level domain names would helpfully reduce behaviors such as *cybersquatting*. However, it is also worth saying that the layout of the internet namespace is one that generates a enormous amount of emotional heat, whatever the naming scheme selected.

.biz (internet term)

New top-level domain name announced in November 2000 to group business-orientated websites. An alternative to *.com*.

.com (internet term, business term)
Internet services and websites are generally identified by *domain names.* A simple example of a famous `.com` domain name is:

www.amazon.com

The www component refers to the world wide web, meaning that this domain name identifies a website. amazon is the unique part of the name and the suffix `.com` denotes a commercial organization. This whole name, of course, identifies *Amazon*, which is probably one of the most well-known commercial organizations on the web. Domain names therefore represent a simple hierarchical structure for classifying groups of internet addresses (i.e. websites and other services).

The `.com` part is also one of the most familiar symbols of the internet and e-commerce in general. It is one of seven original generic *top-level domain* names (the others being .org, .gov, .edu, .mil, .net, and .int) dating from when the internet was a vehicle for connecting non-commercial websites, and had a mainly US focus. There are also many two-letter top-level domain names that identify countries (.us, .uk etc). And, at the time of writing, there are official moves to increase the number of these top-level domain names (see the entry on .aero).

.com is an international domain name used to refer to commercial services, and usually those with a US or global focus. With the enormous increase in e-commerce and commercial use of the internet, .com names have become valuable real estate. What they offer is a global and unique identifier for a specific company's website, and by implication, the company itself. For all major corporates, their .com name is therefore seen as a critical part of their *brand*. Research has also shown that some users try to find a website by guessing at the domain name, rather than using a *search engine*. A natural and intuitive domain name is therefore an important part of an organization's identity.

One obvious consequence is that .com domain names have become a tradable commodity. Although initial registration costs are generally very low, names are sold often, and very occasionally for millions of dollars. The fact that .com names have intrinsic value leads directly to the practice of *cybersquatting.* This happens where names that might have value are speculatively purchased in the hope that some major organization or wealthy individual will then spend a large sum of money acquiring the .com version of their name. As a practice, this is of increasingly questionable value – since there have been a variety of legal cases round the world to protect names and trade marks, and various arbitration procedures have been introduced by regulation authorities. Many prime names have been taken, given the raw and potent power of the .com symbol. In fact available names have been purchased in their millions. At the time of writing, all two-letter .com names (eg. **www.if.com**) and all three-letter .com names (e.g. **www.egg.com**) have gone, and there aren't many four-letter variations left. The .com domain has also become stretched beyond its original purpose. For example, many UK companies – who typically use the suffix .co.uk – also purchase the .com variants of their names (**egg.com** is just such an example). There are a great many individuals who have also purchased their own names in .com form leading to suggestions for a .nom or .name domain. The latter is currently proposed by *ICANN.*

The suffix .com itself has been turned into both a noun and adjective as *dot com.* The phrase "a dot com" is a common short-hand for an internet start-up company. As an adjective it refers to internet and e-commerce as a whole. So: "dot-com company," "dot-com boom," dot-com bubble," and "has the dot-com bubble finally burst?" are all examples of phrases you will see with monotonous regularity.

.coop (internet term)
New top-level domain name announced in November 2000 to group web-sites linked with co-operatives.

.edu (internet term)
Top-level generic domain name originally intended for all educational institutions. Now focussed on US "four year colleges" and universities.

.gov (internet term)
Top-level domain name for a non-military US federal government site, e.g. **www.whitehouse.gov**. Not intended for international (i.e. non-US) use.

.info (internet term)

New top-level domain name announced in November 2000 to group information-providing websites.

.int (internet term)

Rarely used domain name for an organization established by international treaty.

.mil (internet term)

Top-level domain name for a US military site. Again, not intended for non-US uses.

.museum (internet term)

New top-level domain name announced in November 2000 to group museum websites.

.name (internet term)

New top-level domain name announced in November 2000 to group websites associated with personal names. (Others wanted .nom.)

.net (internet term)

Top-level domain name originally reserved for a network provider, or *ISP*. Intended for international use. Now .net is freely used, as with **www. britneyspears.net**.

.NET (technical term)

Note the capital letters. This term covers a recent architectural initiative from *Microsoft* that allows developers to build applications by integrating collections of web-based "services", which may be built by the developer, or drawn from an external source over the web. A key element of the approach is the use of the fashionable *XML* language to allow services to communicate in a standard way. This represents a strong marketing push from Microsoft to take the architectural high-ground in the development of web-based solutions.

.org (internet term)

This suffix should be used for organizations that don't fit easily within other top-level domains, such as non-profit organizations. Intended for international use.

.pro (internet term)

New potential top-level domain name announced in November 2000 to group websites associated with professionals.

.tv (internet term)

The `.tv` top-level domain represents the country of Tuvalu, which consists of nine coral atolls, north of Fiji, in the southwest Pacific and has a population of approximately 10,000 people. However, because of its association with television, there has been great demand for `.tv` domains which are administered by a company called dotTV (**www.tv**).

@ (e-mail term)

The common typographical symbol for "at," this is used to separate *e-mail* account names (which represent individual users) and domain names (which represent the organization to which the individual belongs) to form a complete e-mail address. So:

John.doe@somehostorg.com

means the `john.doe` account at the organization represented by `somehostorg.com`. This symbol dates from the earliest uses of e-mail on *ARPANET* – the precursor of the internet.

100% Pure Java (technical term)

A certification issued by *Sun*, the originator of the *Java* language. This is a badge of conformance to the Java language specification to ensure that the relevant Java code will execute against a standard Java implementation.

In commercial terms, this is intended to offer some protection to the Java standard, and discourage use of proprietary extensions of the language such as those offered by Microsoft.

24 × 7 (technical term)

Describes a service that is available 24 hours a day, seven days a week and pronounced as "twenty four by seven." An aspiration of many online services, this can be difficult and expensive to achieve, since complex systems require maintenance, back-up, and similar housekeeping.

2.5 G (mobile term)

An intermediate step towards third-generation mobile telephony and computing. See *3G*.

3G (mobile term)

Third Generation or 3G is a generic term for the next generation of mobile phone systems that are designed to offer much higher mobile data rates and integrated internet access. The European standard for 3G is Universal Mobile Telephone System (*UMTS*) which is part of a broader global initiative called International Mobile Telecommunications 2000 (IMT-2000).

Advanced marketing for 3G has raised expectations of data rates of 2 Mbps. However, a maximum speed of 384 kbits is more likely for mobile users, and the high cost of spectrum and competition from existing GSM networks may limit the rate at which the new 3G infrastructure becomes available. Upgrades to the existing mobile networks will themselves offer data rates almost comparable with 3G, promoting the somewhat ironic term 2.5G. In terms of previous generations, the first generation of mobile telephony was based around analog systems, and the introduction of digital systems based on GSM in the early 1990s represented the second generation. Some observers have also started talking about a Fourth Generation (4G) of devices (see below).

400, 401, 402, 403, 404 (web term)

These are error codes standard within *HTTP* or Hypertext Transfer Protocol. HTTP is the network *protocol* that binds the nodes in the world wide web together. These errors are returned by an HTTP server when a request from a client system can't be processed. In plainer terms, these error numbers can be displayed by a browser if it fails to get access to a website. Meanings are:

Number	Message	Description
400	Bad Request	The syntax of the client request is incorrect
401	Unauthorized	The user did not have permission to access the page
402	Payment Requested	Self-explanatory
403	Forbidden	Indicates access is restricted
404	Not Found	The server cannot find a true address that matches the URL submitted

Given the way HTTP is used, some of these codes (e.g. 402) are unlikely. However, 404 is very common when a web document refers to a *hyperlink* where the underlying service or site has moved or disappeared.

4G (slang)

Stands for Fourth Generation mobile and is used somewhat ironically to describe Wireless Local Area Networks (*WLANs*) operated in public places to offer users the high-speed internet access promised (but not yet available) via *3G* mobile phone systems. Such services can only support suitably equipped laptop PC users in relatively small areas, but this is "good enough" in many circumstances, e.g. to provide internet access to business travelers in an executive lounge at an airport. A major business advantage to operators is that the radio spectrum used for WLANs is effectively free, in comparison with the £billions spent by the mobile phone companies for *3G* spectrum.

802 (technical term)

The name of a standards committee run by the Institute of Electrical and Electronics Engineers which is responsible for developing standards for Local Area Networks (*LANs*). A variety of different technologies are covered by different working groups within the committee and each working group is distinguished by a number after the "dot," among the most important are:

➡ 802.3 for networks based on *Ethernet*

➡ 802.11 for *Wireless LANs*

802.11 is now getting a great deal of attention as wireless divices become more common, and is the basis for what has been named the *Wi-Fi* industry standard.

90% club (slang)

Slang term that appeared in the media after stock values of many dot-com or technology companies declined steeply from April 2000 onwards. Members of the 90 percent club have seen their valuations drop by 90 percent or more – a very typical decline, given the inflated valuations beforehand.

AAC (technical term)

Stands for Advanced Audio Coding. AAC is an audio format which is an extension and improvement of the much more well-known *MP3* standard (which is now the preferred way of sending high-quality recordings of music across the internet). For this reason, AAC is sometimes called MP4.

Abbreviation (slang)

In the context of *e-mail*, *chat rooms*, and *Internet Relay Chat*, abbreviations refer to shorthand expressions for common English phrases. Here is a selection from a variety of sources, with the more Anglo-Saxon variants edited out.

AAMOF	As a matter of fact
AFAIK	As far as I know
AFJ	April fool's joke
AFK	Away from keyboard
BRB	Be right back
BTW	By the way
F2F	Face to face
GMTA	Great minds think alike
IMHO	In my humble opinion

IMO	In my opinion
IMNSHO	In my not so humble opinion
LOL	Laugh out loud
OTF	On the floor laughing
OMG	Oh my gosh/God
ROTFL	Rolling on the floor laughing
TTFN	Tata for now
TTYL	Talk to you later
WB	Welcome back
WTG	Way to go

The use of text messaging on mobile phones has created a new forum for these abbreviations, and an even more aggressive variety of very short abbreviations. See *text* for more details.

Absolute (technical term)

In the context of absolute *link* or absolute *URL,* the word "absolute" means full or complete. So, in *HTML,* an absolute link specifies the protocol (eg. http://), the name of the target computer, and the location of the particular file referenced in full, rather than just relative to the current page. Similarly, an absolute URL describes a resource's exact location on the internet.

Accelerator (business term)

Similar to, though less used than, *incubator.* An accelerator is an organization intended to drive a start-up company rapidly from early stages to greater business maturity by the provision of a mixture of services, potentially including funding, business advice and technology infrastructure.

Acceptable use policy (business term)

A statement from an *Internet Service Provider (ISP)* or similar organization that describes what a particular service allows, what you aren't authorized to do, and general conditions of use. Essentially this is an ISP's contractual small print. Generally available online.

Access log (technical term)

An access log is a general term for a file that lists all the activities requested of a particular system. In the context of the web, the term will cover a *server-*

based file that lists all the requests for individual files from a website. The log will typically include requests for *HTML* files, embedded images, and any other files accessed. Useful in a security context, the data in an access log can also be analyzed to produce key statistics of website usage and uncover common usage patterns.

Access provider (business term)
Common alternative for *Internet Service Provider*.

Acrobat (product)
See *Adobe Acrobat.*

Active server pages (technical term)
An innovation introduced by *Microsoft*, which inspired *Sun* to create the concept of *Java Server Pages* or JSPs. It is intended for building web applications of more sophistication than simple *HTML* pages, and also supporting *thin-client* approaches where most of the work is done on server systems, rather than a user's PC. Active server pages can contain a mixture of text, surrounding HTML and scripting languages like *JavaScript* and *VBScript* which can do more than HTML on its own. When a *browser* triggers an active server page, it runs on the back-end server, creates a stream of HTML dynamically, which is then delivered back to the user's own PC for display, as illustrated below.

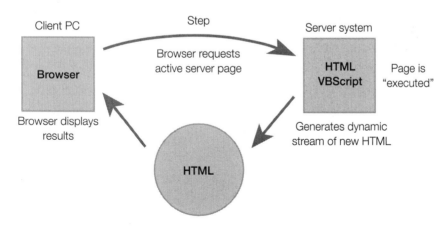

Active server pages

Active-X (technical term)

Essentially, a late 1990s technical marketing term for the distributed architecture provided by *Microsoft* around its family of middleware products (*COM, COM+, DCOM*). A key feature is the concept of Active-X control. Similar to Java *applets,* these are software components that can be downloaded over a network, including the internet. Active-X controls are commonly used for complex user interaction in applications, and can be written in a range of languages, including *Visual Basic,* which is the flagship language originated by Microsoft itself. Some developers don't like Active-X because it allows all features of a PC to be used and accessed, and security relies on electronic signatures being attached to an Active-X control. This puts the onus on the end-user to identify which suppliers of Active-X controls can be trusted.

Ad rotation (business term)

Used in internet *advertising*, where *banner* ads are displayed at the top of a page. Ad rotation describes the situation where a series of different ads are displayed in the same area on screen, with each visitor seeing the next ad in a list that will eventually cycle around.

Address (technical term)

Has a variety of precise meanings, but is always based on the notion of an identifier that tells a computer program where to find something. This is particularly important with networks, and in the case of the internet the term can be used at a variety of levels:

(1) To describe the textual domain name in a readable form that people can understand ...

(2) ... which will then translate into a numeric *IP* address which tells the *TCP/IP* network software where to send data to...

(3) ... which will eventually translate into an even lower-level numeric, machine-readable addresses for a particular Local Area Network (*LAN*).

Address Resolution Protocol (ARP) (technical term)

A member of the *TCP/IP* protocol family. It supports the translation of a numeric *IP* address into an even lower-level physical address on a Local Area Network (*LAN*). In essence, it allows software to turn an IP address – which has global meaning – into a local reference for a particular networked group of machines.

Adobe (company)

Adobe Systems is an important software provider focussed on desktop publishing and similar products. Its main website is at **www.adobe.com**.

Adobe Acrobat (product)

A cross-platform application – available on *Windows*, *Macintosh* and *UNIX* – used to create formatted documents in Adobe's *PDF* (Portable Document Format). Very commonly used for high-quality documents intended for printing.

Adobe Acrobat Reader (product)

A freely available application intended for use as a browser *plug-in* that allows *PDF* documents to be viewed and printed in their original format and layout.

ADSL (technical term)

Stands for either Asymmetric Digital Subscriber Line or Asymmetric Digital Subscriber Loop. This is a technology designed to maximize what can be sent across ordinary phone lines (which are made up of "twisted-pair copper") rather than the rarer and more expensive fiber-optic cable. The "asymmetric" element allows data to be received at greater rates than it can be sent – ideal for most types of internet use. ADSL differs from a *modem* connection in that it only establishes a connection between the user and the local telephone exchange. Therefore, there is no need for an end-to-end connection to be established via dial-up, and ADSL is referred to as "always on." ADSL was originally developed in the early 1990s to allow telephone companies to deliver video over their existing copper infrastructure but was not widely deployed. However, it is now increasingly in great demand for fast internet access.

ADSL contention ratio (technical term)

A traditional dial-up connection establishes an exclusive link between the end user's *modem* and a modem at the ISP location, similar to a voice call. The situation with ADSL is different. The connection is only exclusive between the user and the local telephone exchange. The rest of the trip uses

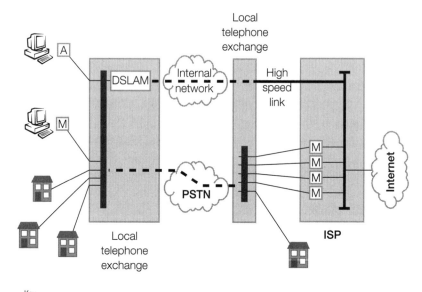

Key
M   Modem
A   ADSL interface
R   Router
DSLAM   Digital Subscriber Line Access Multiplexer
PSTN   Public Switched Telephone Network

ADSL vs. modem connection

shared infrastructure, for which the user is in competition with other ADSL users connecting to the same telephone exchange. The degree of competition is referred to as the "contention ratio" and is typically between 1:20 and 1:50. A ratio of 1:50 means that the telephone company is trying to fit a maximum of 50 ADSL users on to one internal connection. This is not as bad as it may sound, as all users are not active at the same time and internet traffic is "bursty," allowing other users to communicate in the gaps of others' surfing. There are many other potential points of contention (e.g. between the ISP and the internet backbone) which will probably have worse impacts than ADSL.

Advanced Audio Coding (technical term)
See *AAC*.

Advanced Encryption Standard (security term)

See *AES*.

Advertising (business term)

E-commerce has essentially generated a new, large, and complex industry around marketing, branding, and advertising. Advertising has relevance in two main ways:

(1) Use of traditional media (press, television, posters) to market new dot-com businesses. This activity should be apparent to anyone in an industrialized country, and traditional ad agencies went through a late 1990s boom period as many *dot-com* companies used mainstream media to attempt to attract users to their *websites*. With the market correction in the dot-com world of 2000, this type of expenditure is undertaken with much more thought. In essence, such advertising attempts to build *brand* quickly. Brand is a much talked about subject in the e-commerce world. It is also a complex phenomenon where a corporate identity gets linked in the public mind to a set of values and characteristics. Much of the advertising about new dot-com companies succeeds – if it succeeds at all – in creating a degree of awareness, and hopefully placing a *URL* into a potential user's mind. It may not be so successful at building a long-lasting brand. For example, the European sports clothing retailer *boo.com* generated a great deal of awareness that ended up being linked to technical hitches, launch delays, and eventual liquidation and sale of assets.

(2) Use of new media (primarily the web) to create new forms of advertising. We will expand on this below.

The main purpose of web-based marketing and advertising is to attract users to a website, usually by grabbing a user's attention when they are doing something else, and then providing a *link* directly to the destination. Standard routes include:

➡ using banner ads;

➡ having a link embedded in a related website;

➡ through the results generated by a search engine;

➡ e-mail or Usenet postings.

The **banner ad** (sometimes just called banner) has spawned a whole commercial culture in itself. The advertising website allocates a certain amount of space to carry advertising – usually the strip at the top of the page, hence the name "banner." An interested user clicks on this and gets carried through to the destination site that's being promoted (or sometimes, an intermediate **buffer page** actually held on the site doing the advertising for reasons of speed).

There are a variety of ways of paying for banner ads – one such mechanism is to pay a **CPM** (cost per mille), or cost per 1000 views of an ad.

Banner advertising is conceptually very powerful, as banners can be specifically and intelligently targetted. However, they are very common and less and less effective. As a result, there is a focus on "rich media" banners using animation, video, and other techniques to stand out from what is now a very large crowd.

Search engines (which provide the ability to locate pages and sites that contain specific key words) are also fundamental to generating **site traffic**. Even though most general search engines (**Google**, **Yahoo!**, **Excite** etc.) can only index a fraction of what's available on the world wide web, they still remain an extremely popular way of finding interesting sites for many users. As you might expect, search engines have also created a whole sub-industry to help commercial sites get listed early on in a results list after a search. Standard techniques can include:

➡ Using **meta-tags** – descriptive entries placed in the **HTML** that describe the content in a website. Be warned, some search engines don't look at meta-tags.

➡ Using special software designed to submit your pages to specific search engines.

➡ Using a commercial service that specializes in this area.

E-mail is another powerful marketing vehicle, especially when used by a supplier to provide updates on the progress of an order, or distribute offers and news to registered users. However, junk e-mail (or **spam**), or commercially minded postings to non-commercially minded **Usenet** newsgroups will generate torrents of negative emotion.

Overall, web-based advertising is a relatively big business. Summary figures vary widely (for example, IDC estimates US spending on internet advertising at $3.3 billion in 2000, while Forester Research says $5.3 billion and eMarketer suggests $6.1 billion). Nonetheless, there are important caveats. Internet-based advertising is still a small fraction of total advertising: 2.5 percent in 2000, according to eMarketer. In addition, *click-through-rates* – the percentage of displayed banners and other adverts that a user actually clicks on – are falling to less than 0.5 percent. This reflects ad clutter on poorly designed sites, a lack of novelty, and user boredom. A direct implication is that new business models that rely on income from advertising are now viewed with great suspicion by potential investors. For a few well-known destinations – like *AOL* or *Yahoo!* – significant revenues can still be generated, however.

AES (security term)

Stands for Advanced Encryption Standard. This refers to a modern *encryption* algorithm intended to code messages so they can only be read by authorized people, based on use of a shared numeric *key*. This is the successor to *DES* (Data Encryption Standard) which is in widespread use. The algorithm was selected from a competition run by NIST (the US-based National Institute of Standards and Technology). There were five finalists called MARS, RC6™, Rijndael, Serpant and Two Fish. The winner is Rijndael, named after Joen Daemer and Vincent Rijmen.

Affiliate (business term)

In the context of web-based e-commerce, an affiliate website is intended to generate business for another organization's website via the use of *links* – usually for a cut of the generated sales volume.

Agent (technical term)

A background program (i.e. one that keeps quietly busy without the need for user guidance) that performs some automated task – such as searching for and finding information – and reports back when the task is complete. Given the enormous amount of information available on the world wide web, agents seem a natural technique for performing intensive tasks. In truth, it is difficult to build agent processes that are both robust and useful. One successful and substantial use of agents – more commonly called *crawlers*, spiders, or robots in this context – is to create indexes for search engines by searching through the content of websites.

Aggregation (business term)

Aggregation in plain English is simply the act of creating a collection of things, or the collection itself. In terms of e-commerce, it covers websites (or similar) that collect together products, content and services. Good historical analogies might include department stores and mail order companies, both types of business being revolutionary when first introduced.

Online examples include:

➡ Online grocers (like Webvan in the US, or Tesco Online in the UK).

➡ *Amazon* which brings together books, DVDs, videos, auction services, and other elements.

➡ *Portals* like *Yahoo!* and *Excite* which aggregate many types of content and service.

➡ Financial service sites which often allow a choice of similar financial products from a range of product providers, and provide supporting data and tools.

➡ Some types of site (e-Trade in share trading, and various travel portals) which bring together information related to complex decisions that would usually have involved a physical third-party intermediary.

The underlying value to the end-user of this type of site will vary, but often covers elements of convenience, discount pricing, the ability to select and match, and easy fulfillment.

Agora (business term)

Used by Dan Tapscott and others in the book *Digital Capital*. Not in wide usage, but this is a very useful term covering types of e-commerce where price is not pre-set, but agreed during a process of electronic negotiation. Agora is derived from the ancient Greek term for marketplace.

Agoras fall into the following categories:

➡ Open markets (such as a job site) set up for one-to-one negotiations and most suited to one-off goods or services.

➡ Sell-side auctions (the best consumer example being *eBay*) that are essentially one-seller to many buyers. A popular and often successful model.

➡ Buy-side auctions which enable a buyer – usually of some substantial item or service – to receive multiple bids. An approach most suited to the *business-to-business* world.

➡ *Exchanges*, which have been at the heart of certain types of commerce for centuries. Many traditional types of exchange (e.g. stock markets) have used electronic support for a decade or so. The internet makes the wider use of exchanges a cost-effective option, and there are many *B2B* exchanges now in existence, although there are big and valid questions about the long-term potential of all such sites.

The key characteristic of a successful Agora is liquidity – i.e. are there large enough numbers of sellers, buyers and sufficient volume in transactional and/or monetary terms to make the market place attractive?

Alias (e-mail term)
Alternative *e-mail* name for a person or group.

Allen, Paul
One of the original founders of *Microsoft* with *Bill Gates*, and once head of research and new product development. A well-known and selective investor in high-tech companies.

Alliance (business term)
In business an alliance is some kind of formal link between organizations, with varying levels of contractual support. For example, a systems integrator may have an alliance with a software product supplier to use that supplier's product on certain types of project. The payback may be services, support or warrants that give the integrator equity in proportion to sales volume. Advocates of the new economy put a great deal of emphasis on networks of businesses, so alliances are increasingly common.

alt. newsgroups (internet term)
One of the most distinctive features of internet culture – certainly prior to the dominance of the web – is the *Usenet* distributed discussion system.

Usenet is divided into a hierarchy of **newsgroups** to which articles or messages can be "posted" for reading by others. The alt. prefix is the start of the alternative hierarchy within Usenet which isn't controlled in the same way as other newsgroups, and often covers topics that are seedy, bizarre, obscure, or all three.

Alta Vista (company name)

Alta Vista is one of a number of well-known internet companies that started life around a **search engine**. It began in 1995 as an initiative from **DEC** – a once proud manufacturer of mid-range computers – that exploited DEC's Alpha hardware technology. The Alta Vista name apparently emerged from a confusion of phrases on a white board. Ownership has passed through **Compaq** – who acquired DEC – to **CMGI**. Services provided at the time of writing include the original search service, news and entertainment content, shopping, and various portal services. Available at **www.altavista.com**.

Always on (technical term)

Many consumers access the net via a clumsy process of dial-up and logging on. An "always on" service provides immediate connection to required services. For home users, new phone services, like **ADSL**, can provide "always on" access. While not having to wait for a connection to be established is undoubtedly a benefit, it does increase the potential to be compromised by **hackers** if a system is left idle (but connected) for long periods of time.

Amaya (product)

Distributed as freely available **open source** software, Amaya is a **browser** developed by members of the World Wide Web Consortium (**W3C**). It is intended to be a practical tool and testing ground for W3C concepts. It includes an **HTML** editor as well as a viewer, and support for more recent technical innovations.

Amazon (company name)

Amazon is one of the strongest global brands to be created on the web. Initially created to sell books, it now offers a broad range of consumer products and services.

Amazon was founded in legendary, and low-key, fashion in 1994 by Jeff Bezos, Shel Kaphan and Paul Barton-Davis, in a converted Seattle garage. It grew in a few years into probably the most well-known **B2C** or business- to consumer site. Although in retrospect it feels like Amazon had first-mover advantage, it wasn't the first B2C site, or even the first seller of books over the internet. What Amazon did display early on was a number of important characteristics typical of the **dot-com** world of the late 1990s. These include:

➡ a strong initial idea (based on completeness of list … "if it's in print, it's in stock");

➡ a focus on both service *and* discounting;

➡ a focus on growth and market position, at the expense of initial profit, driven by external funding (and covered by the phrase "Get big fast").

Amazon has become a classically powerful brand, and generates genuine customer loyalty, although its discounts are usually not the most generous available. When it enters a new market, it tends to gain significant market share quickly. As well as books, it now offers a range of goods and services including CDs, videos, DVDs, auctions, and even tools for home improvement.

At the time of writing, Amazon had lost some of its shine through patenting its one-click payment system – which to some seems a little like an attempt to patent the concept of **cookies**. And the model of growth driven by external funding rather than profit is under greater scrutiny than ever before. For example, Amazon's fulfillment costs (i.e. the costs of getting goods to customers) can be higher than conventional channels. As a result Amazon and companies with similar models are encountering much more scrutiny and skepticism by the media and investors than in the boom period of the late 1990s. At the time of writing, Amazon is following a strategy based very firmly around the now popular notion of "Path to Profit."

Amazon sites are available in a wide range of countries (**Amazon.com**, **Amazon.co.uk**, **Amazon.au**).

Amazonned (slang)

Sometimes used when a traditional business loses sales to an e-commerce competition – which naturally enough rises from Amazon's early success in capturing a large chunk of the book-buying marketplace. Already a little archaic sounding.

America OnLine (AOL) (company name)

AOL is an internet mega-brand. Founded in 1985 as Quinton Computer Services, it offered a range of proprietory (and non-internet) interactive services when the internet itself was a network supporting mainly academics and researchers. Initial services were based on technologies including Commodore machines and variants of the PC over a proprietory network. In 1991, the name America OnLine Inc. was introduced. In 1993, users exceeded half a million for the first time. In the mid-1990s, AOL made a major shift to pure internet technologies, although it maintains its own look and feel to users. In 1996, it reached 7 million members and the year after passed 10 million. In 1999, it acquired *Netscape* and exceeded 20 million users. At the start of 2000, it announced its striking merger with Time Warner – a significant and controversial mixing of old and new economies.

At the time of writing, AOL supports around 22 million members in the US, UK, Germany, Japan, and other countries, and supports more than 5 billion messages a day. It is the world's number-one internet online service, and has demonstrated an impressive record of corporate re-invention.

Andreesen, Marc

One of the major contributors to the early development of the *world wide web*. While still an undergraduate, Andreesen and Eric Bina built a *browser* called *Mosaic* at the University of Illinois. The concept of browsers predates Mosaic, but Mosaic was the first to display images beyond plain text, and focus on user friendliness. Mosaic turned the web into a visual medium accessible to average users. It became available to the wider web community in 1993, and achieved fast take-up.

Mosaic came to the attention of *Jim Clark*, founder of Silicon Graphics, and with Clark, Andreesen became a founder of Mosaic Communication, which is rather better known these days as *Netscape*. Netscape's key product is the Netscape Navigator – one of the world's most popular browsers and at least a conceptual descendant of Mosaic. In many ways, Netscape in its hey-day represented one of the first internet-style start-up and IPO successes – see the article on Netscape for more details. Andreesen, at the time of writing, is involved with a company called *Loudcloud*.

Angel (business term)

Or sometimes: *business angel.* A term borrowed from the theatre and similar domains. Describes a private investor who supports new dot-com companies, typically at an early stage before *venture capital* funding has been obtained.

Angry fruit salad (slang)

A *web page*, or other type of user interface, which is remarkable for its overuse of color, graphics, and other multimedia delights.

Animated GIF (or GIF animation) (technical term)

GIF stands for Graphics Interchange Format which is a simple compressed format commonly used to display images on the web. By combining multiple images in a loop, a clumsy animation can be shown. The advantage of this is that more sophisticated animations will require third-party *plug-ins* (like *Flash*) to a browser, while standard browsers can already handle GIF.

Anonymizer (web term)

An utility or service designed to provide anonymous browsing – used in situations where, for example, an employee wants to search the web without the details of searches being monitored by their employer. This highlights one of the tensions between the personal and corporate world that the web generates. Many organizations provide relatively easy access to the web – it is, after all, an awesome research and communication tool. Organizations will tolerate a reasonable level of personal use (reasonable, of course, being hard to define). However, the *formal* policy of the majority of companies is often strict, prohibiting or heavily restricting personal internet use.

Anonymous FTP (internet term)

Allows users to connect to an internet server and download files when they have no true access rights. Sometimes controlled uploading is also permitted.

Anonymous remailer (e-mail term)

One of the great debates created by the internet concerns privacy, freedom of speech, and freedom of action. We will offer no judgments in this particular text, but it isn't an easy area, since the internet represents all aspects of human life, including its seedier side. Closely aligned to this debate are issues of *intellectual property.*

If an individual wants to send e-mail that can't be traced to them (and is this protecting privacy, or failing to take responsibility?) then anonymous remailers can be used. In most cases, they will strip your name and e-mail address from your original message and send it on.

Pseudo-anonymous remailers require an account on the relevant server – so ultimately you will be known to the people who manage that server. Other types offer greater theoretical anonymity, but are hard to use.

These are free services, usually linked to the internet's *hacker* sub-culture and subject to frequent change and disappearance.

AOHell (slang)
Not-so-friendly slang version of AOL.

AOL (company name)
See *America OnLine*.

AOLer (slang)
Somewhat derogatory term for a user who discovered the *Usenet* as part of the popularization of the internet by *America Online*, and then posts naïve statements.

Apache (technical term)
A free, *open source*, and popular *web server* designed to present data from a server system to an end-user running a *browser*. Typically found on *Linux* and *UNIX*-based servers, it was apparently named because it started as "a patchy server" – i.e. it was based on existing code and a series of modifications or patches.

Given the fact that Apache is both a good tool, and free, it is the most popular web server software, particularly for small sites. Some estimates say roughly two-thirds of all websites use Apache.

Apache Group (organization)
A non-profit volunteer organization that supports the development of *Apache*.

API (technical term)
Stands for *Application Programming Interface.* A common, non-internet-specific term for the way a software developer can use technical services from a technical product or service. It is of relevance here because internet technical

solutions are often complex – based on multiple products, programming languages and standards. APIs glue these elements together. A good example in this area is the *Java* platform which offers the programmer many standard services, as well as the core programming language.

Apple (company name)

Apple is a well-known computer brand, and a major influence in the development of personal computing, although it hasn't always reaped the full benefits of its track record of commercial innovation.

Founded in the late 1970s by Steve Jobs and Steve Wozniak, Apple was initially famous for the Apple II computer, which was the first commercially successful personal computer. (The IBM PC standard became dominant a few years later.) Apple then introduced the Apple Macintosh in 1984 – the first popular machine to offer a modern graphical user interface. Although never as popular as the conventional MS-DOS/Windows/Intel de facto standard, the family of systems started by the original Macintosh has always had a loyal following. One of the strongest elements of Apple's current generation of products is the *iMac* range, which are Macintosh derivatives designed for easy internet use and famed for their translucent and modern styling.

Applet (technical term)

A program or software module that can be dynamically downloaded from the internet and executed locally on the end-user's PC, typically within a *browser*. Most often associated with the *Java* programming language. Typically used to add flair, complex behavior, and unusual interaction to a website. Over-enthusiastic use of applets can impact performance, unfortunately.

Application (technical term)

Commonly used term for a software program that serves some end-user purpose – ranging from a word-processor to an accounting system. Many aspiring software suppliers are, of course, searching for the legendary "killer app" which will take a market segment by storm, or define the use of a technology.

Application Programming Interface (technical term)

See *API*.

Application server (technical term)

In the most general sense, an application server is any computer that supports the execution of application code and processing requests from a client computer (e.g. a PC). In the context of the web the term is used more specifically, and typically refers to specialized software running on a server that supports the execution of software components written in *Java* (e.g. Servlets, Enterprise Java Beans, or Java Server Pages) or similar languages. However, the boundary between a webserver and an application server is foggy and often depends more on marketing whims rather than product architecture. In addition, Microsoft has integrated many of the functions of an application server into the Windows 2000 operating system. Other examples of application server products include:

➡ BEA Weblogic

➡ IBM Websphere

➡ Oracle Application Server.

Application Service Provider (business term)

Often abbreviated to ASP, an Application Service Provider provides networked access – typically via the internet – to a suite of applications that can essentially be rented rather than purchased. The end users of these "apps on tap" will be other businesses. The heart of the business proposition here is a mixture of:

➡ **Speed**: gaining access to applications that are already live on the ASP's servers.

➡ **Cost**: through savings on license costs, infrastructure and implementation effort, which are shared across users.

➡ **Adaptability**: since end-customers don't have time to manage their own server environment, and upgrade costs are shared.

ASPs represent one type of *netsourcing* where business services are provided over networks. Early entrants to the ASP market include SAP, Peoplesoft and Siebel, already well-established software suppliers. The ASP market has a lot to prove, but is attracting a great deal of attention. In concept, ASPs are strikingly similar to computer bureau services common in the 1970s and 1980s.

Archie (internet term)

A somewhat antiquated, but amusingly named utility for finding useful files in publicly available archives.

Architecture (technical term)

With computer and e-commerce systems, the term architecture refers to the conceptual structure and organization of the system, or even major components of a system. As computer systems have got progressively more complex, the notion of having an overarching design and a chief designer (or architect) is often a key feature of a successful software or hardware development. This is especially true with complex e-commerce applications which have many elements in terms of hardware, network and software. A software architect would usually worry about the following aspects of a serious system or website:

➡ Specification of server hardware (e.g. the choice of microprocessor and manufacturer, amount and layout of disk and memory, choice of *operating system*).

➡ Design of the network (e.g. selection of network *protocols* and amount of *bandwidth* required). With an e-commerce solution, some of this will be given. Even so, the choice and configuration of equipment such as routers, design of the connections between backend servers and optimization of use of the internet remain hard tasks for big systems.

➡ Design of the application software (e.g. selection of programming language(s) and indentification of common *components* which can be reused).

➡ Decomposition of a complex system into different *layers* and *tiers* so that the work can be successfully split between different people, and complex processing can be isolated and written only once.

➡ Ensuring that a system is scalable to handle maybe an unknown number of additional users and easily extensible to include new functionality.

Ariba (company)

A well-known supplier of software solutions and services for certain types of *B2B* sites. The Ariba B2B Commerce Platform covers tools for e-procurement, the creation of e-marketplaces, and other applications for buyers, suppliers, and market markers.

ARP (internet term)
See *Address Resolution Protocol.*

ARPA (organization)
The US Department of Defense Advanced Research Projects Agency, respon-sible for *ARPANET*, the direct forerunner of the internet. Renamed DARPA – with the D standing for Defense – in the 1970s.

ARPANET (technical term, organization)
The ancestor network of the internet, and the first undertaking of its kind, ARPANET grew large from small beginnings and generated many things we now take for granted (like modern forms of *e-mail*, the *TCP/IP* network protocol family and the internet itself). ARPANET's history is complex, but some highlights include:

- 1958   ARPA created, partly in response to Sputnik.
- 1960 on   Various papers published on packet-switching and network designs that have no single point of failure.
- 1965   ARPA sponsors early studies on co-operative networks.
- 1967   ARPANET design discussions.
- 1968   Request for proposals for ARPANET. Bolt, Beranek and Newman (BBN) get key contract for building Interface Message Processors (IMPs).
- 1969   First four nodes on line at UCLA, Stanford, and other universities. First attempt at connection fails when letter G of LOGIN is typed.
- 1971   15 nodes, 23 host machines. Ray Thomlinson invents inter-sys-tem e-mail (and later selects the "@" sign for e-mail addresses).
- 1973   First international connections to the UK and Norway. Bob Kahn and Victor Cerf start work on "internetting" concepts. E-mail makes up 75 percent of ARPANET traffic.
- 1974   Victor Cerf and Bob Kahn publish design of a Transmission Control Protocol (TCP). The *TCP/IP* protocol family is destined to become the common technical language of most computer net-works and the internet itself.

➡ 1982 First uses of term the "internet".

➡ 1983 TCP/IP becomes standard ARPANET protocol.

➡ 1984 *Domain Name System* (DNS) created.

➡ 1985 Symbolics.com becomes first registered domain name.

➡ 1987 Number of connected hosts exceeds 10,000.

➡ 1989 Number of connected hosts exceeds 100,000.

➡ 1990 ARPANET as such ceases to exist. The American National Science Foundation takes over responsibility and funding for NSFNET, the physical network which has been at the heart of ARPANET and continues to serve the internet.

ASCII (technical term)

Stands for American Standard Code for Information Interchange – although only the abbreviation is ever used. It is a coding scheme that uses numeric values from 1 to 127 to stand for letters, numbers, punctuation characters, and the like. This is a highly efficient way of coding text, needing 7 *bits* per character (although each character is usually stored in a field 8 bits wide). It is used in most *e-mail.* This is why plain e-mails don't allow multiple fonts and graphics.

Ask Jeeves (company name)

Essentially offering a type of *search engine*, Ask Jeeves (named after the fictional butler) aims to deliver a "humanized online experience." Input is in the form of English language questions, although answers are given in a traditional search engine style. Ask Jeeves has websites at **ask.com**, **AJKids.com** (intended, as you might guess, for children), **DirectHit.com**, and offers regional variants like **ask.co.uk**. Ask Jeeves also provide software and services to businesses for content searching within information offered by a particular website.

ASP (business term, technical term)

One abbreviation, two meanings. Can stand for *Application Service Provider* – a business term, or *Active Server Pages* – a technical term. These terms are explained under the expanded headings.

Asymmetric Digital Subscriber Line (technical term)
Asymmetric Digital Subscriber Loop (technical term)
See *ADSL.*

ATM *(technical term)*

Stands for Asynchronous Transfer Mode. A fast, low-level network standard, but with somewhat less flexibility in terms of *routing* than other approaches.

Attach (e-mail term)

Add an *attachment*, or external file, to an e-mail.

Attachment (e-mail term)

A file – which might be a document, a PowerPoint presentation, a compressed (*zipped*) archive of many files, or an executable program – that is linked to an *e-mail* message. Since an attachment can be a program and since some mail systems (such as *Microsoft* Outlook) can be fairly permissive in what they allow an opened attachment to do, e-mail attachments have become a prime vehicle for spreading viruses, such as the "I love you" virus in early 2000.

Auctions (business term)

The success of online auctions was initially surprising, but they now represent one of the most obvious – and sometimes successful – aspects of e-commerce. Online auctions mimic and extend the types of auction seen in the non-wired world. Many auction sites are available in both the business-to-consumer and business-to-business marketplaces. A typical consumer-based auction process consists of the following steps:

➡ A seller creates an entry on the auction website, describing the article for sale; setting a minimum bid (or reserve) price and timescale for the auction.

➡ Prospective buyers place bids (sometimes with a maximum limit to which a bid can be automatically incremented).

➡ At the end of the auction period, the highest bid above the reserve price wins.

There are now many auction sites and services. However, the paradigm site is **eBay.com** (with local variants such as **eBay.co.uk**). Founded by Pierre

Omiden in 1995 – after a conversation with his wife, an avid collector – this site supports a full-feature auction service. At the time of writing, eBay can be used to buy and sell items in more than 4,000 categories, ranging from collectibles and antiques, through to automobiles and computers. It offers a number of features to support personalization and build community. Indeed, the community aspects of eBay – which include a much-used feedback facility to allow people to record their views of buyers and sellers – is one of the prime reasons for eBay's popularity. Followers in the auction space have included Amazon, who invested $45 million in Sotheby's in June 1999 to create **sothebys.amazon.com** which trades in collectibles, art, and similar items.

Auction-like concepts are increasingly common in business-to-business applications in areas such as procurement, or disposal of excess inventory. A related and big concept is the notion of electronic online *exchanges*.

An interesting twist on the auctions concept is offered by **priceline.com**, which became very quickly established as a major internet brand after its creation in the late 1990s. **priceline.com** is centered round the "Name Your Own Price" internet pricing system. (The name is trademarked, and the concept is protected by patents.) Here consumers set their own discounted price and through aggregation of requests, priceline attempts to match the requested price. The main **priceline.com** site offers service in areas such as airline tickets and hotels.

Auction aggregators (business term)
A growing trend since 1999, where relevant companies search auction sites and multiple auctions with *crawlers* to find the best auctions for a particular item. As you might expect, such an approach has resulted in the odd lawsuit from auction sites protecting their own content.

AUP (business term)
See *Acceptable Use Policy.*

Authentication (security term)
The process of checking if someone is who they claim to be, usually before granting access to a particular service or system. A general computer security term, the most obvious authentication mechanism on the internet is the log-on dialog, which generally requires a user name and a password. The

name (often just the user's e-mail address) and password are first entered when a user registers on a website. Since this is a common feature of most e-commerce sites, and since there is little standardization, the internet is of course littered with forgotten passwords.

Author (web term)

In the context of the web, to author describes the task of creating content, often multimedia content.

Authorization (security term)

A general computer security term that describes the right of a user (or a program) to access a particular service or set of data.

Automagically (slang)

Refers to an application performing a function in a mysterious way. Essentially a technical variant of "act of magic."

Autonomy (company)

A European company, Autonomy was founded in 1996 by a Cambridge University Ph.D student named Michael Lynch. It was an offshoot of another company called Cambridge Neurodynamics. Autonomy offers infrastructure products focussed on automatically linking very large amounts of unstructured information sources (like e-mails) together, using a variety of pattern matching algorithms and probability theory approaches. Using text patterns, Autonomy calculates a probability that a document is about a specific topic – allowing, for example, links between documents to be automatically generated in real-time. As Autonomy are fond of saying, much of their approach is based on the statistical work of the Reverend Thomas Bayes from the 18th century.

Autonomy is headquartered in Cambridge, UK, and San Francisco, USA.

Auto responder (e-mail term)

A utility that generates an automated response, usually an acknowledgment of receipt or pre-scripted information, to an inbound e-mail.

Availability (technical term)

A general computing term that describes for how much of a given period a system is available for use. Most serious commercial systems are designed to be available 99.5 percent of the planned service hours (or higher). This is a major factor in building a robust e-commerce system. Users expect to be able to use internet sites when they want, often outside working hours. However, true 24 × 7 systems – meaning 24 hours availability, 7 days a week – can be difficult and expensive to build. Some major internet sites have tarnished their names by unexpected *downtime* (i.e. periods where the underlying website was not available).

AvantGo (company)
AvantGo provides software and services that allow browsing of web content on a mobile device such as a *Palm Pilot* or Windows-CE handheld system, or latterly *WAP*-enabled phones.

Avatar (technical term)
A picture or animated picture used to represent a user in virtual-reality-style environments, including some types of internet chat room.

B2B (business term)

B2B is a very well-known, almost-abbreviation for 'business-to-business', the "2" being a common shorthand for "to." This is a general term for e-commerce businesses that aim to support other types of business, rather than consumers (who are served by **B2C** solutions). B2B companies and services generate significant interest because of the scale of current business, and its future potential. For example, commentators such as IDC and eMarketer have predicted global transaction volumes growing from around $150–$200 billion in 2000 to over $1,000 billion in the next few years, which will probably represent around 80 percent of e-commerce revenues.

Although discussion at any one time tends to focus on fashionable niches (such as, in 1999/2000, *exchanges*) B2B is a loose term covering many types of service. An non-exhaustive list of examples include:

➤ **Exchanges:** support industry markets for many types of goods and services (see entry on *exchanges*); a very dynamic area with major interest from existing corporates.

➤ **Business trading communities:** normally targeted at vertical markets and industry sectors, these provide a mix of business-focussed content and services.

➡ **Application Service Providers(ASPs):** ASPs rent out software-based services. A natural play for owners of package software, ASPs should be attractive to small companies who cannot afford to buy their own equivalent dedicated system.

➡ **Trusted intermediaries:** provide fundamental services in a trusted manner – e.g. secure messaging, secure payments etc.

B2B initiatives span all scales of business. Some of the world's largest corporations are investing in exchange systems to reduce their procurement costs, and they bring tremendous potential liquidity to such markets. As another example, Cisco – itself one of the world's largest companies by share value – undertakes the majority of its trading over the internet. At the other end of the scale, online services are often targeted at *SMEs* or small to medium-sized enterprises – the rationale here being that small companies can benefit from services they could not afford individually. In fact, at this end of the market the B2B and B2C boundary becomes blurred.

B2B (slang)

With the decline in e-commerce company stock values in 2000, the migration of professionals from traditional corporates to dot-com companies started to reverse. So B2B was somewhat corrupted to stand for "back to banking" and B2C for "back to consulting"!

B2B exchange (business term)

See *exchange*.

B2C (business term)

Simple almost-abbreviation for business-to-consumer. Business-to-consumer websites are focussed on direct contact between a business and consumers.

B2C sites represented the first major wave of e-commerce business, and given their accessibility to ordinary members of the public, have generated a significant amount of media coverage. This coverage has ranged from the wild and wide-eyed in the glory days of e-commerce stock valuations, to something much more pessimistic and questioning after the collapse of B2C valuations in early 2000. Types of site include:

- **e-tailers:** selling goods to consumers in a style similar to an intelligent mail order catalog. Good examples include *Amazon*, *Webvan* and *eToys*, which made their names in books, groceries, and toys respectively, although Amazon's set of offerings is now much broader.

- **Auction or similar type of sites:** where price isn't pre-fixed but in some way negotiated. *eBay* is the prime example of an auction site, targeted to individual rather than business buyers.

- **Marketing-led sites:** where the aim is simply to promote an organization or its products. Almost any scale of company now has some kind of web-presence – which may or may not offer the ability to transact some kind of business. A good example of sites with a pure marketing purpose are those written for film releases, which offer information, trailers, and sometimes games. The *Blair Witch Project* generated some of its initial publicity through such a website.

- **Content plays:** where the digital content is the goods being offered – in the form of text, music or video. Income for the business here is often based on advertising and subscription – a business notoriously hard to make work. In fact, for entertainment providers, the internet has been described as a "zero-revenue" channel by the consultancy Jupiter. A few high-end publications (like the *Wall Street Journal*) still pursue a subscription model, however. Subscription is also being used for *MP3* audio content.

- **Consumer services:** includes examples such as *e-banking*, where either a pure internet bank or a traditional bank offer services over the internet.

- **Substitution of traditional third parties:** where a website offers services traditionally offered by a third party in a physical location. Good examples include share-trading normally done through brokers, and travel sites. The value proposition here is often the provision of much more choice and information to the end-user.

- **Portals and community sites:** providing a way of identifying and navigating to other sites in a particular area. Examples include general services like *Yahoo!* and more focussed sites like the US-based Thirdage, which caters for older people.

The B2C space is now crowded, and in the case of e-tailing still takes up only a fraction of overall retail activity, although penetration of some particular markets is much higher. Characteristics of successful B2C companies are often said to include:

⇒ Winning underlying business proposition (e.g. combination of discounting/high-service as with Amazon, addressing otherwise unmet needs as with eBay).

⇒ Early mover in relevant niche and a strong brand.

⇒ Building or accessing a natural community.

⇒ Good understanding of end-customers and their desires and behaviors.

⇒ Understanding the issues that go with fulfillment getting physical goods to customers.

At the time of writing, the goods most often sold through B2C sites include computers, software, books, CDs, videos, and DVDs. Popular services include certain types of financial services (share-trading) and travel. Sales of items that people like to touch and feel (e.g clothing) haven't worked nearly so well.

The B2C marketplace generated enormous levels of interest in the late 1990s, resulting in extraordinary valuations of B2C companies on stock markets around the globe, many new entrants, and a great deal of excitable media coverage. In 2000, something of a hangover descended on the sector after the initial party. Stock market valuations fell significantly – including the valuations of the most well-known players, such as Amazon – and other companies simply failed as their venture capital funding ran out. Reasons? The stock market was displaying its own natural cycle. Online purchasing in retail goods is significant, but still only a relatively small fraction of all retail activity. The market is crowded, with many me-too ideas. And many traditional organizations now offer their services over the internet (and sometimes other *channels* such as *digital television* or *mobile* telephones). A good European example is Tesco, a large UK supermarket chain, which is now one of the world's largest on-line grocers. All in all, B2C business models are now regarded with a huge amount of skepticism, and the market is characterized by a mix of delayed *IPOs*, mergers and acquisitions, and out-right failure.

B2C (slang)
In classic gallows-humor style, B2C is also used for "back to consulting" for those disillusioned with a move to the dot-com world. See also the second definition of *B2B*.

B2D (business term)
Stands for business-to-distributor, although this term is not often used. It represents a specific type of *B2B* site where a core business communicates with its own distribution network. It has also been used to stand for busi-ness-to-device in anticipation of a world of highly distributed access to services across a wide range of special devices (think of intelligent fridges or medicine cabinets that can automatically re-order).

B2E (business term)
Stands for business-to-employee. Not nearly as widely used as the phrases *B2C* and *B2B*, this term describes sites that aim to provide services to employ-ees, i.e. consumers who are at work. The business aim is to generate business for the site provider, and allow an employer to offer perks to its people.

Backbone (technical term)
General term for a network link, usually built for speed and throughput, that connects other networks together. In a large building or campus, individual *LANs* (Local Area Networks) are often connected with a fast, fiber-optic back-bone. In the context of the internet, the term covers members of a complex hierarchy of different major links that connect the millions of users, and many thousands of LANs, that make up the whole internet.

Bandwith (technical term)
Strictly speaking this should mean the range of frequencies that can be trans-mitted over a transmission media (e.g. a cable) and is measured in Hertz (Hz). However, it is commonly used to describe how much data can be trans-mitted over a network, often measured in some form of *bits* per second, e.g. *megabits* or *gigabits* per second. The term also has common currency as a

metaphor for intelligence or personal time as in "he doesn't have the bandwidth to handle this."

Banner, Banner ad (business term)

An advertisement on a website, typically a strip at the top of a page that links to the advertiser's own site, or an intermediate *buffer page* held on the original site. See also *advertising*.

BBS (technical term)

Stands for Bulletin Board Service. Something of an historical term, it was typically used to cover small-single online services set up by a specific community (often computer enthusiasts) and accessed via modems that dial up a *PC* set up for the purpose. Many such communities have migrated to the internet, and BBSs can be seen as part of the internet's cultural heritage.

Bcc (e-mail term)

Stands for blind carbon copy (or sometimes blind courtesy copy). Used to copy e-mails to others without the main or *cc* recipients knowing. To be used with tact.

BEA Systems (company)

Formed in 1995 by Bill Coleman, Ed Scott, and Alfred Chuang, and taking its name from their initials, BEA Systems is a leading provider of *middleware* products and e-commerce infrastructure products such as *application servers* and *Enterprise Java Bean* platforms. BEA has built its product set largely by acquiring the venerable *Tuxedo* transaction processing monitor from Novell, TopEnd from NCR and WebLogic from the vendor of the same name.

Bell Labs (organization)

Influential research organization that developed important platform technologies such as the *UNIX* operating system, and the *C* programming language.

Berkeley University (organization)

The University of California at Berkeley, like Stanford University, has been a major influence in the development of computing technologies in California, and is particularly famous for the *BSD* version of *UNIX*.

Berners-Lee, Tim

Tim Berners-Lee created the concept of the world wide web. Although similar concepts had been discussed since at least the 1940s, it was Berners-Lee who created and popularized the first successful architecture for connecting information and knowledge into a global web.

An Englishman, and graduate of Queen's College Oxford, Berners-Lee devised the underlying concepts behind the world wide web while based at *CERN*. He designed the first world wide web server "httpd" and the first browser called unsurprisingly "WorldWideWeb" in 1990–1. Through 1991 to 1993, he developed the fundamental architecture concepts of the web: *URIs/URLs*, *HTTP*, and *HTML*. After CERN, he joined MIT, and is also director of the World Wide Web Consortium (*W3C*) which focusses on developing new common standards for the web. Berners-Lee has written a very readable history of his experiences and ambitions for the web in his book *Weaving the Web*.

Beta (technical term)

Term used when software is ready for testing with real customers or users (after an internal *alpha* phase). So, *beta* software undergoes *beta* testing. It is very common practice among some major suppliers where trusted and friendly customers are given early versions of software.

Bezos, Jeff

Jeff Bezos, founder of *Amazon*, is one of the most well-known and publicized figures in e-commerce. Bezos co-founded Amazon in Seattle in 1994 after a Princeton education and a spell in roles that combined financial markets applications and technology. A driven, engaging, and playful personality, Bezos is, in many ways, the archetypical new-economy entrepreneur.

Big Blue (slang)

Common nickname for *IBM.*

Binary (technical term)

Refers to the base-2 number system used by computers internally, where 10 represents 2, 100 represents 4, and so on.

Since machine-readable information – like a program in executable form – is unintelligible to people, such data is often loosely described as being binary data. The term "binary" as a noun often refers to the machine-runnable version of a program.

BIND (internet term)

Stands for Berkley Internet Name Domain which includes an *open source* implementation of a name server – a piece of software which converts domain names (such as **www.amazon.com**) into Internet Protocol (*IP*) addresses (see entry on *DNS* for more details on this magical process). BIND is implemented on very many systems connected to the internet (including many ISPs) and represents an important part of the internet architecture. It is a good example of successful open source development. Unfortunately some sites continue to use older versions of the BIND software which contain a number of well-known security vulnerabilities. These have been fixed in later releases.

Bit (technical term)

A fundamental computing term, referring to the smallest unit of storage of information. A single bit can take only the values of 0 or 1, and from this the *binary* arithmetic at the heart of computing technology is built. So the binary number 10 represents the number 2 in 2 bits, the binary number 100 the number 4 and so on. Internally, computers store numbers or references to parts of memory as words that contain a series of bits. A computer with 32-bit words can therefore represent numbers up to 2^{32}, and one with 64-bit words up to 2^{64}. Larger word sizes mean greater information-processing capacity.

Bits are used as a measure of network capacity through some form of *bps* or bits-per-second. Example measures include Kbps (kilo-bps), Mbps (mega-bps), and Gbps (giga-bps)

Bitlegging (slang)

Stealing intellectual property and content from the internet.

Biz. newsgroups (internet term)

Usenet term for *newsgroups* that are part of the newsgroup hierarchy focussed on discussions related to business matters.

BizTalk (product)

Microsoft product designed to support the exchanging of data and documents between businesses (and within businesses) over the internet, with business user friendly tools. Part of a range of server-side products from Microsoft. Like many such products, supports the fashionable XML language.

Black hat, Black-hat hacker (slang)
Someone who attempts to break into, or disrupt, computer systems for illicit purposes. A white-hat hacker, on the other hand, does the same thing as part of a system's testing lifecycle.

Blind carbon copy (e-mail term)
See *bcc*.

Bloatware (slang)
Slang for software that takes up large amounts of a systems resource – typically memory.

Blowfish (security term)
Popular, unbroken, and free encryption algorithm devised by *Bruce Schneier* in the early 1990s.

Blue Martini (company name)
A company that supplies software and services to build e-commerce applications with a focus on customer management. Well-known toolset among those who build websites.

Bluetooth (technical term)
Bluetooth (named after a Danish king) is an emerging standard for replacing physical cables with radio links over short distances. It uses radio frequencies at the top of the UHF (Ultra High Frequency) range, occupying approximately 80MHz of radio spectrum at around 2.4GHz. To prevent interference with other devices operating at this frequency, Bluetooth broadcasts at comparatively low power levels that will not travel long distances, and so is designed not to compete with cellular telephone networks for wide-area mobile access.

A collection of up to eight bluetooth devices (seven slaves and one master) can work together to form a "piconet," which communicates at rates of approximately 1Mbps. Bluetooth only defines how raw data is carried over the wireless link and is able to carry other higher data level protocols such as *TCP/IP* or *WAP* (Wireless Application Protocol).

Typical uses might include:

➡ replacing serial cables between peripherals;

➡ supporting cordless telephony handsets;

➡ providing a connection between portable devices and a LAN (although Bluetooth is not itself a Wireless LAN protocol);

➡ replacing infrared for communications between handheld devices and PCs.

boo.com (website)

One of the most well-known European startups, and an unfortunate symbol of the nature of the internet business world at its riskiest. Founded by two young Swedes, **boo.com** was focussed on sports fashion retailing and had a distinguished set of backers who provided funding on an epic scale. It was one of the first well-funded B2C startups to fail. Analyses of why boo failed vary, but the organization tried to launch in 18 countries simultaneously, was delayed by its complex technology, and then did not generate sufficient cash flow to sustain itself. It folded in mid-2000.

As a footnote, it is worth saying that at the time of writing boo has been relaunched under new management, and with a stripped-down business model.

Bookmark (web term)

A simple method – provided as a feature of ***browsers*** – of recording a ***link*** to a specific ***site*** or ***page*** within a site so you can return later. This is done by simply clicking on the specific saved link which is stored as part of a list. ***Microsoft's Internet Explorer*** – a very common browser – calls bookmarks ***favorites***.

Borgware (slang)

Commercial software that requires other software products from the same company to work.

Bot (slang)

Short for ***robot***. It is a program that does a task in the background without needing user interaction. One class of internet bots – also called spiders – searches the web for keywords in web pages, and then create indexes for ***search engines***. ***Agent*** is an alternative term for bot.

Bounce (e-mail term, slang)

An e-mail that bounces is one that is returned because it could not be delivered. This can happen for a variety of reasons. For example, the destination address doesn't exist, the relevant server is unavailable, and so on.

Bozo (slang)

Term of abuse. A fool.

Bozo filter (slang)

Loose term for a feature provided in some *e-mail* and newsgroup readers to filter out messages from specified, and unloved, individuals.

Bps (technical term)

Bits per second. A measure of network speed. See the entry on *bit* for more detail.

Brand (business term)

Brand is important in most business contexts, and is seen as especially important for e-commerce businesses. This is because attracting visitors to a website is fundamental to both the actual success of a site, and its perception by investors and industry observers. The name of an e-business needs to be known to its potential users and associated with positive attributes.

A brand is a complex construct made up of several components:

- **Legal:** identifying symbols and words.
- **Perceptual:** a personality, image, and set of values in the minds of customers.
- **Economic:** brand is an intangible but valuable asset.

Brand in fact is sometimes given a concrete value. For example, Interbrand/Citibank valued, in July 2000, the brands of Coca-Cola and Microsoft at over $70 billion. The biggest internet brands were Yahoo! ($6.3 billion), AOL ($4.5 billion) and Amazon.com ($4.5 billion).

Bricks and mortar (business term)

A term that describes a traditional business that has physical assets, such as shops, depots or factories, as opposed to an online business that interfaces with its consumers electronically. Somewhat misleading, of course, since many e-tailing businesses will require some sort of warehouse space. The term *clicks and mortar* is used to describe businesses that use a mixture of traditional *channels* (such as stores) and online channels.

Bridge (technical term)
A networking device that connects two networks. Also see *router*.

Broadband (technical term)
Short for "broad bandwidth" and usually associated with a highspeed connection that may use several parallel channels. There are no hard and fast rules that determine when connections become "broad," and the term is widely abused in marketing materials.

Broadcast (technical term)
A data transmission sent to multiple users or devices. For the web, where text updates, audio, and video can be sent easily to multiple users, the term *webcast* is often used, particularly for audio and video.

Broadvision (company name)
Supplies technical products and services for building large-scale e-commerce/ internet businesses.

Brochure-ware (slang)
A website that does no significant processing but contains marketing content only.

Browser (web term)
The concept of a browser is a cornerstone of the underlying architecture of the world wide web. A browser is, in essence, a program designed to view a website's content and a navigation tool to move between content. Browsers are the way humans interact with the web.

Early browsers displayed plain text, but the use of the web really took off with the introduction of *Mosaic*, developed by *Marc Andreesen*, that could display graphics. The history of browsers is relatively complex, but the two most popular browsers today are *Microsoft Internet Explorer* and *Netscape Navigator*, which are both at least conceptual descendants of Mosaic.

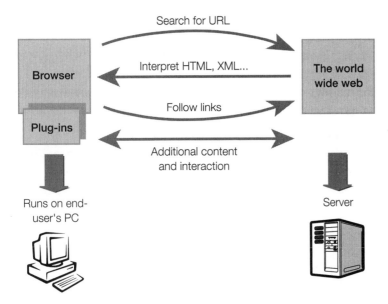

The functions of a browser

Modern browsers are very rich in function, and highly configurable, but the diagram above shows their bare-bones features.

The following explains these functions in more detail.

(1) Search for **URL** – the most basic feature. Given a URL (Universal Resource Locator), a browser will use the **Domain Name Service** to translate this into a numeric **IP address**, and then connect to the appropriate website. Browsers also provide straightforward access to **search engines** for retrieving data based on **keyword** searches.

(2) Once connected to a website, a browser then interprets and displays its content. Nowadays, a browser has to interpret a multitude of content formatting languages including:

➡ **HTML:** Hyper Text Make-Up Language, the original content language of the world wide web, which mixes text and formatting instructions.

➡ **XML:** eXtended Mark-Up Language, a more powerful descendant of HTML.

➡ **CSS:** cascading style sheets, a formatting standard that helps separate display and style instructions from content.

Modern browsers will also be able to run *Java Applets*, *JavaScript*, and other programming constructs.

(3) A key feature of the web – perhaps *the* key feature – is the *hyperlink* represented by convention with underlined text: **some reference**. Clicking on a hyperlink within a page displayed by a browser will take you to the indicated web page. This is what connects information together in a useful way.

(4) Browsers can typically also be extended through additional software modules called *plug-ins*. These are generally downloadable – often for free – over the internet itself. A plug-in will allow special data formats to be interpreted and displayed. Examples include plug-ins for desk-top publishing, and playing of video and audio clips.

New kinds of browsers are also appearing for use in mobile devices, television set-top boxes, or internet appliances, which may one day be more common than the computer-based browsers we are currently familiar with. Examples include:

➡ UP.Browser from *Phone.com* for mobile devices using *WAP* (Wireless Application Protocol);

➡ Fresco from ant.co.uk for use internet appliances such as the Bush internetTV;

➡ Device Mosaic from OpenTV for use in *digitial TV* set-top boxes.

BSD (technical term)

Stands for Berkeley Software Distribution and refers to a very influential version of the *UNIX* operating system developed at the University of California at Berkeley. Since BSD UNIX was strong on networking, being the first version of UNIX to support *TCP/IP*, many of the academic systems connected to the early internet were based on BSD UNIX.

BSP (business term)

Stands for Business Service Provider – a more general extension of the *Application Service Provider* or ASP concept which focusses on renting software solutions. A BSP instead will focus on providing both systems support, and *outsourcing* options for business processes. A BSP could, for example, out-source a company's HR system, but also provide people to undertake some the core HR administrative processes.

Bubble (business term)

A well-known, historical term that refers to a period of manic over-optimism and over-valuation of company shares, or similar. The original bubble was started when the South Sea company was founded by the Earl of Oxford in 1711 to exploit business opportunities in South America. An extremely popular stock, it made Exchange Alley and Cornhill in London impassable, given the vast numbers of people and carriages attracted to the associated rampant speculation. The success in raising funds this way inspired schemes based around perpetual motion, trading in hair, improving the art of making soap, extracting silver from lead and – famously – one scheme focussed on "a company for carrying an undertaking of great importance, but nobody to know what it is." Millions were invested, inevitably to be lost.

Many comparisons between the worlds of e-commerce and the South Sea Bubble, or earlier Dutch tulip mania, have been made – supported somewhat by the steep decline in valuations of some e-commerce and internet companies from April 2000 onwards.

Perhaps more fruitful comparisons can be made with those market shifts based on technological innovation. A good example of this is the British great railway mania of the 1840s. Another is the early development of the automobile industry. Such periods are typified by a profusion of start-ups, a great deal of speculation and failed investments, consequent failures, merger and acquisition activity, and eventual survival of a smaller number of very successful companies.

Buffer page (web term)

In web advertising, a *page* that is accessed via a *banner* and which is stored ("buffered") on the site on which the ad is running. Most banners will take you instead to another site. A buffer page allows for focussed messages and speed of response.

Bug (technical term)

Well-known technical term for an error in a computer program. It covers problems that are due to bad design (i.e. failing to complete a transaction because a user takes an unexpected navigation path) to more subtle problems caused by performance problems or incompatibility with versions of browsers. Given the focus on speed in the internet world, a surprising number of websites are produced that have obvious bugs.

Bulletin board (technical term)

Used interchangeably, if inexactly, with *BBS*. See *BBS*.

Burn rate (business term)

In the context of *dot-com* startups, generally refers to how fast the funds obtained to start the business – usually from outside sources such as *venture capitalists* – are being spent. Too high a burn rate, relative to revenues, is not good news, and many dot-com companies have failed when their external funding ran out.

Bush, Vannevar

If you research the history of IT and the web, you will soon come across the name of Vannevar Bush. Bush was a scientist who invented the Differential Analyzer in 1931: a machine that could mechanically solve differential equations. Perhaps more well known these days is his unrealized concept for a device called the Memex, which is seen by many as a conceptual ancestor for both the PC and the world wide web.

With the Memex, Bush was searching for a technical solution to managing knowledge and information. While some of his concepts date to the 1930s, it was a 1945 article by Bush called "As We May Think" (published in *Atlantic Monthly*) which is best remembered today. The Memex was to consist of a workdesk with viewing screens for microfilm, a keyboard, and other control devices. The Memex would allow users to build associative trails, analogous to the processes of the human mind, and similar to the linking ideas in *hypertext.* In 1959, Bush proposed Memex II, which was intended to use magnetic tape for the storage of data, and storage of sound.

Business angel (business term)
A very early-stage private investor in a dot-com startup. The word *angel* is sometimes used on its own for the same purpose.

Business archangel (business term)
A business angel with significant funds and/or a degree of industry fame and recognition.

Business-to-business (business term)
See *B2B*.

Business-to-consumer (business term)
See *B2C*.

Business-to-distributor (business term)
See *B2D*.

Business-to-employer (business term)
See *B2E*.

Business model (business term)
A general business term which will normally cover the essence of a particular business – its core value proposition, what it sells, how it sells it, and how it makes money. The e-commerce world is interesting because it is hard to predict which business models will work, and which won't. For example, some early online businesses were based on the notion of interesting content with revenues generated by a mix of advertising and subscription. This is very hard to make work, and almost all web content is now free. On the other hand, the auction site *eBay* filled a niche that few would have predicted as being worthwhile.

Business-web (business term)
See *b-web*.

Button (technical term)
Button-shaped graphic on websites (and many other types of program) that

can be activated with a mouse click. Generally, it launches some type of processing within the program or site.

Buyer-driven (business term)

In a traditional business-to-consumer transaction, the seller is often in control, setting the basic parameters of the transaction, especially price. A buyer-driven business model is where the authority resides with the purchaser. Whatever doubts one might have, the internet does offer a medium where such business models can be trialled, and interesting experiments have included **priceline.com** and **letsbuyit.com**, where purchasers can influence price.

In the *B2B* world, of course, many companies already have enormous power as purchasers given their scale, and many B2B *exchanges* are formed around consortiums of similar companies on the demand, rather than the supply side.

B-web (business term)

A term introduced by Dan Tapscott to cover communities and alliances of content providers, suppliers, distributors, and infrastructure providers that are brought together to service some particular business purpose. The equivalent terms "economic network" or "economic value network" are in more common use.

Byte (technical term)

A fundamental computing term that refers to a unit of storage of information that is 8-*bits* long, and can therefore represent numbers from 0 to 255. This is enough to hold the numeric coding for the *ASCII* character set that forms the basis of, for example, most e-mails.

Bytes are most commonly used to measure available memory size or disk space – usually with a multiple of kilo-, mega-, or giga-.

Bytecode (technical term)

In the context of *Java*, refers to the compiled form of a Java *applet* or program that isn't readable by people, but which can be executed by a *Java Virtual Machine* or JVM.

C (technical term)

Name for a programming language originated by Dennis Ritche at *Bell Labs* alongside the development of the *UNIX* operating system, and popularized in the 1970s and 1980s.

It is hard to overstate the importance of C. It gained incredible popularity, is almost universally understood by generations of technologists, and has been widely used for application development and systems programming. The many variants of the UNIX operating system – widely prevalent on the internet – are written in C.

The reasons for C's influence include:

➡ The popularity of UNIX among first academics and technicians, then commercial systems developers and end user organizations. C is the systems programming language of choice for UNIX.

➡ True portability between PCs, servers and other types of machine – easy to take for granted in the era of *Java*; C was one of the first real successes in this area.

➡ Simple structure, combined with real power.

C has a daughter called *C++* which is much more complex and supports object orientation. *Java* has similarities to both.

C++ (technical term)

A version of *C* designed to support *object-orientation*, which was developed in the 1980s at *Bell Labs* by Bjorne Stronestrup. Influential and much used, C++ is a complex language that requires real expertise to use properly. It is used for complex server processing in some e-commerce applications.

C# (technical term)

Pronounced C sharp, this is a derivative of the *C* programming language developed by Microsoft, possibly to be positioned as a competitor to *Java*, and part of Microsoft's .NET initiative.

C2B (business term)

Stands for consumer-to-business. Not often used, but does describe a particular type of site where consumers drive transactions with businesses. The best example is probably **priceline.com** where consumers set an acceptable price for a good or service, which is aggregated with the needs of other consumers in a kind of reverse bidding process with potential suppliers.

C2C (business term)

Stands for consumer-to-consumer, a term sometimes used for websites that put consumers in contact with other consumers. The *auction* site *eBay* is one example.

Cable (technical term)

Has a variety of meanings, including the basic shielded wiring used in all computer systems. From an e-commerce perspective, it is most often used as a shorthand reference to cable television systems that can support high levels of network bandwith. Increasingly, cable operators are using their infrastructure – in conjunction with specialized hardware (set-top boxes) – to offer *digital TV (DTV)* and interactive internet services.

Cable modem (technical)

Cable modems are *modems* (a network device that imposes a digital signal over an analog line) designed specifically to work with the coaxial TV cable, which anchors a home to a cable television network. Their advantage over conventional modems connected to copper telephone lines is much higher speed.

Cache (technical term)

A general IT term that covers use of main system memory in a computer (which has high access speeds) to store commonly used data that would otherwise be referenced much more slowly over a network or from disk. This is a technique used in many internet components, including *browsers*.

Café Babe (technical term)

All compiled Java class files start with the unique "magic number" 3405691582. In hexadecimal (a numbering system used by the deeply technical) the representation of 3405691582 is CAFEBABE. In a posting to the Usenet newsgroup **comp.lang.java**, one of the original members of the team that created Java wrote:

Strangely enough the magic number for class files was chosen long before the name Java was ever uttered in reference to this language. We were looking for something fun, unique and easy to remember … It is only a coincidence that the oblique reference to the cute barristas at Peet's Coffee was foreshadowing for the name Java.

Caldera (company name)

One of a number of companies (like Red Hat Software and VA Linux) that specialize in supplying and supporting *Linux* software. Linux is an *open source* version of the *UNIX* operating system, which has become very popular among web developers and other types of computer user.

Call center (business term)

A call center is a group of people that serves a defined business purpose using telephones – such as processing customer enquiries and sales – with dedicated resources, typically supported by purpose-built IT systems. Many types of business now offer a mix of call-center and online services. Creating *multi-channel* systems that properly support online, e-mail, and telephone processes can be complex, and this complexity drives a growing group of software suppliers who specialize in multi-channel architecture.

Cannibalize (business term)

Used when a new initiative (an online sales service, for example) threatens to take work and value away from another component of the same business (an existing sales force). This situation often presents a dilemma for established businesses, when faced with investing in a new area at the expense of their traditional business model.

Carbon copy (e-mail term)

Often referred to as cc. E-mail systems will copy *e-mails* to those on a cc list in a way that's visible for the main recipients. *Blind carbon copies* will be copied invisibly to their intended recipients, without others knowing.

Carpet bomb (slang)

An alternative term to spamming. See the entry on *spam*.

Cascading style sheet (web term)

A powerful addition to *HTML* and *XML*, developed by the *World Wide Web Consortium* (W3C). Style sheets – expressed in an HTML-like syntax – allow typographic styles, spacing and similar instructions to be specified separately from the main content. This allows:

➡ greater control over the look of web pages;

➡ separation of style and structure;

➡ easier maintenance where a big site's overall style sheet can be changed quickly to create a new look.

Why "cascading"? The CSS standard contains rules for what happens when rules in different sheets have a contradictory meaning for a single text element. Usually, element-specific rules over-ride general rules.

To imagine how CSS could be used, imagine a single stream of report data – in XML format – being displayed dynamically in different layouts achieved by simple adjustments to a style sheet.

Case, Steve

Well-known chairman and CEO of *America OnLine* (AOL), with a strong con-sumer-focussed background from Procter and Gamble and Pizza Hut, who has been instrumental in turning America OnLine into one of the few internet mega-brands.

Category descriptor (web term)

A domain name that clearly identifies the business category in which it operates, e.g. a word with "pets" in the name. This helps to identify the nature of the business. However, it also runs the risk of becoming indistinguishable from the hundreds of other sites also with "pets" in their name.

Cc (e-mail term)

See *carbon copy*.

CCITT (organization)

Stands for Comité Consultatif International Télégraphique et Telephonique. Old name for what is now the *ITU* (International Telecommunication Union). It controls major pre-internet networking standards such as *X.25*.

Cerf, Vinton

Major figure in development of the *internet* (through the *ARPANET* project), and co-developer of the *TCP/IP* family of network protocols with *Bob Kahn* in the early 1970s. Seen as one of the technology founding fathers of the internet. With Kahn, he was awarded the US National Medal of Technology by President Clinton in 1997. Currently he works for WorldCom and sits on the Board of *ICANN*.

CERN (organization)

Stands for Conseil Européen pour la Recherche Nucléaire. Based in Geneva, and mainly a place where physicists smash fundamental particles together. It is also where *Tim Berners-Lee* created the *world wide web*.

CERT (organization)

Stands for Computer Emergency Response Team. CERT is a US government funded organization to co-ordinate the reporting of internet security problems, specifically vulnerabilities (e.g. bugs in software products that may compromise security), current malicious activity and countermeasures which are reported through "advisory" postings on its website (**www.cert.org**).

Certificate (security term)

A certificate (or digital certificate) is an electronic *public key* for a specific encryption algorithm combined with an electronic signature of a trusted third party. In simple terms, it is a mechanism to allow data to be securely encrypted in a public arena like the internet. Online businesses often acquire such certificates to allow them to use public encryption algorithms in dealing with customers. This technique is at the heart of the popular *SSL* (Secure Sockets Layer) standard. SSL is much used in e-commerce when details like credit card numbers are processed.

Certification authority (security term)

A certification authority is an organization that electronically issues *public keys* for public key encryption algorithms, with an electronic signature to ensure authenticity. *Verisign* is one well-known such certification authority.

CESG (organization)

Stands for Communications/Electronics Security Group, part of the UK Government Communications HQ at Cheltenham. Provides recommendations on the use of electronic cryptography in the UK. See its website **www.cesg.org** for more information.

CGI (technical term)

Stands for Common Gateway Interface. Simple standard method of getting a webserver to call another program that does something useful, and then returns results for eventual display on the end-user's browser. A way of creating dynamic content and using programs written with a variety of languages and technologies.

Chambers, John

At the time of writing, president and CEO of *Cisco* – the internet world's premier supplier of networking equipment – with prior experience at IBM and Wang. Said to have a strong set of business ideals that underpin the Cisco machine and focus on customer service, strong recruitment policies and willingness to adopt the successes of other technology companies.

Channel (web term, technical term)

A term that is used often, which has multiple meanings. For example, some websites use it for describing groupings of content and links. In the context of customer-facing organizations, "channel" often refers to a mode of interacting with customers. Standard channel types include phone/call centers, normal mail, e-mail, websites, WAP phones, and so on. For many kinds of business, channel proliferation is a real issue and the holy grail is to produce a multi-channel business and technical architecture that can handle information presentation and consistent business process control across multiple channels.

Chat (internet term)

Real-time conversation between users of a system or network through typed messages. On the internet, it is often implemented via a program called *IRC*.

Chat room (internet term)

Informal term for the electronic forum or channel through which chat-type conversations take place.

Check box (technical term)

A graphic control or element found on many websites that allows options to be selected from a list using a mouse.

Churn (business term)

The rate of change in the user or subscriber base of a website (or indeed any business). Many users of online services are fickle and will leave if tempted by better offers. For this reason, website providers strive to create "sticky" websites and build a sense of *community* to reduce churn.

CIDR (internet term)

Stands for Classless Inter-Domain Routing. CIDR is a replacement for the original concept of address classes for the Internet Protocol (*IP*) and was introduced to help meet the enormous demand for IP addresses caused by the popularity of the web and also the increased complexity of managing the routing information that binds the internet together. The original class A, B, and C address system allocated 8, 16, or 24 bits of the 32-bit *IP address* to identify uniquely the network to which a computer was attached. CIDR can identify variable-length network IDs using 13 to 27 bits and therefore offers much greater flexibility. (To understand this entry fully, see the entry on IP addresses.)

With the standard approach, organizations that were allocated an old-style class-B network address seldom used all 65,000 possible host IP addresses, effectively "wasting" the unused addresses. Similarly every class-C network needed to be known about by routers in the internet backbone, even if several thousand of these "networks" were in fact allocated to the same organization. CIDR breaks this "lumpiness" and allows multiple old class-C addresses to be aggregated and single class-B addresses to be broken up and distributed to different organizations. CIDR is something of a stop-gap until IP version 6 (see *Ipng*) is implemented, and although an elegant solution to the problem of allocating IP addresses, coexistence with the older class-A, B and C addresses has increased the complexity of managing IP addressing.

The written format of CIDR addresses is a standard IP address followed by a forward slash (/) and a number between 13 and 27 which represents which portion of the address represents the network. For example, 158.152.0.0/16 means that the first 16 bits of the address represent the network and the remainder are for hosts on that network, e.g. any IP address in the range 158.152.0.0–158.152.255.255 belongs to this network (which happens to be the company Demon internet). By comparison 158.152.0.0/27 would limit the address range to just 32 addresses (158.152.0.0–158.152.0.31), hypothetically allowing some other network to use the 158.152.0.32/27 range (158.152.0.32–158.152.0.63).

The table shows how the scheme works:

/n	Number of equivalent class-A,B,C networks	Approx. number of host addresses
/27	1/8th of a class C	30 hosts
/24	1 class C	~250 hosts
/19	32 class C, 1/8th of a class B	~800 hosts
/16	256 class C, 1 class B	~65,000 hosts
/13	8 class B, 1/32nd of a class A	~524,000 hosts

Cisco (company)

It has been said that in the American gold-rush, most money was made by supplying products, services and entertainment to prospectors, rather than by prospecting itself. The e-commerce equivalent of this is the supply of infrastructure products and services, and in many ways Cisco is the internet infrastructure supplier par excellence.

Founded in 1984 out of Stanford University, Cisco shipped its first product in 1986. It provides many of the networking products that make up individual networks within the internet, including *routers*, LAN and WAN switches, bridges and associated software (in other words, the fundamental network plumbing). Like Microsoft, Intel, Sun and Oracle, Cisco is one of those technology companies that dominates and defines its market. Around 80 percent of internet routers – a fundamental component of the internet – are supplied by Cisco. Part of Cisco's own vision is the idea of a modern enterprise as a "Global Networked Business" supported by networking technology. Cisco certainly lives up to this concept itself, with most Cisco products being ordered over the web.

Cisco revenues have grown from $69 million in 1990 to not much less than $20 billion in 1999. Even more impressive has been its extraordinary valuation in stock-market terms, which made Cisco one of the world's largest companies by market capitalization. As a result, Cisco has used its own stock as currency to support a wide range of acquisitions. However, even Cisco has been hit by the downturn of 2000 and 2001.

Clark, Jim

Archetypal Silicon Valley entrepreneur, who was instrumental in the creation of Silicon Graphics and Netscape. Subject of a book, *The New New Thing*, by Michael Lewis.

Class (technical term)

The word "class" has a specific meaning in the context of developing software using *objects*. A class is the code a programmer writes to define the contents of an object in terms of necessary data and the basic functions or methods used to process that data. When an object is created in memory, the class definition is used as a kind of template. One of the benefits of an object approach is the ability to reuse common classes for routine functions such as user interaction. Libraries (or frameworks) of reusable classes are becoming common. They are an important part of the *Java* language (and hence the e-commerce world).

Click (business term, web term)

A term originating simply from the action of depressing ("clicking") a mouse button. It is used as a general term signifying the act of interacting with a website – and so finds its way into general, slangy terms such as *clicks and mortar*, company names, or trademarked service names such as Amazon's one-click. In web advertising, it can be used as a shortened version of *click-through* which describes when a *banner* ad is used – i.e. clicked – by an end-user.

Click-rate (business term)

In web advertising, the percentage of impressions or views of a *banner* that result in a *click-through* by the end-user. When banner advertising started in the mid-1990s, click rates of around 10 percent were sometimes seen, but now this has dropped to an average level of fractions of 1 percent. Some-times also referred to as click-through rate or CTR.

Click-stream (web term)

The navigation path of a user through a given set of web pages. Some sites record click-streams for analyzing usage patterns.

Click-through (business term)

Describes the act of clicking on a *banner*, or similar, web advertisement. Sometimes a click-through is just called a plain *click*.

Click-through rate (business term)

See *click-rate*, which means the same.

Clicks and mortar (business term)

The term *bricks and mortar* is used to describe traditional businesses that need physical presence – particularly stores or branches. The derivative "clicks and mortar" covers businesses that use both physical assets such as stores, and online interfaces. Currently, clicks-and-mortar businesses are seen as generally more viable than many online "pure plays."

Client (technical term)

A "client" is typically shorthand for a client program (or piece of hardware on which client software runs) which accesses a server process. In the context of the internet and world wide web, the client hardware is usually a user's *PC* and client software a variety of *browser*, but could cover a micro-browser embedded in a mobile telephone or a set-top box connected to a *digital tv* network.

Client–server (technical term)

A technical term of some vintage which describes a type of *distributed system* where a "client" program requests services from a "server" program. The server program typically runs on dedicated equipment, serving multiple clients. The internet and the web applications that sit on top are very much based on this concept. When a *browser* accesses a website, a piece of *webserver* software will typically generate a stream of data (in, for example, *HTML*) which the browser interprets and displays. For serious e-commerce sites, there are usually other server processes and hardware behind the scenes to handle database access, financial transactions and the like.

CMGI (company name)

CMGI was actually founded in 1968 as College Marketing Group but evolved into one of the new types of company found in the e-economy. Describing itself as a "leading global internet operating company," the organization focusses on investing in, developing, and managing companies that are aimed to take roles in a broad business network. One of the more well-known brands in the network is *AltaVista*; other companies specialize in fulfillment, infrastructure, marketing, and professional internet services.

CNET (company)

Runs a well-known and popular website (with millions of hits each day) at **www.cnet.com** that covers content on technology, computers and the internet. Responsible for a number of other services, including the also-popular *ZDNet*.

Cobweb site (slang)

A *website* that has not been changed for a long period.

ColdFusion (product)

ColdFusion is a well-known software developer's toolkit to support the construction of websites made by a company called Allaire. It allows developers to build a content database where the contents can be extracted dynamically and displayed to users, and eliminates the need to write raw *HTML*.

COM (technical term)

An abbreviation with a variety of technical meanings. Here it stands for Common Object Model, a Microsoft specification of its own model for connecting software components on *Windows* platforms. One version of the specification – called DCOM, for Distributed COM – allows distribution of components across a network. COM is the foundation underneath Microsoft's *Active-X* framework.

Commerce One (company name)

Well-known supplier of products and services for the construction of B2B (business-to-business) solutions. Strong in the online exchange marketplace.

Common Object Model (technical term)

See *COM*.

Community (business term, web term)

Humans, some would argue, are the most social of animals. It is certainly clear that online communities are one of the most natural consequences of internet-like technologies. From the earliest days of *ARPANET* (the ancestor network of the internet), the most distinctive use of the new networked service was to support e-mail. When the web was then conceived, it was initially seen as a way of linking knowledge, but with the graphic features of *Mosaic*, it soon became a way of linking people as the first personal home pages were developed. In parallel with these developments, many computer enthusiasts joined a *BBS*-style community. And as the internet developed, one natural focus of community was *Usenet* – a vast, distributed discussion group system that supports many types of community. Usenet has more than 30,000 discussion groups at the time of writing. Another early influential online community was the WELL, or Whole Earth 'lectronic Link.

Community building is now seen as a fundamental part of constructing a successful website. With business sites, the aim is firmly to attract the maximum number of visitors and return visitors. Examples of businesses at least partly built around the idea of community include the online *auction* site *eBay*, which encourages active buyer and seller participation, and Geocities, which organizes itself into virtual neighborhoods and provides a broad range of facilities to encourage community behavior. These include free tools for the construction of personal home pages.

Compaq (company name)

Compaq, or more formally, Compaq Computer Corporation, is one of the major names in computer hardware supply. It was founded in Houston, Texas, in February 1982. The first product – a portable, if heavy PC – was launched in late 1982. Initially focussed on business PCs, Compaq manufactured its one-millionth PC in 1987 and achieved sales of US$1.2 billion. In 1993, Compaq entered the consumer marketplace with a range of home computers: Compaq Presario PCs. Early in 1995, Compaq reached its stated goal – obtaining the number-one slot in worldwide PC market share. Very much known for its PC workstation and server products, Compaq spent much of the late 1990s on a sometimes tough journey to become "a world leader in the manufacture of servers, workstations, networking products, desktop PCs, and portable PCs." Among highlights of this process were the takeovers of Tandem – a supplier of fault-tolerant hardware – and the once-mighty *DEC*. Although Compaq wouldn't be the first hardware supplier many would think of in terms of the e-commerce revolution, it remains a very large and important manufacturer.

Comp. newsgroups (internet term)

In *Usenet*, newsgroups whose names start with `comp.` focus on all aspects of computing.

Component (technical term)

The term component is often used loosely to represent any element of a computer system. However, in software development, component can have a much more specific meaning. Although exact definitions vary, a software component is an encapsulated piece of business or technical functionality that can be reused without detailed knowledge of its implementation.

Components are a step towards allowing new applications to be assembled by "clipping together" standard bits of functionality rather than writing custom code. Similar in meaning to *object*, although a higher level concept.

Compression (technical term)

Bandwidth is precious, and it pays to reduce or compress the amount of data to be transmitted. This works because most text or graphics data streams contain repeating data (e.g. spaces or blocks of color). One technique is to use a program to compress (or *zip*) file attachments. Certain networking protocols also have the ability to compress data. In these cases, the compression algorithm is "lossless" and no information is lost. Standards like *MPEG* allow for compression of video and audio by throwing away information that is normally invisible or inaudible to the user, although if done too aggressively the image or sound quality will suffer.

CompuServe (company name)

Actually founded in 1969 as a computer time-sharing service and based in Columbus, Ohio, CompuServe was one of the earliest commercial pioneers in the online service industry. In 1979, CompuServe became the first such service to offer e-mail capabilities and technical support to personal computer users. Shortly afterwards it introduced real time "chat." Its consumer services anticipated what the internet would offer considerably later.

Still a major and well-known high-end brand, CompuServe has been a wholly-owned subsidiary of *America OnLine* since early 1998, targetted at what the CompuServe website calls "adults seeking a reliable tool for business and personal reference."

Confidentiality (security term)

A general computer security term which simply means that transmitted information is kept secure through, for example, *encryption*.

Console (technical term)

Sometimes used to denote the master, controlling terminal attached to a multi-user computer system. More popularly used these days to cover a *games console* – such as the Nintendo N64 or Sony Playstation. Some of the emerging generation of games console – such as the Playstation 2 – are powerful computer systems in their own right and can offer networking functions, including internet access.

Consumer-to-consumer (business term)
See *C2C.*

Content (web term)
The information, in its broadest sense, provided by websites and other types of online service. Content can consist of formatted text, graphics, full motion video, audio – in fact all forms of multimedia delight. The use of the term dates from a period where the types of business supplied by e-commerce were seen to fall into two natural categories: infrastructure providers (e.g. ISPs) and content providers. Content is obviously fundamental, as recognized in the well-worn phrase "content is king." However, what has proved hard is to build a sustainable business model for "content-only plays." Most information on the web is free and it is notoriously hard to persuade users to subscribe to online periodicals, although some with more of an elite focus (e.g. the *Wall Street Journal*) do rely on subscriptions. And because of current technology limitations, the use of the internet as an alternate channel for mainstream entertainment content still remains a novelty.

Content management system (web term)
A system and set of tools used to manage the content of a website, rather than relying on a set of raw *HTML* pages. This type of toolset is good for complex, dynamic websites and also websites where content is being authored by people without a technical background. A content management system provides tools to create and manage a database of content, possibly in a variety of different formats, and tools to display that content dynamically over the web. It will usually provide features to standardize look and feel, manage changes, maintain a history of revisions, and provide configuration management for multiple authors. *Vignette* is one well-known product with content management features.

Convergence (technical term)
Covers the coming together of different types of technology. For example:

➡ Voice and data can both be transmitted over common telecoms infrastructure.

➡ Computers can now display – bandwidth allowing – streamed video.

➡ *WAP*, *iMode* and other types of mobile access allow phones, Personal Digital Assistants (*PDA*s) and other devices to access the internet.

➡ Television is going digital. More to the point, the first interactive services are being provided to satellite and cable users.

The serious commercial question raised by convergence is which of the equipment manufacturers, service providers and software companies will own the end-user in the future.

Cookie (web term)

Simple websites have no "memory" of a user's interaction with them. Any "hit" on a site to download a page is completely independent of any other. A cookie is a special file created on a PC by some websites, which allows the site to store information that may be useful next time the user visits (for instance simple information about who the user is). Technically this kind of information is known as "state" and the official name for cookies is the HTTP State Management System (specified in the internet specification document *RFC* 2109).

This can be a great convenience, but it can also represent a potential invasion of privacy (with cookies providing a record of the sites you have visited) or a potential security risk if important information has been stored within the cookie.

The location where cookies are stored will vary depending on the operating system of the client machine being used, but with Microsoft Windows versions you should be able to find them in the directory **C:\Windows\ Cookies** – you may be surprised at quite how many there are!

In theory your browser will only present cookies to a webserver if:

➡ the site created them in the first place;

➡ the site was specified when the cookie was created.

However, cookies are simple text files and are visible to any application or user of your PC.

Copyleft (slang)

Sardonic play on "copyright", originated by *Richard Stallman* and associated with the *General Public License* found in software such as GNU *EMACS* as distributed by the Free Software Foundation. Such a license grants reuse and reproduction rights to any user, and supports the notion held by some that software should be essentially free.

Copyright (business term)

Having copyright in some form of intellectual property means you have the right to control and get economic benefit from its duplication and distribution. In most countries the originator (you, or more likely the organization you work for) has copyright automatically in a work as soon as it is fixed in a tangible medium (which usually includes electronic media).

Given the nature of electronic data, which can be copied with trivial effort, computers have always caused trouble. In the area of copyright and intellectual property they can cause trouble squared or cubed. Commercial organizations want to protect their rights to works they own. This isn't a view universally shared, of course, and the internet has a multitude of sites where copyrighted data can be obtained without payment. Specific areas where copyright problems occur include:

- ➡ *warez*: slang for bootleg copies of software products which are posted on to the internet.
- ➡ *MP3*: an MPEG standard for audio which allows near-CD quality music tracks to be shipped across the internet in highly compressed form

Some of these issues came to a head with *Napster.* Napster doesn't offer MP3 files directly, but it does allow users to swap MP3 files easily – and many of the files swapped are copies of tracks by major music artists. As a result Napster has been at the center of a fierce legal battle triggered by the band Metallica and the major record companies.

CORBA (technical term)

Stands for Common Object Request Broker Architecture. A specification from the *OMG* (Object Management Group) dating from 1992 onwards to allow *objects* to communicate and interact in distributed environments.

Objects are a modern way of building systems using potentially reusable components. An important technical standard, which has influenced much of the *middleware* used in building e-commerce solutions.

Core dump (technical term)

An ancient computing term, dating to the days when computers had metallic cores for memory. When a computer crashed, an image of what was in memory (the core) was saved (dumped) for *debugging*. The term was perpetuated in the *UNIX* operating system and the technique is used by programmers when a program crashes with a catastrophic error.

Cornea gumbo (slang)

A badly designed web page, or user interface. Synonymous with *angry fruit salad*.

Cost per mille (business term)

See *CPM*.

Counter (web term)

A graphical object on a web page that counts the number of times the page has been visited. Favored by writers of personal websites.

CPM (business term)

Used in web advertising, CPM stands for cost per mille – and refers to the cost of buying *banner*-style advertising per 1,000 views (To those of a certain age, also irrelevantly refers to an early PC-type operating system.)

CPU (technical term)

Stands for central processing unit – a term from the beginnings of computing. A CPU is the part of a computer that executes instructions derived from a software program. These days CPUs are microprocessors or "chips." For example, Intel's Pentium processor powers most current personal computers, acting as the CPU.

Crack (security term, slang)

A slang(ish) term describing the act of gaining unauthorized access to a system, or breaking a particular *encryption* scheme.

Cracker (security term, slang) ·
Someone who breaks into systems – often illegally. In the media, the term *hacker* is used synonymously, although some people who call themselves hackers, and see themselves as part of a positive technical sub-culture, object to the confusion.

Crawler (web term)
A type of bot, or robot, that reads through many websites classifying content for the index of a *search engine*. Sometimes also called a spider.

CRM (business term)
See *Customer Relationship Management*.

Cryptography (security term)
Covers the use (and study) of *encryption* to protect information.

CSS (web term)
See *cascading style sheets*.

CTR (business term)
Short for *click-through rate*. See the equivalent *click-rate* for full explanation.

Cuckoo egg (slang)
Has been used to describe an unexpected and unpleasant surprise in a computer system, and *The Cuckoo's Egg* is the title of a well-known book on computer security by Clifford Stoll. More recently the term describes an *MP3* audio file that has maybe 30 seconds of the original song followed by white noise, cuckoo clock noises, or unexpected messages. It is designed explicitly to waste the time of those who download illicit copies of music files using websites such as *Napster*. It reflects a movement started by a professional musician who does not like the original Napster model, which allows the sharing of near-CD quality music tracks without royalties.

Custom domain name (web term)
A domain name where customers would intuitively expect to find your personal or corporate presence, without having to resort to a search engine. For example, you would expect to find IBM at **ibm.com**. Organizations that don't move fast enough to register all relevant custom domain names may find

them taken by other legitimate businesses or *cybersquatters*. For example, **bigblue.com** does not belong to IBM.

Customer-centric (business term)

Linked to the ideas in *Customer Relationship Management* or CRM – customer-centric describes a mode of business where maximum focus is given to end-customers and their perception of the services they receive. Given the importance of attracting customers and, above all, return visits to *B2C* sites, most B2C companies would claim to be customer-centric.

Customer Relationship Management (business term)

A set of business practices and models that focusses on understanding, attracting, developing, and retaining customers of any enterprise. From CRM comes such simple but fundamental insights as the notion that the majority of disgruntled customers don't complain – they just go elsewhere. CRM and e-commerce are linked in obvious ways. The focus of any successful *B2C* business must be the experience of the "C" in CRM. The internet is also increasingly a major channel for customer servicing for any modern business.

CRM has become a major theme for many businesses that deal with customers on a large scale – and certainly not just e-businesses. At its broadest, it covers customer-centric business strategies, culture and business processes designed around efficient, high-quality and consistent handling of customers. It can span marketing, sales, servicing customers after they have purchased something and the multiple channels that customers can use to contact an organization (personal contact, mail, e-mail, the web, call centers and more). From a technology perspective it touches on usability design, management of multiple channels and content, automating work flows and gathering and using information about customers. Use of technology is a key part of many CRM initiatives and there is a growing market in CRM software products, services and spin-off sales of hardware (since data collection and analysis can result in large databases).

Cutler, Dave

Architect of two of the IT industry's most influential computer operating systems:

➡ VMS for the DEC VAX minicomputers (a ground-breaking system in its day);

➡ Microsoft Windows NT.

Cyber- (slang)
Once upon a time, cybernetics was a simple, respectable term for the study of control systems. Cyber- was later adopted through terms such as *cyberpunk* and *cyberspace*, to describe a fashionable 1980s sub-genre of science fiction. Now (with *e-*, *online*, and *i-*) it acts as a prefix to common words to indicate they are being used in an online or computer-based context.

Cybercafé (slang)
Either a physical café with internet access, or a virtual, online gathering place.

Cybercash (slang)
Describes various terms of electronic money. Not often used.

Cyberchat (slang)
An alternative term for *IRC*, and other online chat mechanisms.

Cyberchondria (slang)
Covers misdiagnosis of one's personal symptoms through use of online medical resources.

Cybercitizen (slang)
Means the same as *netizen* although it is seen much less often. Describes someone who uses the internet or similar on a frequent basis.

Cybercop (slang)
Someone who investigates *cybercrime*.

Cybercrime (slang)
Crime committed electronically (and a big topic in itself).

Cyberculture (slang)
The culture of the online world.

Cybernaut (slang)

Someone who spends time – probably a great deal of time – online.

Cyberphobia (slang)

A term used by some psychotherapists to describe an irrational fear of computers.

Cyberpunk (slang)

The science fiction sub-genre typified by the works of *William Gibson*, which involve mythical, virtual-reality worlds.

Cybersex (slang)

Sexually orientated use of *e-mail*, *chat* and other online technologies.

Cybersiren (slang)

Has been used to describe the lure and excitement of *dot-com* startups which attracted talent en masse from more traditional forms of employment, particularly in the late 1990s.

Cyberspace (slang)

Once used to describe the virtual-reality worlds of *cyberpunk* novels, but now much more commonly used to describe the content of the internet.

Cybersquatter (slang, business term)

Probably the most well-known cyber-word, referring to the well-established practice of buying internet domain names speculatively, targeting existing company names and trademarks – or the names of famous people. The ambition of most cybersquatters is to encourage the original owner of a name to buy the domain name at an inflated price. Cybersquatting is a much-frowned-upon activity, and increasingly hard given new forms of regulation.

Cyberstalker (slang)

A cyberstalker is an individual who pursues others via online means (*e-mail*, *chat*, *instant messaging*) – an unpleasant and sometimes dangerous intrusion of privacy.

Cyberwar (slang)

Has been used in the press to cover *cracker*-style attacks on computer systems as part of overt or covert hostilities between nations.

Cybrarian (web term)

This term is a compound of "cyber" and "librarian" and describes an information science professional who uses the web as a resource and research tool.

Cypherpunk (slang)

Derivative of *cyberpunk*. Someone who is interested (and usually adept) in the uses of electronic ciphers.

Dark Fiber (technical term)

Optical fiber allows data to be transmitted at high speed by sending pulses of light. Dark fiber refers to optical fiber that has been installed for use in the future, but is not yet in use, i.e. there are no pulses of light being sent so the fiber is literally "dark".

DARPA (organization)

Defense Advanced Research Projects Agency. See *ARPA* and *ARPANET*.

Database (technical term)

A structured collection of data held on a computer system. Today, almost all serious databases are based around the "relational" database model where data is stored (logically at least) in a tabular format (see diagram on page 72).

Databases are of course fundamental to almost any type of e-commerce solution and this is especially true where large volumes of product, customer and transactional data need to be stored. The actual physical structure of databases is much more complex than the user view of simple flat tables shown here. Databases will need to contain large amounts of index data for fast access, be structured to enhance management of disk space, and so on.

Book id	Title	Pub. date
⋮ ⋮		
32107	UNIX System Programming	1987
43198	Digital Lexicon	2001
⋮ ⋮		

Rows or records

Database fields

For these reasons, databases are normally managed by a self-contained *database management system* or DBMS.

Database management system (technical term)

A database management system is intended to manage databases of information. They are typically implemented as a family of software products, at the heart of which lies a core engine that deals with:

➡ layout of data on disk

➡ indexing for fast access

➡ security control

➡ search optimization

➡ handling updates across multiple server systems

➡ recovering from failed or canceled updates

➡ handling concurrent updates from multiple users

➡ ensuring a "transaction" completes in full or is "rolled-back" if a problem occurs.

Modern, serious database management systems support the standard SQL (Structured Query Language) for database access, and offer good network connectivity for e-commerce-type distributed applications. They will also support complex multimedia data formats.

The major vendors in this space include *Oracle* and Microsoft with SQL* Server. Other contenders include Informix and *Sybase*. IBM's mainframe database system DB2 is still also much used.

Data Encryption Standard (security term)
See *DES.*

Datagram (technical term)
The internet is a *packet-switching* network where data is split up into small chunks or packets and then sent packet by packet to the end destination for re-assembly. A datagram is another term for packet, often used when discussing the *TCP/IP* family of network *protocols* that support the internet. A datagram consists of data and delivery information such as the destination *address.*

Data mining (technical term)
A large transactional website will generate huge amounts of data on, for example, customers, customer preferences and buying patterns. Data mining covers a set of techniques and software tools for analyzing such data – usually after it has been copied to a special database server system. Data mining techniques can support customer research and cross-selling activities.

Data server (technical term)
A software process, typically running on a dedicated server system, which handles access and requests to data. Usually implemented using a *database management system.*

Data warehouse (technical term)
A database intended to store a great deal (possibly all) of the data associated with a given enterprise. It offers a platform for activities such as *data mining*. It is a popular suggestion from providers of *database management systems* and disk arrays.

Davies, Donald Watt
British researcher at the UK's National Physics Laboratory who was a leader in the development of *packet-switching* in the 1960s.

Day-trader (business term)
Someone who trades on their own account using internet trading systems, looking not at long-term investment but at making a turn on market volatility on an hour-by-hour basis. Inspired by the enormous technology stock values

of the late 1990s, the vast majority of day traders (maybe up to 80 percent) lose money.

DBMS (technical term)
See *Database management system.*

DCOM (technical term)
Microsoft term that stands for Distributed Common Object Model. See *COM* entry for more details.

Debugging (technical term)
The process of removing errors (bugs) from software programs, including websites. Usually done through a series of structured testing phases around business functions, and technical considerations like performance testing.

DEC (company name)
Stands for Digital Equipment Corporation, a name looked on with fond sadness by those who developed their technical skills in the 1970s and 1980s. DEC equipment (in particular PDP and VAX systems) underpinned the early development of *UNIX* and internet technology. Unfortunately, their then chief executive famously compared UNIX with snakeoil, and DEC failed to capitalize on a natural lead. Once a company that had the same kind of buzz as *Sun* at its best, it was purchased by *Compaq* after a troubled time in the 1990s.

Deep linking (web term)
Covers the situation where one website has a hyperlink that points to content "deep" inside another website, i.e. "underneath" the target site's home page. Actually relatively common, for example, when a reference is being made to a specific article on a news site. This can cause legal friction, however, when the operators of the target site think that their content is being effectively stolen. There have a variety of court cases in several countries – for example between ticket-sales sites in the USA.

Dell, Michael
Founder of Dell Computers, an important player in the PC market which made its mark through direct sales (rather than use of retailers) and custom-building each PC for a customer order, rather than building costly inventory.

Denial of service (security term)

A denial of service attack aims to prevent users from accessing a particular computer service. It doesn't necessarily damage the underlying system or data, but just makes it unavailable. Since the internet is an open network, websites are vulnerable to this kind of attack, which normally involves swamping a site with a vast amount of data and processing requests.

DES (security term)

Stands for Data Encryption Standard. A relatively old, but proven, method for electronic encryption, i.e. coding data for added security. At the time of writing, work is progressing on an updated standard called *AES* or Advanced Encryption Standard.

Designing for awards (slang)

Usually occurs when web design agencies are given a free rein to build sites without an appreciation of the underlying product, processes, or economics. The resulting presence can often be visually rich and operationally poor, resulting in awards for the agency and financial difficulties for the business.

Destroy your own business (business term)

Popularized within the mighty GE corporation, this was a headline for an initiative to encourage managers to think of ways to re-invent their business areas using new technology and business models.

Device (technical term)

General computing term for any item of equipment connected to a computer or network. So, in a mundane sense, disk drives, printers, web cams, and scanners are types of device. Continuing technology developments, such as mobile computing, and the increasing ubiquity of embedded microprocessors, are encouraging the development of many more types of device – these include intelligent phones and handheld PDAs with internet connectivity. And the day of the internet-enabled fridge or medicine cabinet is already here, if not at volume.

Device-independent (technical term)

Describes a way of performing a particular task independently of the underlying hardware device. This is an increasing challenge, given the vast array of different devices now accessing the internet (as one example, think of the very different screen sizes between PCs, PDAs and WAP-enabled mobile phones).

DHCP (internet term)

Stands for Dynamic Host Configuration Protocol. Part of the *TCP/IP* software set that allows a network connected to the internet to assign a temporary *IP address* to a given machine that is using the internet at a particular time. It can impact programs that record a user's internet address for later reference.

DHTML (net term)

Stands for Dynamic Hypertext Mark-up Language. Plain *HTML* (without the dynamic) is the original content language of the web. An HTML document consists of the text that will end up being displayed, and formatting instructions written in a simple programming syntax.

DHTML builds upon HTML and allows web pages that move or incorporate some sort of animation, without inefficient calls back to the *webserver.* The graphical impact can be dramatic. DHTML works through a combination of HTML, *JavaScript* or similar, *cascading style sheets* and the *Document Object Model.* All of these are component technologies in the *world wide web.*

Dialogbox (technical term)

A feature of many programs and websites, this is a pop-up box designed to get a very specific response from a user within a graphical user interface.

Dial-up (technical term)

Relates to connections to an Internet Service Provider (*ISP*) or similar type of online service using a *modem* over the telephone network, or, to be precise, the Public Switched Telephone Network (PSTN). A typical dial-up internet connection establishes a telephone connection between a modem connected to a PC and one at an Internet Service Provider. Instead of a voice conversation, the call carries tones generated by the modems representing the data being transmitted to the internet. The rates at which data can be transmitted depends on the quality of the connection and are typically between 28 and 56 Kbits per second.

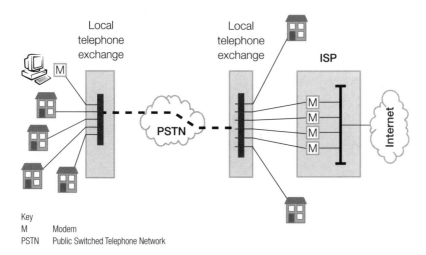

Key
M   Modem
PSTN   Public Switched Telephone Network

Dial-up connection via a modem

Digerati (slang)

A term derived from *digital* that covers the elite of e-commerce and the new economy.

Digital (technical term, business term)

In a technical sense, the term digital has a plain meaning and describes information processing based on numeric coding rather than analog processing of continuous values. Digital is now used as a general adjective to refer to things related to IT, or business models and ideas that arise out of IT and most specifically e-commerce. So it is an alternative for *e-*, *cyber-* and other prefixes that brand a concept as being new, exciting and shiny. You will therefore come across phrases (and book titles) such as the "digital economy," "digital capital," "being digital," and so on.

Digital certificates (security term)

See *certificate.*

Digital divide (general term)

Now used on both sides of the Atlantic to describe the difference between the more affluent who have access to, and knowledge of, technology and e-commerce services, and the poor who do not. This divide is especially pronounced if you take a global view, looking at developed versus developing worlds.

Digital economy (business term)
A synonym as broad – and vague – as "new economy." Covers economic activity related to IT and e-commerce.

Digital Encryption Standard (security term)
See *DES*.

Digital Equipment Corporation (company name)
See *DEC*.

Digital signatures (security term)
A technique to allow messages (including e-mails) to contain information that securely and reliably identifies who it came from. Digital signatures have two main uses:

➡ Ensuring messages really did originate from the person who appears to have sent them (*authentication*).

➡ Preventing people subsequently denying that the message was from them (*non-repudiation* of message origin).

US legislation in 2000 – signed electronically by Bill Clinton – gives digital signatures the same legal force as physical signatures, to support the development of *e-commerce*.

Digital television (technical term)
Also sometimes covered by the abbreviation DTV. Digital television covers the replacement of analog systems – which maximize quality at the expense of bandwidth – with digital systems where the television signal is compressed with limited impact on quality, but large benefits in terms of network demands. The result – whether delivered via the airwaves, satellite, or cable – is the ability to provide many more channels and extra features.

A natural extension is to provide internet or internet-like services as an adjunct to the main television content. In the case of conventional or satellite broadcast technology, this will require an additional outbound phone link for user input. Cable can handle both input and output. DTV is therefore seen by some as an important potential technical channel for *e-commerce*, and the first services are already well established. However, a television is not a PC – offering, for example, lower screen resolution than a conventional computer display. As always, use of a new channel requires some thought and serious design effort.

Disintermediation (business term)
Refers to situations where an *e-commerce* solution removes the need for some form of intermediary – a way of cutting out the middleman. Probably most common within organizations where direct/online sales channels can, for example, disintermediate an existing sales force.

Disruptive technology (business term)
Covers technology innovation that brings fundamental change to a business area, thereby creating new businesses, and destroying old ones. The continuous nature of IT development means that disruptions occur frequently and many major IT suppliers have been in existence for a small number of years (with major exceptions like IBM or HP). Such innovations include the microprocessor, personal computers, new forms of external media, networking innovations, and so on. The internet/e-commerce wave is distinctive because of its visibility to the public at large, but in some ways it is not unique.

Distributed system (technical term)
Any computer system that consists of components on multiple computers, connected by some sort of network. The internet is of course the paradigm example of a distributed system.

DMZ (technical term)
Stands for Demilitarized Zone. It is a logical "buffer zone" between an organization's internal network and the internet, typically used for hosting enterprise applications which need to be accessed from the internet without exposing all of the organization's internal systems.

DNS (internet term)
Stands for Domain Name System. DNS is the internet's equivalent of the telephone directory, turning (relatively) intelligible destination names (such

as **www.amazon.com**) into the numeric *IP* (Internet Protocol) addresses that the routers and computers attached to the internet understand. Every machine attached to the internet knows about a special server called a name server, usually held at the local *ISP*, which is able to able to translate readable names into IP addresses. In the very early days of the internet, the list of machines was small enough for the mapping to be held in a single file and for this file to be copied to every name server. Today, the size of the internet makes this impossible, and instead a hierarchical system of name servers is used. When asked for a machine it doesn't know about, a name server first asks one of the 13 "root" name servers located around the world (these machines are probably the closest things the internet has to a centralized component). The root name servers don't know about all the machines on the internet, but for a given domain they know who to ask, e.g. for any machine in the amazon.com domain (e.g. **www.amazon.com**), they know to ask a machine called ns-1.amazon.com at a specific IP address.

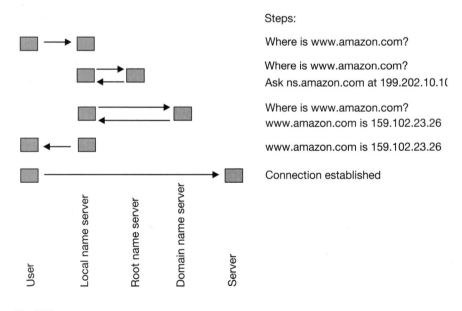

Steps:

Where is www.amazon.com?

Where is www.amazon.com?
Ask ns.amazon.com at 199.202.10.1(

Where is www.amazon.com?
www.amazon.com is 159.102.23.26

www.amazon.com is 159.102.23.26

Connection established

The DNS process

This hierarchical process continues until a name server is reached that actually knows the IP address of the destination machine in question. The result is then cached by the original name server for a defined period to avoid having to repeat this process the next time someone asks for the same machine. All this happens between you typing a *URL* and the page starting to load. The process is shown in the diagram opposite.

The hierarchical nature of DNS also means that an error in the configuration of a name server responsible for a certain domain will make that domain "unreachable" to the whole internet. This has led to several high-profile outages. For instance many of Microsoft's sites became unreachable on January 24 2001 due to an error in the name servers for the `microsoft.com` domain.

Document Object Model (web term)

Often abbreviated to DOM. A World Wide Web Consortium (*W3C*) specification that outlines a general structure for documents containing dynamic HTML, XML, etc. This allows easier manipulation through treating a document as a hierarchical collection of component objects rather than just flat text and tags. Of limited concern to users, DOM is a tool for developers of state-of-the-art websites.

DOM (web term)

Stands for *Document Object Model.*

Domain, Domain name (internet term)

A way of dividing up the internet in a hierarchical fashion, using understandable names rather than the underlying numeric *Internet Protocol addresses.*

Let's take an example using the domain name:

www.accenture.com

Domain names work from right to left, so

.com   is an example of a big *top-level domain*, which divides up the internet name space into continental size groupings. Other top-level domains include .org, .edu, .mil, .net, .int, .gov and two letter codes for countries (like .us and .uk).

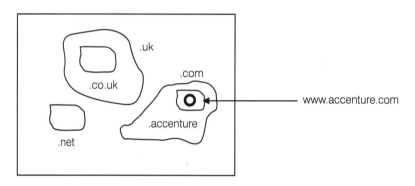

Domain name space

accenture.com   is a sub-domain within .com which denotes systems belonging to Accenture.

www.accenture.com   denotes the master website within accenture.com.

This is shown graphically in the diagram above, although not to scale!

See also the *DNS* entry on how domain names are used in practice.

Domain Name System (internet term)
See *DNS.*

Domino (product)
A family of products from Lotus, originating out of Lotus Notes mail and knowledge management software. Domino products support internet mail services, tools for building web applications, and integration with the original Lotus Notes software – a favored choice of many corporates.

DoS (security)
Common abbreviation for *denial of service.*

Dot address (internet term)
An internet or IP address in its dotted quad format (n1.n2.n3.n4). See *IP address* for more details.

Dot bomb (slang)
A poor e-investment in a dot-com business, or a failed dot-com business.

Dot com (slang, business term)

The way ".com" is pronounced; variously spelt as dotcom or even dot.com. Has a variety of uses:

➡ As a noun, a "dot com" generally means a *start-up* company wholly focussed on the internet.

➡ As an adjective to link a concept to the internet, or e-commerce. As in: "Dot com revolution", "Has the dot com bubble burst?".

".com" is one of the *top-level domains* of the internet and is therefore an important concept in its own right. See the *.com* entry in the Standard Terms glossary.

Dot com companies are a lot less fashionable than they once were, leading to the term "not com" to describe more traditional companies.

Dot corp (slang)

A spin-off internet business established by a *bricks and mortar* company, i.e. a traditional company. An interesting difference between the US and European e-commerce markets is that many European e-commerce success stories fall into the dot-corp category. In fact many observers expect dot-corp-style approaches to dominate over dot coms in the future.

Dot corpse (slang)

Same as *dot bomb*.

Dot gone (slang)

Means the same as *dot bomb* and *dot corpse*. A failed dot-com company. Endless fun.

Dot hon (slang)

A successful *dot-com* business executive.

Download (technical term)

To copy data – and in particular data held in files – from a remote system on to a local system, often a user's PC. Occurs, for example, when copying an upgraded version of a free *plug-in* module down to your PC.

Downtime (technical term)

Covers a period – planned or unplanned – when a computer system or website is unavailable.

Dreamweaver (product)

An enterprise-level product for website design and construction from Macromedia, with features supporting workflow, and integration with other types of web application, Microsoft Office, and e-commerce and application servers.

DSL (technical term)

Stands for Digital Subscriber Line or Digital Subscriber Loop, and covers a family of services that are intended to support high-speed transmissions over conventional copper phone lines. Since there are several varieties, you will often see the term xDSL to cover them. The leading member of the family is *ADSL*.

DSLAM (technical term)

Stands for Digital Subscriber Line Access Multiplexor. This is the piece of equipment at the telephone-exchange end of an ADSL connection, and combines multiple ADSL lines on to a single internal link on the operator's internal network. The number of ADSL connections combined on to a single link is called the contention ratio. For a third party to operate an ADSL service, they must be able to install and operate equipment located within a telephone exchange. Since the telephone operator controls access to the exchange and is also likely to be offering an ADSL service, this can lead to complex negotiations.

DTV (technical term)

See *digital television*.

Dynamic Host Configuration Protocol (internet term)

See *DHCP*.

Dynamic HTML, Dynamic Hypertext Mark-up Language (net term)

See *DHTML*.

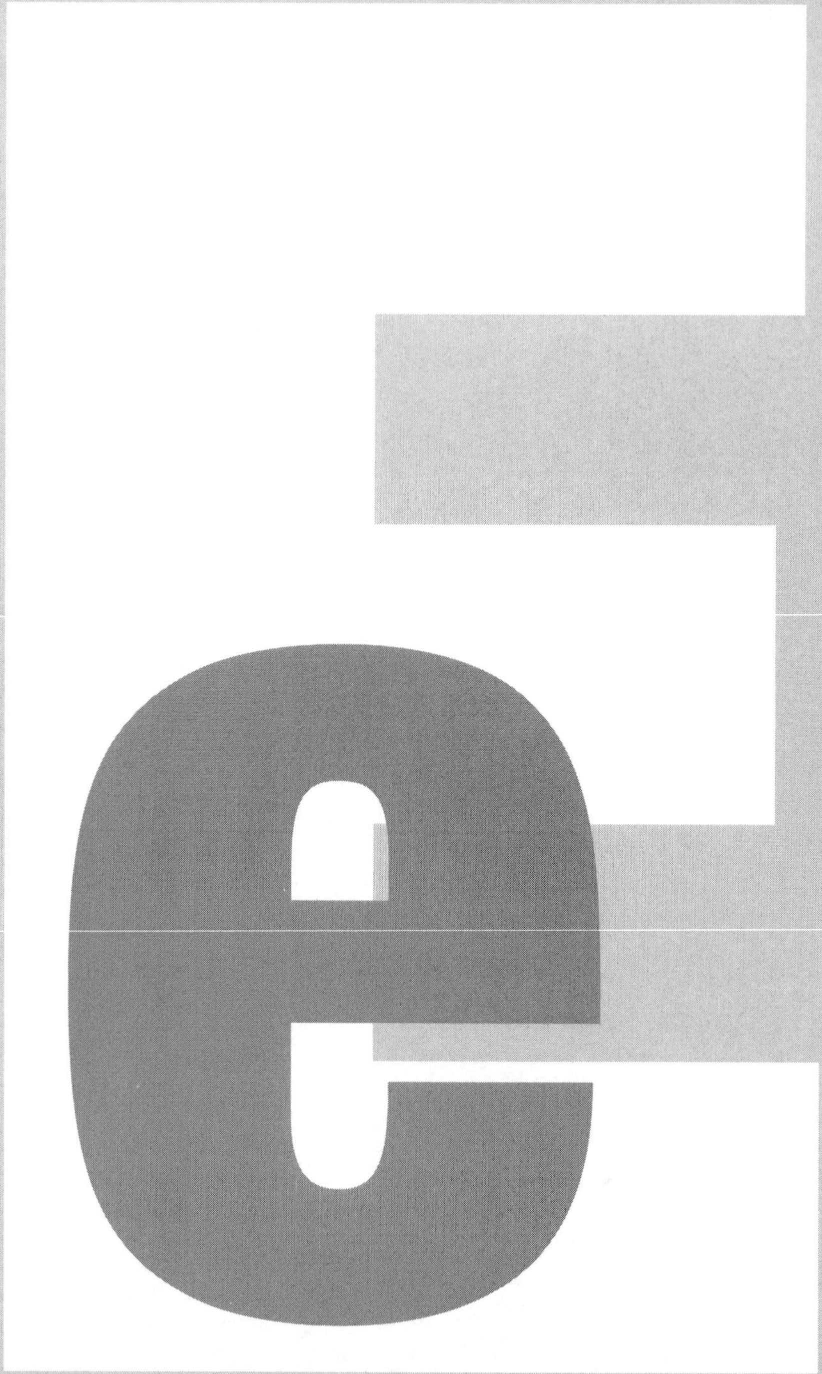
E
e

e- (business term)
The universal prefix for things related to e-commerce (or eCommerce, the hyphen being wholly optional). The "e" stands for electronic, and in fact has a long history through terms such as EDI (Electronic Data Interchange). The use of a small "e" is what usually denotes a term used in the e-commerce or internet areas. Very often used, it seems tired, but it is a convenient shorthand nonetheless. Other general-purpose prefixes include *i-* for internet, *cyber-*, and *online*.

eAI (business term, technical term)
Stands for e-Application Integration and covers software which is designed to join other software applications together so they can exchange data. Such software is a type of "middleware" and the market is a large and growing one.

Easter egg (slang)
A hidden surprise in a program, or website. For example, a picture of the development team accessed through an unlikely series of keystrokes.

e-banking (business term)
Providing banking services online. Most major banks now offer this in some way for personal and, increasingly, corporate customers.

eBay.com (website)

One of the world's most popular websites, eBay essentially created the concept of a consumer-to-consumer auction service. See *auction* for a broader perspective.

e-bill presentation (business term)

Covers the sending and processing of bills and invoices electronically, which can reduce costs for a business.

e-book (business term)

Devices that act as electronic books, into which novels or magazines can be downloaded. Success is limited to date, and research shows reading speed is slower with computer screens than old-fashioned paper. However, there is significant ongoing research into electronic paper substitutes which will have the same reflective qualities as paper.

e-brand (business term)

A brand that is used online, not just to distinguish one set of products or services from another, but to generate a mental picture of the particular experience to be had by visiting that online presence. As online businesses often have fewer physical assets than their off-line counterparts, a greater percentage of their overall valuation will be attributed to intangible assets such as the e-brand. Failure to live up to the e-brand "promise" during customer interactions across any channel often results in customer defections. See also *brand*.

e-brokerage (business term)

An e-brokerage allows users to buy and sell stocks (that is, shares) and obtain investment information from a website. Some e-brokerages are provided by traditional and well-established brokerage houses. Others are online only.

e-business (business term)

A general term for online business activities, successfully used by IBM in its marketing. Means the same as *e-commerce*, although a few argue that e-business is a more general term.

e-cash (business term)
A commonly used synonym for what is also called e-money, electronic money, or digital money. These days it is also the trademarked name of a supplier of products in this area. See *e-money* for a longer description of the general concept.

ECN (business term)
Stands for Electronic Communications Network. Although this sounds like a general technical term, it isn't. ECNs are a growing feature of world financial markets and are securities trading systems that are usually privately owned and offer automated order routing and trade execution services. They are alternatives to traditional stock exchanges with fewer services, but potentially lower costs and other benefits. Some also automatically link to true stock exchanges. Examples include Archipelago, Instinet, Island, and Strike. In the USA they already account for significant volumes of trading in shares listed on NASDAQ or the NYSE (New York Stock Exchange).

Ecology (business term)
Used to describe the complex landscape of e-commerce businesses, of which there are a great many, and their inter-relationships.

e-commerce (business term)
At its broadest, this covers the carrying out of any commercial activity using electronic means, with a particular emphasis on promoting, selling, and buying products and services.

Historically, various types of commercial activity have been long supported by electronic means – banks have been swapping tapes since the 1960s, and use of pre-internet networking has been prevalent in financial markets for some time. E-commerce as a term was introduced around 1990 as a result of the opportunities that technology seemed to offer. At that point the web was just in its toddler stage, and it wasn't until the mid-1990s that the strong link between the internet and e-commerce started to be made.

The initial public face of internet e-commerce was focussed on *B2C* start-ups and *e-tailers* like Amazon in particular. This wave has passed and the big transaction flows of the future will probably revolve around B2B solutions connecting existing corporations. With the advent of channels such as mobile telephony, and the fact that the vast majority of corporations are online in some way, the specialness of the term e-commerce is already being eroded.

Eco-net (business term)
Evocative term describing a specific network of businesses – and particularly e-commerce businesses – that work together in some way.

EDGE (mobile term)
Stands for Enhanced Data Rate for Global Evolution. Broadly based on the architecture of the *GSM* cellular phone network, EDGE is designed to increase normal mobile data rates by a factor of three, up to a theoretical maximum of 48 kbps (using the same resources as a single voice call) or 384 kbps using all the local capacity of the network. Upgrading GSM with EDGE requires significant modification to the network and may be overtaken by the rollout of *UMTS* (Universal Mobile Telecommunications System), the long-term replacement for GSM.

EDI (technical term)
Stands for Electronic Data Interchange, a very broad term covering the transfer of structured business data from computer to computer, avoiding the effort and errors introduced by having to re-key information (e.g. purchase orders, bills). In some ways EDI was a precursor to business-to-business *(B2B)* e-commerce. Although some EDI implementations relied on exchange of magnetic tapes, most used private value-added networks (VANs) which linked participants in a particular industry (e.g. automotive parts), defined the message formats and transmission protocols to be used, and provided central audit functions. Messages were typically defined using a syntax called EDIFACT (*EDI* for Administration, Commerce and Transport) which was similar in intent to *XML* (eXtensible Mark-up Language). The internet and XML have removed the need for proprietary communications networks. However, the need to establish a common meaning for messages among participants remains (which these day means commonly understood XML *tags*).

e-entertainment (business term)
Sometimes used to cover the provision of "normal" entertainment – in video, audio, and multimedia form – over the internet. Given the state of cur-

rent technology, which means streamed video is still a poor user experience in most cases, and the general pattern of internet usage, the internet has not yet proved the bright, new channel for entertainment some hoped.

EFF (organization)
See *Electronic Frontier Foundation.*

Ego-surfing (slang)
Searching for references to your own name on the web.

e-government (internet term)
Used by multiple governments to cover the provision of government services (information, tax return filing, etc.) over the internet.

EJB (technical term)
Stands for Enterprise Java Beans. A standard for server-side software components which (at least in theory) should allow complete portability of applications. An EJB is hosted by an application server within a software "container" that supports all of the EJB's interaction with the host system. Therefore, provided vendors make the same interfaces available within their container implementations, it should be possible to reuse the same EJB on a variety of platforms. Why are EJBs needed? *Java* goes some way to supporting "write once, run anywhere" but enterprise applications typically need access to databases and transaction processing systems, which are not standardized by the core Java language, but are covered by the EJB specification.

e-lancer (business term)
A freelance worker in the e-commerce world.

Electronic Communications Network (business term)
See *ECN.*

Electronic Data Interchange (technical term)
See *EDI.*

Electronic Frontier Foundation (organization)
A public advocacy organization founded in 1990 by Mitch Kantor and John Perry Barlow that campaigns for civil liberties, free speech, and privacy for online users.

Elevator pitch (slang)

A speech promoting a *dot-com* business concept that lasts no longer than an elevator ride. A term invented because of the legendary short attention span given to new ideas by *venture capitalists*.

Ellison, Larry

Flamboyant CEO of *Oracle*, which he founded in 1977 and which is (depending on fluctuations in stock market valuations) probably the second largest software company in the world after Microsoft. As well as being an outstanding businessman, Ellison is an accomplished sailor, winning the harrowing 1998 Sydney to Hobart race in his yacht *Soynara*. He also owns his own Italian jet fighter aircraft (apparently he tried to buy a Russian MiG jet fighter, but US customs wouldn't allow it).

EMACS (technical term)

Derived from Editing MACroS, EMACS is a famous, powerful and highly programmable text editor program originally created by Richard Stallman and available in freeware form as GNU EMACS. Of interest because it was probably the best example of good free software before *Linux*.

e-mail (e-mail term)

E-mail is such a ubiquitous form of communication that it hardly seems to merit an entry. However, it had to be invented. It is also technically harder to get right than one might think, and some approaches and standards (such as *X.400)* haven't gained mass approval.

Current forms of e-mail really date back to the early days of *ARPANET* (the research network that eventually gave way to the modern internet) when Ray Thomlinson introduced the first inter-system e-mail system. Once invented, e-mail quickly became the dominant use of the ARPANET and is still the prime reason many, many people use the internet.

Behind the scenes of any e-mail system there is a complex arrangement of server processes – often based around *POP* (Post Office Protocol). At the front end, there is a wide choice of client programs for sending and reading e-mails, including Microsoft Outlook, Netscape Messenger and Eudora. Most such mail systems are rich in features, although the majority of users only access and use a tiny fraction.

As a form of communication, e-mail has its own distinctive characteristics. It is informal (how many people spell-check e-mails?) It is also somewhat impersonal, which causes some people to write things they would never say. Aggressive *flames* are one of the downsides of e-mail, which leads directly to the notion of *netiquette* to encourage good behavior.

One aspect of the internet and web worlds is freemail. Services such as Hotmail – the trailblazer in this space – allow anyone with a *browser* to set up and use their own free e-mail account. Free mail services are often provided to attract users to sites that offer a broader range of services or are advertising-financed. They are typically used for personal (outside work) use, and by travelers or students.

e-mail address (e-mail term)
An e-mail address denotes a specific user within a specific organization and conventionally takes the form of **username@organization.suffix**.

e-mail filter (e-mail term)
Most e-mail systems allow filters to be configured that file and manipulate incoming e-mail based on information included in the message. A particular type of filter (sometimes called a *bozo* filter) can be used to block spam or other unwelcome messages from specific sources.

e-market, e-marketplace (business term)
General term for a website or online service that aims to draw buyers and sellers together. Increasingly used since it has a broader although less precise meaning than *exchange.*

EMC² (company name)
Perhaps less well known than companies like Sun, Cisco or Oracle, EMC is a major supplier of storage technology for e-commerce and other types of businesses. EMC describes itself as a company that builds "the world's most robust, secure and trusted information storage infrastructures," and at the heart of its product range are a set of reliable and scalable disk arrays for storing large mission-critical databases.

e-money (business term)
e-money or electronic money is in some ways an old concept. Banks have

processed electronic transactions between each other for many years, and the world's financial infrastructure moves trillions of dollars between financial institutions each year – often using closed, secure and relatively old network protocols like *X.25*.

Consumer access to e-money is a different matter, and there are many current initiatives that aim to mimic physical cash, or paper-based processes like cheque writing. This is a complex area and a non-exhaustive list of types of e-money include:

- **Online use of credit cards**: this is now familiar and most consumer spending on the internet is driven through entry of credit card details over secure connections such as provided by *SSL*. Although figures for online fraud aren't necessarily that large, online users are often still anxious about security matters.

- **Smart cards**: for example, Mondex which contain a starting cash value which is reduced by each transaction, and embedded security mechanisms. Actually quite an old concept by e-commerce standards, which hasn't ever quite reached critical mass.

- **True electronic money**: the internet now supports features that allow much closer electronic mimicry of physical cash – specifically public–key cryptography and electronic signatures. So blocks of electronic money can be made secure and then signed, rather like cheques. An interesting class of such systems are those that support micropayments – as low as a few pennies – which are intended to allow internet content to be sold at point of use rather than through a subscription fee. There are quite a few active companies in this area, including Cybercash and Digicash/e-cash.

Currently credit cards dominate in online consumer spending and the take-up of alternatives remains low-key. This is a very active area, however, which will continue to evolve. Examples of innovation include Beenz – a scheme where online activities create points or Beenz which can be "spent," and various gift-voucher-like initiatives to allow children who can't get credit cards to shop online. Mobile technologies offer some very interesting possibilities, as exemplified by phones that carry electronic money and enable users to buy from vending machines by simply dialing them.

Emotag (e-mail term)

Adaptation of HTML's *tag* construct. In *HTML* a tag is enclosed in angle brackets (< >) and triggers a formatting or other action. An emotag uses this syntax informally to add commentary to e-mail such as `<joke>` ... `text` ... `</joke>`.

Emoticon (e-mail term)

Also known as smileys, and invented during *ARPANET* days, these symbols are formed from normal ASCII characters and are meant to add emotional tone to a message. Examples include:

- `:-)` smile
- `;-)` wink
- `:-(` sad face
- `:-1` straight face
- `:-0` shock, or bored yawn
- `:-7` tongue in cheek
- `:-/` wry face.

Encryption (security term)

The process of hiding the meaning of a message to prevent it being understood by a third-party eavesdropper. Modern techniques use complex mathematical functions (called algorithms) to convert the message (known as plaintext) into an encrypted form (called ciphertext). For this to be useful, obviously the reverse process must also be possible. The encryption and decryption processes require a key (basically a number) and it is the size of the key that determines how hard a third party would need to work to "crack" the ciphertext.

Two major forms of encryption exist: symmetrical encryption (where the same key is needed for encryption and decryption) and asymmetric encryption (where a combination of two keys is needed).

Enterprise (business term)

Means the entirety of a business or organization. Used to denote something that serves a whole business and is therefore serious and scalable. So an "enterprise server" is a big computer system.

Enterprise Java Beans (technical)
See *EJB*.

e-payments (business term)
Covers systems that support electronic payment and movement of funds. Electronic systems have existed to do this kind of activity for years, generally based on proprietary technology. There is more recent activity using internet approaches. For example, SWIFT (Society of Worldwide Interbank Financial Telecommunications), who run a well-known international fund transfer system, is – at the time of writing – building a "business-to-business internet payment service" for its 3,000 banking owners and their customers in 190 countries.

The term e-payments is also used by some to cover more mundane consumer solutions that allow credit and debit cards to be used in a secure manner, using component standards such as *SSL* or *SET*.

e-servicing (business term)
Sometimes used when an e-commerce solution is built by a business to serve existing customers, rather than generate new revenues. In this situation, technologies like the internet are used to create new channels to interact with customers, alongside branches, call centers, etc. Some observers think the predominant use of the internet in the *B2C* area will in the end turn out to be centered around such servicing for existing companies.

e-tailer (business term)
An online retailer like *Amazon*.

Ethernet (technical term)
Ethernet has (in one form or another) become a very popular form of Local Area Network (*LAN*). It was originally developed in *Xerox PARC* in the 1970s and later became standardized as IEEE 802.3. In its original form Ethernet operated over bulky coaxial cable at a maximum speed of 10 Mbps. However, modern versions operate over cheap UTP (Unshielded Twisted Pair) copper cable and at speeds over 100 Mbps. Ethernet is a low-level standard. It provides the bottom two layers of the *OSI* (Open Systems Interconnection) reference model, and the *TCP/IP* protocol suite (among others) can operate over it.

Ethernet is not suitable for operation at distances over a few 100 meters; however, some equipment manufacturers are hoping to overcome this limitation and make "Global Ethernet" an option for replacing xDSL for use over the existing telephone infrastructure. Standards for operating Ethernet LANs at speeds over 1 Gbps are also being developed.

eToys.com (website)

Well-known *e-tailer* of toys. One of the first big e-commerce names to suffer serious problems after the stock market decline of 2000, this name now points to **KBkids.com**.

ET software (slang)

A piece of software that performs an apparently innocent function but also "phones home" – for example, connecting to an internet server to record the browsing activity of the end-user.

Eudora (e-mail term)

Well-known e-mail package that originally started life as *freeware* for Macintosh computers.

Evergreen (slang)

Occasionally used by designers and web ad agencies to describe a website that is kept up to date and fresh and therefore is more likely to attract repeat visitors.

Exchange (business term)

Exchanges – as buildings, infrastructure or platforms for the transaction of business or monetary exchange – have a long history and have been a key component in the growth of modern capitalism in Europe and the USA. Many traditional exchanges (such as stock exchanges) have had electronic trading platforms – typically not based on internet-style technologies – for many years.

In this entry, we will cover the growth of new types of *B2B* (business-to-business) or online exchange which are seen by many as the killer app of B2B internet-inspired e-commerce. Using the various software solutions now available, online exchanges provide a virtual market space for bringing multiple buyers and sellers together and allowing them to buy and sell through dynamic agreement of prices. Key characteristics that make an exchange different from other types of B2B site should include:

- multiple buyers and sellers
- centralized matching of buy and sell orders
- neutrality in dealing with buyers and sellers according to the rules of the exchange.

The services to users that can be bundled around an online exchange include identifying potential sourcing, negotiating, transacting and payment, and more complex valued-added services. Traditional exchanges tend to focus on financial instruments and commodities. Now there are hundreds of exchange initiatives. Many were started in 1999 and 2000 and are at the time of writing still in the early stages of development and usage. These variously offer trading in energy, paper, chemicals, freight space on aircraft and trucks, manpower, advertising space, whole aircraft, and much more.

The potential value to buyers in such an exchange can include cost reduction (through more price competition between suppliers), and – potentially – more cost-effective procurement and supply chain processes. The value to suppliers is a bigger market and indeed the key general success factor of any type of exchange is liquidity and volume, which means there is sufficient trading to allow fast matching of buy and sell orders, and an "efficient" price-setting mechanism.

The first online exchange initiatives tended to be driven by software suppliers, but now many are being created by groups of buyers. Examples include Covisint for major car makers, Aeroxchange for major airlines, and Traderanger for oil companies. The key feature that such consortium-style initiatives bring is immense potential liquidity – sometimes in the tens of billions of dollars.

Online exchanges do face challenges. There are a great many of them in flight. The volumes in some initiatives remain low. One reason for this is that traditional "spot" exchanges traded in items that do not need complicated surrounding contracts, while some types of B2B exchange attempt to do just this. Integration between a participant's own systems and processes and those of the exchange can be hard. In addition, regulation bodies like the US

Federal Trade Commission and Department of Justice are reviewing several exchanges, including Covisint. This is because the new types of exchange lie outside the long-established regulation frameworks of, say, stock exchanges and there are perceived dangers of collusion, excluding competitors and allowing inappropriate access to commercial information.

Nevertheless, the sector is very dynamic at the time of writing and B2B software suppliers such as Commerce One, I2 Technologies, and Ariba have benefited.

excite.com (website)
Popular and well-known *search engine* and *portal* service.

Execute (technical term)
To run a program. A general computing term.

Executable (technical term)
The compiled, runnable form of a program. A general computing term.

Exodus (company name)
Founded in 1994, Exodus Communications led the internet data center market – providing a network of managed buildings across the globe where companies can place their website computer hardware, while Exodus manage the networking. This is a crowded market, but Exodus is a good example of a company that has occupied the kinds of infrastructure niche created by the internet.

Explorer (product)
Shorthand for Microsoft's *Internet Explorer*, one the of most common *browsers*.

Extranet (internet term)
A network that is built using internet technologies and extends an organization's *intranet* to selected outsiders such as suppliers and customers, but without providing access to the outside world via the general public internet.

e-zine (slang)
Sometimes referred to just as "zine," this covers an electronic publication or magazine in internet or e-mail form.

FAQ (general term)
Short for Frequently Asked Questions. A document, or web page, listing common questions and standardized answers. An FAQ document is found in many internet newsgroups and on many websites.

Farm (slang)
Used to refer to a data center room filled with impressive amounts of some form of hardware. So, in the e-commerce world you will come across *server farms* that contain multiple servers. Also called *web farms*.

Fat client (technical term)
In the first generation of *client–server* solutions, the client program running on a PC or workstation was often a large, complex beast. Most modern web-based systems are instead typically *thin-client*, with the majority of processing being undertaken on back-end servers. This allows more control of the service by the website developer.

Favorite (web term)
In *Microsoft Internet Explorer*, describes a recorded shortcut (link) to a page on a website. The equivalent term *bookmark* is used in *Netscape Navigator*.

FIL

File (technical term)
The concept of file is a fundamental computing term that should be understood by anyone who has used a computer. A file is essentially a collection of data identified by a file name. The web was created out of the *UNIX* environment, and the *URLs* (Universal Resource Locators) used to identify websites and web pages are ultimately extended forms of UNIX file names and directory structures.

File extension (technical term)
A suffix at the end of a *file* name indicating the *file type*.

File Transfer Protocol (internet term)
See *FTP*.

File type (technical term)
Files generally fall into one of a standard set of categories or types. The type of a file is, by convention, identified via a short extension or suffix at the end of a file name. Common types found on the internet are:

File-name extension	Description
.exe	Runnable program (executable)
.gif	Graphic in GIF format
.htm	HTML document that can be read by browsers
.jpg	Graphic in JPEG format
.mid	MIDI audio file
.mcr	Quicktime movie
.mpg	MPEG movie
.piv	Perl source file
.swf	Shockwave Flash file
.wav	Waveform audio file
.zip	Compressed (zip) file

Filo, David
Co-founder of *Yahoo!*

Filter (technical term, e-mail term)
Filter is a general technical term for a program that removes or changes items in its input data stream. In the context of *e-mail*, a filter is a configurable

mechanism that takes specific actions when incoming mail meets certain criteria. A filter can be used, for example, to:

➡ delete repetitive or unwanted messages, such as spam;

➡ sort messages and place them into designated folders.

Finger (technical term)

An internet tool – originally written for just the *UNIX* operating system – that produces information on what other users (who may be at other locations) are doing.

Firewall (security term)

A firewall is a kind of electronic security guard that separates one network from another (one of these networks often being the internet). A firewall is designed to enforce a defined level of control over the kinds of information that pass between these networks. It is often used to protect an organization's *LAN* (Local Area Network) from open access from the internet. Firewalls are typically implemented on dedicated server hardware, although the important aspects are provided by software.

Examples of firewall use include:

➡ Blocking certain inbound network *protocols* (e.g. *telnet*), which ensures that machines inside the firewall aren't threatened by direct connections from outside.

➡ Limiting external access to selected internal machines (e.g. so all the computers on the inside of the firewall will not be visible outside).

➡ Collaborating with other firewalls to create *Virtual Private Networks*, so that networks can be coupled across the internet, and still have a degree of protection.

➡ Scanning incoming content for malicious programs like viruses.

➡ Authenticating incoming users.

Firewalls therefore have an important part to play in repelling attack, but on their own do not guarantee security. See *security* for a more complete view of this area.

First Tuesday (organization)

An informal grouping that for a time became a major movement. Started in London by John Browning, it then became international. First Tuesday met on the obvious day each month and acted as a forum to bring together aspiring entrepreneurs and investors in the e-commerce arena.

Fixed wireless (technical term)

Wireless is generally seen as a mobile technology. However, in some circumstances using radio frequencies rather than wire to communicate between fixed locations can be useful (e.g. where cabling infrastructure is too expensive to put in place). Radio spectrum in the SHF (Super High Frequency) range of approximately 28 GHz is typically used and requires an unobstructed "line of sight" between the two ends of the link, together with small dish aerials. Such high frequencies can support broadband transmission speeds of 1 Gbit.

Flame (e-mail term)

An aggressive, or insulting, e-mail, or newsgroup posting. Can also be used as a verb describing the act of sending such an e-mail. Some people seem to enjoy flaming as a recreation. It is better to observe appropriate *netiquette*.

Flame bait (e-mail term)

An e-mail or posting designed to trigger a *flame war*.

Flame fest (e-mail term)

See *flame war.*

Flame war (e-mail term)

An e-mail or newsgroup conversation made up of flames, generally of increasing intensity. See also *Goodwin's Law*.

Flamer (e-mail term)

Someone who sends flames.

Flash (product)

One of a number of well-known and much used products from Macromedia, Flash (which was once known as Splash) is a product used to create high-impact websites, with features to support creative use of animation, audio, and other features. It is based on vector rather than simpler but bulkier bit-map graphics and so should normally download faster. In many ways, Flash has become a de facto standard and "Flash Player" is pre-installed on most computers, as it is included with all copies of Windows 98, Netscape Navigator, and the Apple Macintosh operating system. In fact, more than 90 percent of web browsers already have Flash Player installed as a *plug-in*.

Float (business term)
To float all (or part of) a company means to put shares up for public sale, typically through an *Initial Public Offering*.

Folder (technical term, e-mail term)
General term for a collection of files or e-mail messages held on disk.

Forte (product)
The Forte range is owned by *Sun*, although the core products come from compa-nies called Forte Software and NetBeans taken over by Sun in recent years. Some of the Forte products have a history spanning quite a few years, but Sun ownership and the adaption of Forte for internet applications have given the product range a new lease of life. Forte products are intended for developers – typically serious developers – and offer an Integrated Development Environ-ment (IDE) for building high-end, complex applications. Some Forte products support the more traditional computer languages (C, C++, Fortran). Others are very much oriented towards internet and web technologies. These products include Forte Fusion, which is XML-based, and several product sets for *Java* development, including products specifically oriented towards internet and web applications.

Forwarding (e-mail term)
Common feature provided by e-mail packages. Allows messages and attach-ments to be copied on to other recipients.

Frame (web term)
Frame is one of those words that has a variety of technical meanings. In the context of the web, frames are used to divide a browser window into smaller, sub-windows, each displaying a different HTML document.

Free Software Foundation (organization)

Founded by *Richard Stallman*, the Free Software Foundation (FSF) is dedicated to the development of software which users are free to copy, redistribute and enhance, the most well known element being the *GNU* (GNU's not UNIX) software initiative.

The FSF uses "free" in its wider libertarian sense rather than simply meaning free of charge. On its website (**www.gnu.org**) the FSF defines four main characteristics of free software:

➡ Freedom to use for any purpose (e.g. personal, commercial, academic, military).

➡ Freedom to make copies and redistribute.

➡ Freedom to study the source code and adapt it.

➡ Freedom to onward distribute modified versions of the code.

The FSF is not opposed to charging for the distributions of "free" software, which represents one of the foundation's main sources of income. However, users must be free to share, copy and modify what comes on the distribution media. Free software and *open source* are in many ways comparable but advocates of free software argue that the term "open source" does not embody the spirit of freedom central to the principles of the FSF.

Freeware (internet term)

Freeware is a term for software that is offered free of charge and typically downloaded fron the internet. Freeware is not necessarily free to all types of user (e.g. commercial users), nor is it necessarily provided free from copyright or complete with source code. Therefore Freeware has a different meaning from *Free Software* or *open source*.

Frequently Asked Questions (general term)

See *FAQ*.

Frontpage (product)

Microsoft website authoring tool that supports the creation of impressive websites, but can require specific "extensions" on the webserver which originally were only available for Microsoft's IIS webserver product. Microsoft now provides support for other web servers, including *Apache*.

FTP (internet term)

Stands for File Transfer Protocol – a widely known and used *protocol* used to copy files across computers connected via *TCP/IP*. Also used as a verb for the act of transferring files.

Fulfillment (business term)

Fulfillment refers to the process of satisfying an order (shipping goods) once it has been placed. This is a large business topic and needs serious attention for anyone building an e-commerce business around sales of physical goods. It is a particular challenge for some US sites, given the scale of the country. It is an equal challenge for sites that aim to be pan-European given different laws, customs regulations etc.

Funding (business term)

An e-commerce business can be an expensive undertaking with significant investment needed before hopeful future profit. Many startups therefore need external funding from private investors, *venture capitalists*, and other sources. Funding is often given in stages (to control investors' risk) and you will come across phrases such as "seed capital," "first stage funding," "funding round," and so on. In return for supplying funding, an investor expects to receive equity based on the current valuation of an organization. The hope is that when the company is floated, or sold, the investor makes a capital gain. Most such investments actually fail, and professional venture capitalists therefore invest in a broad portfolio to spread risk. The availability of funding is, of course, linked to normal business cycles, and is now harder to acquire than during the "bubble" period of the late 1990s.

G (technical term)

Symbol for *giga* used in sizing (large) quantities related to IT systems. Can also stand for generation in the context of mobile telephony (e.g. 3G meaning third generation).

G2C (web term)

Stands for government-to-citizen and is sometimes used to describe sites that provide the general public with greater access to the workings of government departments.

Gates, Bill

Chairman and chief software architect of *Microsoft.*

In some ways, we hardly need to say more, but a basic biography is always interesting.

- Born October 28, 1955, and grew up in Seattle.
- While at Harvard, developed a version of the BASIC language for the Altair, the first microcomputer.
- Dropped out of Harvard and founded Microsoft, with *Paul Allen*, in 1975.

➡ Through a mixture of technical insight and sharp business sense, acquired rights to operating system software that evolved into **MS-DOS**, and then persuaded the goliath of IBM to use it on the **IBM PC** platform, while retaining the right to licence it to other suppliers.

➡ After a brief detour with an operating system called OS/2, led Microsoft through the creation of the **Windows** family of operating systems, and the now ubiquitous Microsoft family of application programs.

➡ Turned Microsoft on a dime in the mid-1990s to focus on internet technologies. Although he was following an already established market trend, this was a rapid and impressive refocussing.

Microsoft is a dominant and powerful organization, and as a result the company and Gates himself attract a great deal of comment and strong opinion. Microsoft was – in June 1999 – a company that generated $20 billion a year, employed nearly 32,000 people, and had touched the lives of tens of millions of users. This is achievement on a gigantic scale.

Following the tradition of previous hyper-successful industrialists, Gates has a strong philanthropic streak and has contributed hundreds of millions of dollars to charities in areas such as world health.

GB (technical term)
Shorthand for **gigabyte**.

Gbps (technical term)
Stands for gigabits per second – a measure of network speed for high-capacity networks.

General Public License (business term)
The type of agreement that controls distribution of software from the **Free Software Foundation**. Explicitly allows redistribution of software, and represents a key influence for the **open source** movement.

Generation text (slang)
A slang term for the 15–25-year-old mobile phone users responsible for the explosive growth in exchange of simple text messages, using the Short Message Service (**SMS**) mobile standard (see also **text**).

Geocities (company name)

Large web-based publishing community now owned by *Yahoo!* Aimed at ordinary users, Geocities allows individuals to build their own personal websites. A place where you can find family photos, an individual's own genealogical research, or even just an individual's collection of favorite links.

Gerstner, Louis

Gerstner has a strong old-economy heritage (Nabisco and American Express), but is credited with turning around *IBM* – as Chairman and CEO – after a difficult period in the late 1980s and early 1990s.

Get big fast (business term)

A mantra associated with *Jeff Bezos* of *Amazon*, this describes an Amazon-like business strategy where the prime driver of organization behavior is gaining scale and market share – normally requiring significant external funding and delayed profits. In the current business climate, there is now much more focus on early profit, although Amazon on many counts can be said to have succeeded.

Get it (slang)

Used in the sense of "do you get it?" – that is, understand the opportunities and dynamics of the e-commerce world. Now almost all observers think the future of e-commerce lies in the hands of enlightened traditional corporates rather than pure dot-com companies, and the phrase is used much less frequently.

GHz (technical term)

Stands for gigahertz – a measure of frequency measurement meaning 10^{12} cycles per second. (Since this is not an IT quantity, giga is being used in the same way as in the metric system.) Where you might come across this is in discussion of the radio frequencies used for mobile communications.

Gibson, William

Popular science fiction writer who helped create the *cyberpunk* sub-genre of science fiction with his novel *Necromancer* (1982).

GIF (technical term)

Short for Graphics Interchange Format – a file format originally developed by Compuserve for transporting pictures in a compact way, and still in common use.

Giga (technical term)

Prefix that multiplies an IT quantity by 2^{30} – a number close to $1,000 \times 1,000,000$ – a billion. This parallels the use of giga in the metric system, but reflects the fact that computers are based around *binary* arithmetic. This is a basic computing term. We have included it because sizing information is often used in describing features of network systems and the internet. Used in terms such as *gigabit* and *gigabyte*. Close relatives include *kilo*, *mega* and *tera*.

Gigabit (technical term)

2^{30} *bits* – a bit being the fundamental unit of computer storage and taking the values zero or one. Gigabits-per-second (Gbps) is an often-used measure of network speed for large, fast networks.

Gigabyte (technical term)

2^{30} *bytes* – a byte being 8-bits of storage, long enough to hold a numeric code for characters from the *ASCII* character set. Used to measure large amounts of disk space and main computer memory.

Global Positioning System (technical term)

See *GPS*.

Global System for Mobile Communications (mobile term)

See *GSM*.

GNU (technical term)

Acronym for GNUs Not UNIX, a recursive (= self-referential) joke that tells you a lot about GNU's cultural (= hacker) origins. Covers a collection of software that is maintained by the *Free Software Foundation* and distributed under the terms of the GNU *General Public License*. This type of license means that anyone who distributes GNU software, or a derivative of GNU software, can charge for distribution and support, but must allow the user to change and redistribute the code on the same basis. A forerunner of the *Linux* movement,

GNU is probably best known for its versions of the *EMACS* editor and the *C* compiler.

GNU General Public License (business term)

See *General Public License.*

Gnutella (web term)

Housed at the website **gnutella.wego.com,** Gnutella is based around a "fully-distributed information-sharing technology." This allows every client machine – such as a PC – to act also as a server system, turning the "Gnutella Network" into a way of locating and sharing files between users, rather than between users and centralized servers. Some of the files exchanged are MP3 audio files, so Gnutella is seen as an alternative approach to the more centralized *Napster*, which has been at the center of a legal storm with the record companies.

Goodwin's Law (slang)

This term belongs more properly to a text like *The New Hacker's Dictionary* (edited by *Eric Raymond*), but we could not resist adding it here since it says something about the intensity of some *e-mail* and *Usenet* conversations. Invented by Michael Goodwin, it basically says that "as a Usenet or online discussion grows longer, the probability of a comparison involving Nazis or Hitler approaches one." By convention, this marks the end of a heated exchange.

Google.com (website)

Popular *search engine* with an uncluttered user interface, efficient retrieval, large index, and a useful system of marking hits by popularity. We like it. Very much. Also used by *Yahoo!* within the Yahoo! portal.

Gopher (internet term)

Somewhat old-fashioned internet utility for finding textual information and files on the internet, made obsolete by the world wide web.

Goto.com (website)

Well-established website at **goto.com** which is a mix of *search engine*, directory service, and online marketplace. Noteworthy for the fact that it changes companies who want to appear near the top of a search list.

GPRS (mobile term)

GPRS stands for General Packet Radio Service. GPRS uses the *GSM* cellular telephone network to allow users to send packets of data rather than establishing dedicated connections. This has the benefit that:

➡ There is no set-up time to establish a connection (hence GPRS is often referred to as "always on").

➡ Gaps in traffic (e.g. between page downloads) can be used by others to send their own GPRS packets, therefore allowing multiple users to share the same network resources.

The data rates available over GPRS depend on:

➡ The amount of capacity (or "timeslots") in a single cell that the network operators configure to support GPRS.

➡ The capabilities of the mobile device to use multiple timeslots simultaneously.

➡ The number of concurrent GPRS users contending for capacity.

The theoretical maximum data transmission rate for GPRS is ~172 Kbps, but this uses all the timeslots in the cell and does not allow for error correction. First-generation devices are likely to give more modest data rates of approximately 14–28 Kbps.

GPS (mobile term)

GPS stands for Global Positioning System and is a satellite-based system that allows a receiver to pinpoint very accurately its own location. This is potentially important as a means of tailoring mobile commerce services to a user's location (e.g. locating nearby restaurants or engineering plant such as buried pipes). However, once determined, the mobile device must retransmit its location to a service provider via a mobile data service such as the similarly named, but very different, *GPRS* (General Packet Radio Service).

Graphical User Interface (technical term)

See *GUI*.

Gray-hat hacker (slang)
Term for someone who is a mix of *white-hat* and *black-hat hacker* who some-times undertakes illicit hacking or cracking (breaking into systems), but perhaps with some kind of imagined noble purpose.

Gripe site (web term)
An internet presence established to complain about another business or individual. Often takes the form of "(name)sucks.com" where (name) is the organization or individual being complained about. Smart businesses and celebrities increasingly register "(name)sucks.com" before others, to take them out of circulation. Hence, a series of names have appeared along the lines of "reallysucks".

Grove, Andy
Well-known industry figure who participated in the founding of *Intel,* steered it into a position of industry dominance, and now is its chairman (having also been chief executive). Intel is the world's most well-known micro-processor manufacturer and makes the fundamental *CPU* component of the current "standard" personal computer or PC architecture – used not only in user PCs, but increasingly in small- to large-scale servers. He wrote a book that reflected his business philosophy called *Only the Paranoid Survive.*

GSM (mobile term)
GSM today stands for Global System for Mobile Communications. However, it was originally the initials of the European special study group on mobile communications (Groupe Spécial Mobile). GSM is the standard for digital cellular telephony in Europe and many other parts of the world, and can support data as well as voice communications, making it a common mecha-nism for mobile internet access.

GSM uses radio frequencies in the UHF (Ultra High Frequency) range at 900 Mhz, with variants operating at 1,800 MHz and 1,900 MHz. The available spectrum is divided into 124 blocks (each of 200 kHz) which are reused in geographically separate "cells." Each frequency block is further subdivided into 8 "timeslots," each of which can carry a single digitized voice call. A single timeslot supports a data rate of 34 Kbps but much of this must be used for error correction, giving an effective of data rate of 9,600 bps available throughout the whole network, and up to 14.4 Kbps where there is good reception.

GSM has been a hugely successful architecture and is being used as the pattern for future mobile communication systems.

GUI (technical term)

Stands for Graphical User Interface – an interface that uses graphics and intuitive methods of interaction, such as that provided by a computer mouse. Very common these days and the way almost all people interact with the world wide web through the major browsers such as **Netscape Navigator** and Microsoft's **Internet Explorer**.

Hack (slang)

Normally means attempting to gain access to a computer system for which you do not have permission, often to cause some form of damage.

Hacker (slang)

To the popular press a hacker is a shady individual who maliciously attempts to access computer systems without permission. In the software industry it can also mean an enthusiastic (but possibly unstructured) programmer with a love of technology. The internet supports a thriving and creative community of this kind of person. For this reason, some people prefer to use the term "cracker" to describe a malicious individual, but this also has a special meaning to cryptographers who use it to describe someone who breaks codes.

Hacktivist (slang)

Refers to a politically motivated hacker who makes some kind of moral or political point by, for example, breaking into a corporate website and altering the content.

Handheld Device Mark-up Language (mobile term)

See *HDML*.

Hard launch (business term)

See *launch*.

HDML (mobile term)

Stands for Handheld Device Mark-up Language. A mark-up language for displaying text designed by the company *Phone.com* for use on mobile devices, it was a precursor to *WML* (Wireless Mark-up Language) which has now largely superseded HDML.

Hertz (technical term)

A hertz is a unit for measuring frequency or ranges of frequency and is equivalent to one cycle per second. Hertz are used when referring to the internal speed of a computer's *CPU* or an allocation of radio spectrum for mobile communications. The symbol for hertz is Hz.

Hewlett Packard (company)

Founded in 1939 by Bill Hewlett and Dave Packard in a Palo Alto garage, Hewlett Packard (HP) are probably best known in the e-commerce world as a supplier of high-performance *UNIX* servers (and the laserjet printer). However, other achievements include giving the industry the term "garage startup," creating the first handheld scientific calculator (the HP35), and manufacturing very high-quality test and measurement equipment.

In 1999 HP announced a strategy to split out the test and measurement side of its business to form a new organization called Agilent and also to focus on developing infrastructure to support e-services over the internet.

As for the garage, it was officially designated a California State Historical Landmark in 1987, and a picture can be found at **www.hp.com/abouthp/hpgarage.html**.

History (web term)

A *browser* on a particular PC will typically maintain a "history" of websites its user has visited within some pre-set period of time. This allows users to backtrack, or helps a browser make suggestions after the user has typed the beginning of the name of a commonly visited site. It also allows anxious parents to see what their offspring have been doing on the web.

Hit (web term)

This is a broad measure of how often a website is accessed, and usually refers to a request for each major component of a page, including text, graphics, and other items. Since the number of hits can vary according to the complexity of a page, this is a fairly opaque measure of site traffic. Typically, a view of a single web page results in six or more hits.

Home (web term)

Usually used as an abbreviation for *home page* and employed on websites as a link to take you back to the start.

On a *browser* menu bar the "Home" button takes the user to a defined web page. This is usually the page loaded when the browser first starts.

Home page (web term)

The first main page displayed when accessing a website. For personal websites, the home page is often the entire site.

HomeRF (technical term)

Home RF is a *wireless* network technology aimed at the home and promoted by *Intel* in their AnyPoint range. The need for any sort of network in the home may seem a little estoteric, but in households with more than one PC, being able to share a dial-up internet connection or a printer without trailing cables between rooms has many benefits. HomeRF is designed to be simpler to install and manage than its main competitor (known as IEEE 802.11), which is used in corporate Wireless Local Area Networks (*WLANs*).

Host (technical term)

Host has a similar meaning to *server* and typically describes a computer on which an application is executed. In e-commerce, it usually refers to the computer on which a website is physically located. Website hosting by third parties has become big business, removing the need for a company to manage its own technical infrastructure if it wants to have a web presence.

Hosting (web term)

Running a website on a server – often as a commercial service.

HotBot.com (web site)

Launched in 1996, a popular search engine and portal linked to *Wired* magazine. Part of a collection of "Wired Digital" services, which are currently owned by Lycos.

Hotwired.com (web site)

As with HotBot, a website linked to *Wired* magazine, which covers web technology and culture.

HSCSD (mobile term)

Stands for High Speed Circuit Switched Data. HSCSD uses the existing *GSM* mobile phone network to transmit data at up to 57 Kbits per second by effectively making four simultaneous connections. Unlike General Packet Radio Service (*GPRS*) the network capacity is not shared with other users and is better suited to applications such as the transfer of large files, rather than internet surfing.

HTML (web term)

HTML stands for Hyper Text Mark-up Language. It is the basic and essentially universal language that tells a *browser* both what text to display and also how to display it. This latter formatting aspect is really what the term "mark-up language" means. HTML works in a manner that is independent of the type of browser and end system. Along with the *HTTP* protocol and the concept of *URLs*, HTML is one of the technical foundations of the original web. HTML was originated by *Tim Berners-Lee* with other aspects of the web in the early 1990s, made popular initially through early browsers like *Mosaic*, and is now controlled by the World Wide Web Consortium (which you can read about at **www.w3.org**). Like many of the foundation components of the web, interoperability across software platforms (essentially different kinds of browsers) and display devices (PCs, mobile devices like PDAs, etc.) is a key theme of HTML.

Its core has been stable for some years, and at the time of writing the latest standard version is HTML 4.01, which has new features related to internationalization, accessibility for those with disabilities, upgraded technical facilities, and the like. It is also worth saying that the architecture of the web is growing in sophistication (at the expense of some simplicity) through initiatives such as **XML**, which supplement and extend the concepts behind HTML. Here we will focus on classic HTML, however. See the entry on **world wide web** for a more architectural view of past and current developments.

As a language, especially when compared against more conventional programming languages, the format of HTML is simple. It is almost trite to say so, but this is one of the critical reasons for the popularity of both HTML and the bigger concept of the world wide web. It is easy to learn HTML and create web pages. It is easy to create links between web pages. It is easy to create web pages that have a common look and feel on different software and hardware platforms. These attributes were at the center of HTML's original design goals.

HTML's structure consists of a mix of plain text – which is intended to be displayed – and **tags** (special commands) which contain formatting instructions. HTML is a simplified descendent of **SGML** – a much more general mark-up language with similar syntactical features.

Figure 1 shows how HTML works. A stream of HTML instructions can come from a file containing HTML, or perhaps more typically, it can be transmitted from a webserver – a software component designed to support multiple browsers using Hypertext Transport Protocol (**HTTP**).

In simple websites, the webserver itself reads the HTML from a set of files and passes it on. However, this is a static approach, and if the web pages need to contain more dynamic information (such as a share price), then the HTML can be generated "on the fly" as the output of another, more complex

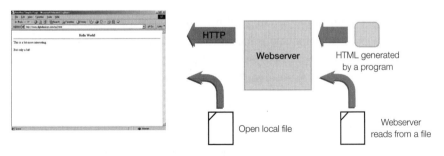

HTML 1: How HTML works

program. These server-side activities are hidden from browsers, which simply issue a **URL** and see a stream of HTML returned over HTTP.

Now for some HTML basics to give a flavor of the language (non-programmers shouldn't worry too much at this point: HTML is a very simple programming language). A whole web page starts with the tag <HTML> and finishes with </HTML>. Note the use of angle brackets (< >) to show the browser what is a tag. Also note that when tags surround a body of text, the notation <sometag> to start, and </sometag> with a backslash to finish the text block is also typical.

An example is always worth a thousand words, so ...

```
<HTML>
    ...contents of the web page
</HTML>
```

The description of each page is structured into a header (which contains summary information about the page) and the body, which is the part actually displayed by the browser. Again the format is very simple:

```
<HTML>
<HEAD>
Header information
</HEAD>
<BODY>
Information to be displayed
</BODY>
</HTML>
```

The header of the page contains information about the page that typically isn't displayed. There is one important exception, the text between the tag pair <TITLE> and </TITLE> will appear in the browser's own banner bar. So if the browser were to receive the following stream of characters:

```
<HTML><HEAD><TITLE>Simple Page</TITLE></HEAD> <BODY>Hello
World!</BODY></HTML>
```

It will display something like the screen shown in Figure 2.

The title

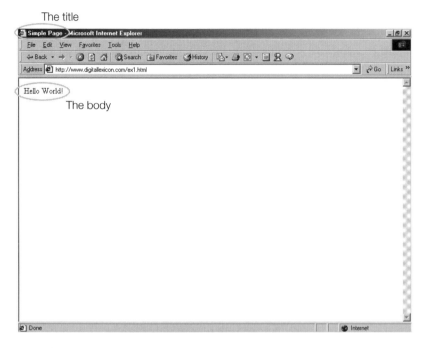

The body

HTML 2: Sample screen

In a serious website, the HEAD section may also contain **meta-tags** using the META keyword. Meta-tags aren't for display, but they do define characteristics and parameters the writer wants to record. Their particular importance is that some (although by no means all) web **search engines** send out **crawlers** to search and collect meta-tags to build search indexes. So, if you want your site to be popular and relatively easy to find, one essential step is to identify relevant keywords using META. For example:

```
<META name="keywords" content="icecream vanilla
chocolate flake ice cream">
```

Body beautiful

The web would be a monotonous (although somewhat speedier) place if all that could be displayed was simple text. There are plenty more tags, which allow the HTML to instruct the browser to:

➡ format text (e.g. use different fonts or layout data in tables)

➡ include "hyperlinks" to other pages

➡ embed images

➡ support data entry

➡ embed other content from other websites.

Some of the simpler tags that support these kinds of functions are described below; a more complete list of tags can be found in the large number of currently available HTML books, or at **www.w3.org**.

Another example:

```
<HTML><HEAD><TITLE>Another Simple Page</TITLE></HEAD>
<BODY><CENTER><B>Hello World!</B></CENTER>
<HR>This is a bit more interesting.<P>But only a bit!
</BODY></HTML>
```

Here, the <B> </B> pair of tags tells the browser to display Hello World in bold, the <CENTER> </CENTER> pair tell it to center the text on the page. The <HR> tag causes a horizontal rule (i.e. a line) to be drawn and the <P> tag tells the browser to start a new paragraph (note that <P> does not need to be paired). So we can use these to liven up our simple page as shown in Figure 3.

This type of tag is useful for improving readability, but doesn't enable surfing between pages. To do this we need a way of including a reference within the page, which a browser can treat specially and (when clicked on by the end-user) follow to a new page. Such a reference is normally called a hyperlink. Returning to our example, one technique to insert a link is to use the <A> </A> tag pair and an "attribute" (HREF). Here the A stands for "anchor".

```
<HTML><HEAD><TITLE>Page With Link</TITLE></HEAD>
<BODY><CENTER><B>Hello World!</B></CENTER>
<HR>This is a bit more interesting.<P>But only a bit!<HR>
<A HREF=www.somesite.com>Link to another place</A>
</BODY></HTML>
```

Note how the destination URL (the destination for the link) is put immediately after HREF, and the text that will be displayed in best underlined style,

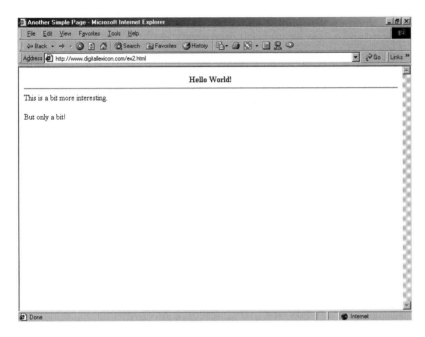

HTML 3: Sample screen

to indicate the link, is put between the `<A>`, `<\A>` tags. The result will look something like the screen shown in Figure 4.

As well as including a link to another page, the browser can retrieve information referenced by a URL and include it within the current page.

For example:

```
<HTML><HEAD><TITLE>Page With Picture</TITLE></HEAD>
<BODY><CENTER><B>Hello World!</B></CENTER>
<HR>Here comes a picture<HR>
<IMG SRC="http://liftoff.msfc.nasa.gov/temp/StationLoc.gif">
</BODY></HTML>
```

Here the tag `<IMG>` (which stands for "image") tells the browser where to get hold of the external content. In this case, it is a graphic of the position of the International Space Station, and the result looks something like the screen shown in Figure 5.

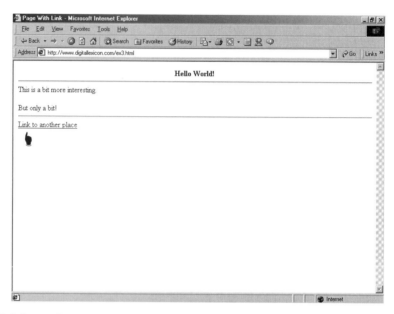

HTML 4: Sample Screen

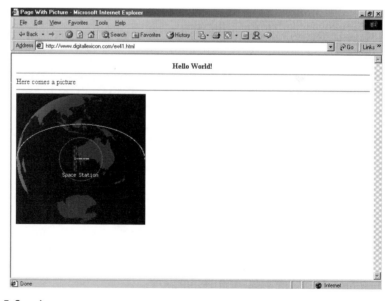

HTML 5: Sample screen

Typically browsers know how to display images in standard *GIF* or *JPEG* formats, both of which are commonly used on the web. To embed different types of media or applications, we need to use the more general <OBJECT> tag. We could have used the <OBJECT> tag in the example above as follows:

```
<HTML><HEAD><TITLE>Page With Picture</TITLE></HEAD>
<BODY><CENTER><B>Hello World!</B></CENTER>
<HR>Here comes a picture (as an Object)<HR>
<OBJECT
data="http://liftoff.msfc.nasa.gov/temp/StationLoc.gif"
type="image/jpeg">
</OBJECT>
</BODY></HTML>
```

This would have produced the same results. <OBJECT> is more powerful than <IMG> since it does not rely on the browser knowing how to handle a certain format. This can be further generalized to support programs that execute within the page (e.g. *Java applets* and *Active-X*), in which case the <OBJECT> tag includes references to the location of the code to execute, the parameters it should be passed, and the visual area on the page it should use for output. This allows very complex web pages to be built. For completeness, you should note that OBJECT replaces a slightly older type of tag called APPLET.

User interaction

So far we have seen how HTML can be used to format text, images and output from other objects (including programs). HTML also allows simple interaction with the user. This is through use of the <FORM> </FORM> tag pair. Within these tags, we can include common data entry "widgets" such as:

➡ text entry
➡ check boxes
➡ radio buttons
➡ dropdown menus
➡ buttons.

Here is an example:

```
<HTML><HEAD><TITLE>Page With Form</TITLE></HEAD>
<BODY><CENTER><B>Hello World!</B></CENTER>
<HR>Here comes a Form<HR>
<FORM>
Type some text: <INPUT TYPE="text" VALUE="UK" SIZE="2">
<HR>
Browsers you use (check all that apply):
<BR><INPUT TYPE="checkbox" CHECKED> MS IE
<BR><INPUT TYPE="checkbox" CHECKED> Netscape
<BR><INPUT TYPE="checkbox" CHECKED> Opera
<HR>
Select a channel
<INPUT TYPE="radio" CHECKED> Hard
<INPUT TYPE="radio"> Medium
<INPUT TYPE="radio"> Soft
<HR>
Year you first used the internet:<BR>
<SELECT>
   <OPTION> 2000
   <OPTION SELECTED> 1999
   <OPTION> Before 1999
</SELECT>
<HR>
<INPUT TYPE="reset">
<INPUT TYPE="submit">
</FORM>
</BODY></HTML>
```

This results in the screen shown in Figure 6 (which has some annotations).

HTML is close to the end of its development path, and Version 4 will be the last major version. The reason for this is that although HTML is a fairly complete standard, the underlying architecture of the web is being extended and generalized. **DHTML** was one step towards this (the D stands for dynamic

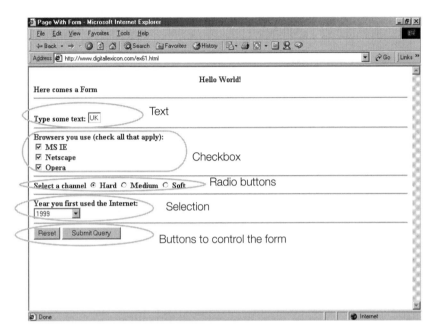

HTML 6: Sample screen

and DHTML does allow more dynamic content, graphic effects, and inter-activity). Current focus however is on XHTML Version 1, which expresses HTML in the much more general **XML** (Extensible Mark-up Language). This will allow developers to extend the features offered by the language in a way understandable to a new generation of browsers and access devices.

HTTP (web term)

Stands for Hypertext Transport Protocol. As the name suggests, HTTP is a network **protocol** for transporting hypertext files between computers. It is the protocol that browsers use to communicate with webservers over the inter-net, and therefore a fundamental building block of the world wide web.

HTTPS (web term)

Stands for Hypertext Transport Protocol – Secure. HTTPS is a version of **HTTP** that uses encryption to protect information passing between webservers and browsers. When used in combination with digital *certificates* it can also pro-vide *authentication* that the other party is who they claim to be. HTTPS uses the standard and very common Secure Sockets Layer (*SSL*).

Hybrid (business term)

Used to describe a business model that combines physical assets – like buildings or people – with online functionality. Similar in meaning to *clicks and mortar*.

Hyperlink (web term)

A hyperlink is a "shortcut" from one place in an electronic document to somewhere else, possibly in another document. The term is often shortened to just "link." The concept in some form has been around since the 1940s (see *Bush, Vannevar*). On the web, the Hypertext Mark-up Language (*HTML*) includes commands to embed links to another place on the web, and *browsers* understand that if the user clicks on the link, the resource refer-enced needs to be downloaded. To the user a link is typically represented by underlined text. Hyperlinks are now so familiar that it's hard to imagine that they were once thought of as something innovative.

Hypertext (web term)

Hypertext can be thought of as information (text, image, and sound) that can be browsed in various orders (rather than starting at the beginning and fol-lowing one path to the end). It is a much older idea than the web or *HTML* (Hypertext Mark-up Language). The actual term was first used by *Ted Nelson* in the famous (but never fully realized) *Xanadu* project.

i-

Sometimes used (in lower case form) as a prefix to stand for "internet". Generally used in commercial names and always in lowercase form. A variant on *e-*, *cyber*, and *online.*

i2 (company name)

Software and services company focussed on tools for building *e-marketplaces* or *exchange* solutions.

IAB (organization)

First, some preamble. The internet is an organic, vast, and heterogenous network of systems and component networks, as well as a home for many different and diverse communities, and there is no real central point of control. Nevertheless there is a variety of international, non-governmental, and non-profit organizations that do impose some degree of regulation and encourage collaboration between interested parties. These groups are interrelated, and their overall structure can seem complicated, although this reflects the scale of the internet community, and the need to get consensus across diverse communities of interest. As an example, one important group is *ICANN* (described below) which supports the *Domain Name System.* Technical development and the setting of standards are supported by a variety of groups organized around **ISOC** (the Internet Society).

The IAB or Internet Architecture Board is one of the groups linked to ISOC. It is a technical advisory and oversight group for ISOC, which selects members of other groups and committees, and oversees the process used to create internet standards, including editorial control and publication of the very important Request for Comments (**RFC**) documents, which are the mechanisms for extending the common technical features of the internet.

IANA (organization)

Stands for Internet Assigned Numbers Authority. Responsible – under the late and much missed Dr Jon Postel – for control of **IP addresses** and similar. Its functions have now been transferred to a much more complicated organization called **ICANN**, which is discussed below.

IAP (business term)

Short for Internet Access Provider, an alternative to ISP or Internet Service Provider. See the **ISP** entry for more details.

IBM (company name)

IBM (which stands for International Business Machines, although the abbreviation is really never expanded) remains one of the most well-known names in the computing industry. IBM's story started somewhat incredibly in 1890, when Herman Hollerith won a government competition with his punch-card tabulating machine. He later formed the Tabulating Machine Co. in 1896. In 1911, this company merged with two others to create the Computing-Tabulating-Recording Company, which would later be renamed IBM. As the computer age took hold, IBM became increasingly dominant with its strong sales culture and range of "big iron" mainframe computers. It was also responsible for the creation of the main de facto standard for personal computers (see below). However, through the 1980s, IBM became increasingly troubled as the computer world shifted from mainframes to microcomputers, servers, and networks. The giant had stumbled.

The company's solution was the appointment of **Louis Gerstner** who became IBM's chairman and CEO on April 1, 1993 – the first leader from outside the company. Widely expected to split IBM into smaller, more dynamic pieces, he kept IBM whole to focus on integrated solutions. However, Gestner did achieve profound change. IBM is now seen as a major player in hardware, software solutions, and services in the e-commerce world (partly achieved through a major long-running ad campaign around the word "e-business"). In 1999, IBM had revenues of almost $90 billion and employed over 300,000 people. It remains one of the most influential companies in the technology world.

IBM PC (technical term)

IBM didn't invent the personal computer. Working prototypes built at Xerox, kits like the Altair, and the first commercially successful personal computer from Apple came beforehand. However, IBM did introduce the systems architecture that evolved into the current de facto standard for personal computers. When people refer to a PC, they are usually referring to a system of this type – sometimes made by IBM, but more usually from a supplier like Dell, Compaq, and so on. The majority of client machines currently connected to the internet are PCs descended from the original IBM PC architecture.

IBM had several false starts with the personal computer concept, including one machine called the IBM 5100 and another plan based around buying Atari. However, success was finally achieved through "Project Chess" – with the new computer codenamed "Acorn." The first IBM PC used an Intel 8088 microprocessor as its CPU, came with just 16 kilobytes of memory (expandable to 256 kilobytes), with up to two floppy disk drives. Shortly after launch, *Time Magazine* named the PC as its "man of the year."

Unusually for the IBM of the period, the IBM PC had an "open" architecture – based on generally available standard components – which launched a new industry, as manufacturers such as Compaq and Dell started producing what were originally called "clones" and now just "PCs." It also served as a launch pad for *Intel* and *Microsoft* – the latter providing the basic operating system software. The technical architecture of the PC has developed significantly and many multi-user servers are built around a PC-like set of components.

The future of the PC is an interesting and much debated issue. Sales have flattened, and new generations of devices such as *PDAs* or even smart phones offer personal computing capability in different ways.

ICANN (organization)

ICANN is part of the administrative infrastructure of the internet. ICANN stands for the Internet Corporation for Assigned Names and Numbers. A private but non-profit organization, its focus is the technical management of the internet's *Domain Name System*, the allocation of *IP addresses*, and key network protocol parameters. This is important stuff, since these areas define how "cyberspace" is laid out. ICANN was founded in October 1998, and replaces previous more informal and ad hoc arrangements.

Underneath its main board, ICANN has three main component pieces: the Address Supporting Organization focussed on the IP address space, the Domain Name Supporting Organization focussed on policy issues relating to the Domain Name System, and the Protocol Supporting Organization which focusses on network protocols.

In November 2000, ICANN introduced a new set of top-level domains – equivalent to .com – which included names such as .biz and .museum. The Domain Name System is an emotional topic for many, and the coverage of ICANN and these new names has been mixed to say the least.

ICANN's main website is **www.icann.org**.

ICQ (product)

A name derived from "I seek you", ICQ is a popular, user-friendly chat/instant messaging tool and service that notifies its users when a friend or contact is online (each user being allocated a unique ICQ number). ICQ supports many forms of communication, including chat, e-mail, voice, message boards, and was developed by a company called Mirabilis. ICQ is now part of the AOL stable, and has around 50 million users.

idealab! (company name)

An *incubator* in the internet/e-commerce world is a company that takes very small startups and grows them into maturer entities through a variable mix of funding and services. In many ways idealab! is the original model of this kind of organization. Examples of idealab!-supported companies include the well-known eToys and Goto.com. Idealab! was founded in 1996 by entrepreneur Bill Gross and remains a privately-held company. It provides access to capital (that is, funding) office space and technical infrastructure, graphic design, marketing, business advice, and other consulting services. Within the e-commerce world, idealab! became a well-known brand and tended to improve the chances for a startup simply by its involvement. With the bursting of the dot-com bubble in 2000, all incubators have of course found the market much more challenging.

IE (product)
Common abbreviation for the Microsoft *Internet Explorer* browser.

IETF (organization)
ITEF stands for the Internet Engineering Task Force and is one of the more important bodies in the development of the internet. It held its first meeting in 1986. Attached to *ISOC* (the Internet Society), it is a large, open, international community of network designers, operators, vendors, and researchers. There is no true membership and anyone can attend any meeting. The closest thing to membership is being listed on IETF mailing lists. Areas tackled by ITEF working groups include: internet applications, the underlying structure of the internet, the IP protocol, network management, operational requirements, routing, and security.

The main IETF website is at **www.ietf.org**.

I love you (security term)
Every so often a *virus* comes along that causes sufficient damage to enough systems globally, that it gets global media attention and name recognition. The "I love you" strain hit the headlines in May 2000. It was manifested as an attachment to an e-mail with a variety of headings (including "I love you"). The attachment was a program that when opened would maliciously overwrite many types of file and then send itself on to addresses in the host PC's Microsoft *Outlook* e-mail address book – a common technique.

IM, IMing (internet term)
Common abbreviations for *instant messaging*.

iMac (product)
A member of *Apple's* Macintosh range, the iMac is a personal computer designed for ease of use and quick internet access. One of its key aspects is its good looks, with translucent styling in colors such as ruby, indigo, sage,

graphite, and snow (Apple's terms). The iMac runs Apple's Mac OS operating system, which doesn't have the same degree of market penetration as Microsoft Windows, but has a loyal following. The iMac is a consumer-orientated product, so some models will play DVDs and all models have software to play MP3 audio files.

IMAP (e-mail term)

IMAP (Internet Message Access Protocol) is a standard protocol for accessing e-mail from one or more servers. The latest version of the standard is IMAP4. IMAP is a client–server protocol in which e-mail is received and held on a server system. Using a client-side e-mail program, the user can look at just the heading and the sender of the e-mail, and then decide whether to download and open the full message. Other facilities allow a user to create folders and mailboxes on the server, and manipulate and search for messages. IMAP is more modern than the very common *POP* (Post Office Protocol) standard, which has a store and forward model based on copying messages to the client system in one go.

iMode (technical term)

iMode is a wireless internet system operated in Japan by NTT DoCoMo. iMode phones include a microbrowser capable of displaying a subset of HTML called compact HTML (cHTML). They access the internet at a relatively slow 9,600 bps via the DoCoMo managed "iMode Center".

iMode has become incredibly popular in technology obsessed Japan, and is a strong competitor to *WAP* (Wireless Application Protocol), which seems to have proved less successful in a broader market.

Impression (web term)

Shortened version of *page impression* – a metric of website usage. See *page view* (a near synonym) for a specific discussion and *measurement* for a more general discussion of common website and web advertising metrics.

Incubator (business term)

Covers a wide range of different businesses that offer a range of services to help "incubate" new ideas and turn them into viable businesses. Services offered include basic facilities (office space) and some technology services, seed capital, business startup and strategic advice, and connection to a greater network of companies in similar positions. Examples of incubators in the e-commerce space include the well-known US-based *idealab!* and *CMGI*, although incubators pre-date the internet as a concept. Many traditional consulting companies have experimented with incubator-like constructs as a natural vehicle for delivery of their services to new businesses, usually for a mixture of fees and equity. Some major companies have trialled similar concepts for internally generated ideas. The incubator space has – like many niches – become crowded, with 200 in the UK alone at peak. This is a number that is proving unsustainable, particularly in the much more pessimistic markets of mid-2000 onwards. Some incubators have moved into working with *dot corps* – spin-offs from existing major companies – rather than the startup *dot com* space that was the original focus of internet incubators.

Infobahn (business term)
Occasional synonym for information superhighway.

Infomediary (business term)
Describes e-commerce companies that act as intermediaries between buyers and sellers. The value infomediaries can offer to customers may be based on discounting, but can also include provision of broader information allowing customers to make more reasoned choices between suppliers. They are potentially important in areas like financial services, and the *B2B* world where buyers and sellers can come together in vertical online communities. They demonstrate a business approach that is directly opposite to *disintermediation* where buyers and sellers can communicate directly, cutting out previous middlemen. The term "infomediary" was first coined in the book *Net Worth* by Hagel and Singer.

Information superhighway (business term)
Term used (and much associated with Al Gore) as a metaphor for the internet. Popular in the mid 1990s.

Informix (company name)
One of a number of companies created around *database management systems* in the 1980s. Informix is a well-established name in this area, although it has

never achieved the level of brand recognition and market penetration that *Oracle* has. As well as the core database engine, the current Informix range includes tools to build e-commerce websites and other software development tools.

Infotainment (business term)

Compound of information and entertainment. Refers to e-commerce offerings that combine the two in some way – although it is used without much precision. See also *e-entertainment*.

Initial Public Offering (business term)

A simple concept: a privately-held company's first sale of stock to the general public, resulting in some kind of stock market listing. This can apply to big established companies, such as Goldman Sachs which famously moved from a traditional partnership-structure to a listed corporate structure. Recently of course, this term is most associated with internet and e-commerce companies. The internet IPO trend could be said to have started with the successful IPO of loss-making *Netscape* in the mid-1990s. For a period, a great many business plans were based on the "liquidity event" and wealth-creation offered by an IPO, and many companies were traded at way above their initial valuation within hours of an IPO. Much greater restraint on the part of investors set in during 2000, and at the time of writing IPOs have become much rarer, and the stock market value of many new companies has tumbled from their original valuations.

Inktomi (company name)

Founded in 1996, Inktomi is a company that supplies infrastructure software to many website operators. Inktomi's products offer support for improving network efficiency, content management, and – most visibly – powering search engines and portals.

Innovators' dilemma (general term)

Title of a well-known book by Clayton Christensen, which pre-dates the mass explosion of e-commerce, but is often referenced in an e-commerce context. The text covers the reasons why successful companies lose their market position (particularly technology companies) and what happens when an approach of continuous improvement of an existing type of product is overtaken by a more fundamental change or "disruptive innovation."

Instant messaging (internet term)

Covers a range of services (for which there is no common standard) that allow immediate communication between logged-on users across the internet. Services are offered by *ICQ, AOL, Yahoo!*, and others.

Integrity (security term)

Not a comment on the personal characteristics of a venture capitalist, but rather a general computing security term that means that a computer system (hardware and software) is thought to be in a well-designed, robust, and secure state.

Intel (company)

Intel – along with *Microsoft, Oracle, Cisco*, and *Sun* – is one of the major technology suppliers that both shapes and dominates their particular market space. Intel's most obvious products are the microprocessors or chips that act as the central processor in industry-standard personal computers (*PCs*). In fact, PCs are sometimes referred to as being based on the "Wintel" standard, a hybrid term combining Windows – the Microsoft operating system – and Intel.

Intel's first microprocessor (the 4004) was produced in 1971 to power calculators. In 1974, the Intel 8080 microprocessor become the core engine of a kit-based personal computer called the Altair, which sold many thousands and inspired the creation of the first true commercial PCs, such as the Apple II. What become pivotal to the development of both Intel, and the now familiar PC marketplace, was IBM's decision to put the Intel 8088/8086 chip into their new PC. IBM's backing made the new-type PC a dominant standard, but it was also – unusually for the IBM at that period – an open standard. This meant that other manufacturers began to produce clones of the IBM PC, creating new markets for both Microsoft and Intel. This moved Intel into the Fortune 500, and *Fortune* magazine named the company one of the "Business Triumphs of the Seventies." Through the 1980s, Intel released successively more powerful developments of the 8086, specifically the Intel 286, the Intel 386, and Intel 486. In 1993, Intel introduced what should have been the 586, but was branded Pentium since numbers were proving hard to trademark. Further releases have continued to be mainly under the Pentium banner. It is worth pointing out that a variety of other microprocessor companies, like AMD, have fuelled their growth by producing chips that can imitate the functions of Intel processors.

Intel's centrality to the architecture of the PC (not to mention servers derived from a PC architecture) has fuelled spectacular growth, with revenues of around $4 billion in 1990 rising to just shy of $30 billion in 1999.

Intel is obviously a core platform technology supplier to the e-commerce and internet worlds – an Intel microprocessor being part of many PCs in use. Intel chips also sit at the heart of increasingly powerful families of servers. As a reflection of this, Intel's mission statement at the time of writing is: "Do a great job for our customers, employees and stockholders by being the pre-eminent building-block supplier to the worldwide internet economy."

Intellectual property (business term)

Covers the ownership of things that aren't physical but related to the realm of ideas and the intellect. Examples include ideas and inventions, literary works, music and art, product names, and logos. Ways of safeguarding intellectual property include patents (for ideas and inventions), copyright (for writing, software, art, and music), and trademarking. The internet, and e-commerce in general, are at the center of a number of intense debates in this area. For example, there is a growing community exchanging MP3-format files, which can contain high-quality copies of copyrighted music tracks (see *Napster*). Conversely, a number of simple business processes – like *Amazon*'s one-click method of buying – have been patented. There is also a strong community that believes software should be essentially free and which has found voice in the *open source* movement. See also *copyright*.

Interactive television, Interactive TV (technical term)

As well as providing many more channels, *digital television* (DTV) also provides a platform for greater user interaction and e-commerce, with the DTV set-top box (STB) taking the place of a PC and using the TV to display information to the user.

Possible models for interactive TV (iTV) include:

➡ using special, highly visual content held on the DTV provider's own servers;

➡ using the STB and DTV network as a means of accessing the web and displaying web pages on the TV;

➡ "enhancing" TV programs by including additional information or integrated advertisements.

The UK market is one in which interactive television is making its mark. Examples of UK services currently launched include:

➡ **Open....:** (the four dots are part of the brand name) operated by Sky Digital (Rupert Murdoch's digital satellite television service). At the time of writing Open is a "walled garden" and does not provide access to the wider web. Custom-developed e-commerce applications are held on Open servers and downloaded to the STB over a satellite channel. The satellite channel is one-way, and feedback from the user is sent via a phone-line modem connection. Since content is specifically designed for the set-top box, the service is not accessible over the internet.

➡ **NTL InteractiveTV:** operates digital cable infrastructure (which can support high speed connectivity in both directions). NTL recently acquired the Cable & Wireless Cable TV business in the UK and plans to integrate the two platforms using common STB software from a company called Liberate.

➡ **OnNet:** operates over the OnDigital terrestrial digital TV network and relies on a modem connection for connectivity in both directions. OnNet provides a browser add-on to the STB and a portal site (**www. ondigital.co.uk/ onnet**) which provides some optimization to assist navigation using a remote control. OnNet provides access through to the web and in theory any website could be accessed by entering a URL. However, some organizations have developed special versions of their sites optimized for DTV.

One early beneficiary in the UK has been Domino's Pizza which (according to the *Financial Times*) was selling pizza worth over £30,000 through interactive TV in July 2000.

Internet (technical term)

The term an "internet" once was a plain reference to an "internetwork" or network of networks where single networks – which may vary different in nature – are coupled together. Messages can be sent from a device or system on one network to another device on a connected, but independent network. See also *internetworking.*

Now of course we talk about "the internet" or even "the Internet" with an upper case I – a single global network. To a home user, it is the world that exists at the other end of a *modem*. Many now use the term "internet" synomously with the web, although the *world wide web* is actually just one type of application that can sit on top of the internet proper. To the more technically minded, the internet is a global collection of networks (and attached systems) which, although very varied, use the *TCP/IP* network protocol family as the main mechanism for exchanging data. The following two definitions are easily found on the internet itself:

The Internet is a global network of networks enabling computers of all kinds to directly and transparently communicate and share services throughout much of the world. Because the Internet is an enormously valuable, enabling capability for so many people and organizations, it also constitutes a shared global resource of information, knowledge, and means of collaboration, and cooperation among countless diverse communities.

The Internet Society main website at **www.isoc.org**, 2000

The Federal Networking Council (FNC) agrees that the following language reflects our definition of the term "Internet".

"Internet" refers to the global information system that –

(i)   is logically linked together by a globally unique address space based on the Internet Protocol (IP) or its subsequent extensions/follow-ons;

(ii)   is able to support communications using the Transmission Control Protocol/Internet Protocol (TCP/IP) suite or its subsequent extensions/follow-ons, and/or other IP-compatible protocols; and

(iii)   provides, uses or makes accessible, either publicly or privately, high level services layered on the communications and related infrastructure described herein.

Federal Networking Council, October 24, 1995

Much of this book is concerned with terms and concepts related to the internet. The rest of this particular article gives a whirlwind tour of some of the structural concepts.

Design principles and characteristics

Some of the design characteristics of the internet arose in the 1960s when researchers began to think of how to make computer networks resilient. Key notions included:

➡ Packet-switching, where messages and data are split up into *packets* (also called *datagrams*) which can be sent independently to a destination computer, arriving in no set order and maybe over alternative routes through the network, to be reassembled.

➡ Having no central point of control, so that networks can grow organically or lose nodes without impacting the function of other components of the network.

These concepts were trialled within the *ARPANET* project – the immediate ancestor of the internet – from the late 1960s. The technology developed was first very much a platform for governmental and other researchers, and academics. However, from about 1988 onwards the use of the internet snowballed, particularly with the appearance of the user-friendly, graphically oriented world wide web in the 1990s. As a result it became a network with hundreds of millions of users, millions of connected systems, and many tens of thousands of interlinked networks which offered a platform for e-mail, other forms of communication, recreation, and e-commerce.

TCP/IP: the protocol engine

One of the key components of the internet is a family of network *protocols* and software that are grouped under the banner *TCP/IP*. A network protocol is a set of rules for exchanging information over a network. These will be implemented through low-level software services that an application program will use, but which are invisible to the normal user. TCP stands for Transmission Control Protocol. TCP takes a message and splits it into packets of data which it then hands to the Internet Protocol or IP. IP has a simple, but fundamental job. It sends each packet across a set of networking links to the destination system. At the other end, another instance of TCP then reassembles the original message. This enormously simplified description is represented in Figure 1 below.

The importance of TCP/IP cannot really be overstated. The actual network and system architecture of the internet is actually rather chaotic and certainly heterogenous (i.e. the internet supports many different types of network and computer). It is TCP/IP that adds a consistent and universally understood (by computers, at least) common language on top of this. As a result, the internet is a very open and adaptable network, which can grow organically and fast. TCP/IP is also relatively simple compared with other networking approaches, and became strongly linked with the *UNIX* operating system – itself a popular platform that influenced several generations of technologists. As a result, TCP/IP gained critical mass as the network protocol of choice in many different types of network, making their connection together into the internet something of a natural act.

TCP/IP was developed in the 1970s by *Vinton Cerf* and *Bob Kahn* as part of the original ARPANET project. Vint Cerf is commonly known as the "father of the internet," and remains an influential figure.

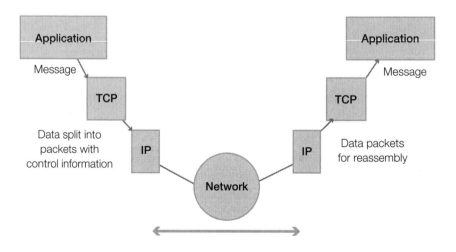

Internet 1: The role of TCP/IP

You may come across a number of other protocols that are related to TCP/IP. For example, UDP or User Datagram Protocol is a variant of TCP that is faster, but does less checking and is therefore less reliable. *HTTP* or Hypertext Transfer Protocol is part of the base architecture of the world wide web and treats TCP/IP as a lower-level service (this type of layering is typical of network-based architectures). Its job is essentially to carry web pages from websites to browsers.

Physical architecture

The architecture of the internet can be viewed in many different ways. One great simplification is shown in Figure 2 below.

The outer circle in the diagram represents the many personal or business users of the internet. These typically access the internet through networking businesses dedicated to the purpose – shown in the middle layer as *ISPs* or Internet Service Providers. At the center of the internet is a complex set of big backbone networks that connect ISPs and offer very high data transmission capacity. The triangle at the bottom indicates that some major corporates may choose to provide their own ISP-like services themselves.

At another level of detail, Figure 3 shows some of the specific networking components commonly found in internet access. The boxes labelled R are routers, the network hardware that glues the internet together.

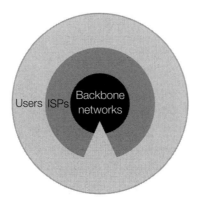

Internet 2: Layers of the internet

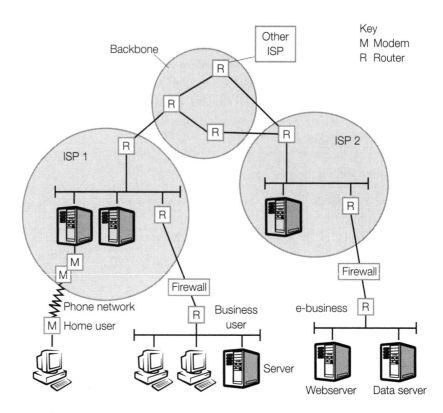

Internet 3: Networking components

Let's decompose this diagram further:

➡ It shows a home user connected to an ISP (labelled M) via a modem and the phone network. The modem will allow a phone line to carry a digital signal. Notice that the ISP has multiple modems to deal with many incoming phones calls.

➡ It also shows a business user – an organization – with a local area network with multiple machines and its own router, a fundamental piece of networking equipment that takes a set of IP packets and sends them to the next stage of their journey across multiple points of interconnection between different networks. The business also has a firewall – a set of software and hardware – designed to protect its network from prying eyes or intrusion.

➡ An ISP – labelled ISP 1 – provides access to both users. The ISP runs its own network, and may offer services such as website hosting (running other people's websites) or its own content (in which case, it might well call itself an *Online Service Provider*). However, the ISP's fundamental job is to route its customers' IP traffic to other points in the internet.

➡ To do this, the ISP offers a "point of presence" that allows it to inter-connect to the backbone networks at the core of the internet. The actual topology of the internet backbone is now extremely complex and some-what dynamic (although influenced by the original US government funded *NSFNET* which underpinned the ARPANET and early days of the internet). Major operators here include MCI Worldcom, Sprint, Uunet (part of Worldcom), GTE and so on. The underlying networks utilize very high-bandwidth media and large routers and switches – the aim being to move around enormous amounts of data at speed, and with great reliabi-lity. There are a number of major "Network Access Points" which allow backbone and ISP traffic to be connected, in places such as San Francisco, New Jersey, London, Paris, and Frankfurt.

➡ A second ISP (ISP 2) is also shown. In this case, it is shown supporting an e-business that runs its own website and associated data servers. Our original users may access this e-business through the multiple links shown in the diagram.

Who plays on the internet?

The internet is now host to all of human life, so it's worth thinking about the various types of organization that use the internet as a primary business or communication mechanism. The following list gives some broad categories. It isn't meant to be exhaustive, but its breadth certainly shows the potential for cultural clash or connection on the internet:

➡ ISPs – Internet Service Providers who provide basic connectivity to most individual and corporate users, usually with a range of value-added services.

- Online Service Providers – like AOL or Compuserve, who provide consumer access and their own distinctive content.

- Hosting companies – like *Exodus* – whose speciality is in running other people's websites within large, carefully managed data centers.

- Telcos – telecommunications companies, who control some of the fundamental transmission media, but often also offer their own ISP type service.

- Regulatory bodies – non-governmental organizations that provide a degree of regulation. Examples include *ISOC* (the Internet Society), which looks after the general technology development of the internet, and *ICANN*, which looks after the controversial areas of the Domain Name System and internet addressing schemes (in other words, the high-level map of cyberspace).

- Many academic and research organizations – who were the original users of the internet before it became a true mass medium.

- e-businesses – like *Amazon, Yahoo!* and a near-infinite number of others who use the internet and the world wide web as their core channel to customers.

- Traditional corporates who use the internet as an additional channel to customers, or a vehicle for a spin-off business.

- Personal users.

- Ad hoc but sometimes powerful communities that form around a particular website or theme. Examples could include the users of a file-sharing service like *Napster*, the various *open source* communities that co-develop software (often very good software), the more local communities that are the target of *Geocities*, the interest groups supported by auction house *eBay*, and so on.

Why did it become so popular?

Computers and networks have been around for decades, and there have been attempts to create something like the internet before. Many of these weren't successful (including various e-tailing schemes in the US) and some have had a degree of local success (like Minitel in France). So what explains the success of the internet? What follows is our opinion of the key factors, although we have left out obvious general trends such the growth in the power of computers.

- The internet is not only a network of networks, it looks and feels like a single network. Its architecture is specially designed to support, and thereby encourage, *internetworking*. If any system was to going to achieve critical mass through organic growth, it was the internet.

- It is based on open and accepted standards (e.g. TCP/IP). It supports many types of constituent network and system and provides a common language for them to exchange data.

- The internet, and associated technologies like TCP/IP or UNIX, have been popular in academia and technology communities for a long time. As a result, generations of graduates have moved into hardware and software companies with a predisposition towards the internet and its surrounding technologies.

- As a service, it is essentially free or close to it – with no charges related to distance. This seems easy enough to understand now, but is a remarkable shift in the way communications services are priced. (Although we must not forget the vast number of people in the world who cannot afford PCs or basic telephony services.)

- Although it doesn't always seem so, since scale has bought some very large problems, some of the key architectural features of the internet – like the Domain Name System – are simple, and support expansion.

- The internet has a history of loose regulation. Although there is very significant and heated debate about privacy and control, the internet has been well served by both its open technology and open culture.

- Although the explosive growth in the use of the internet predates the world wide web, the web is in some ways the ultimate *killer app*, introducing a method of interaction that is suited to all types of user, and – like the internet – based on a simple, but profound set of architectural concepts. It is the web that introduced the concepts of browsers and HTML – which define the primary way most people now use the internet (at least in addition to e-mail).

Internet2 (technical term)

Started in 1996, Internet2 is a non-profit consortium involving around 180 US universities, with support from a large number of commercial organizations. It is not a separate physical network intended to replace the current internet (although it does have a high-speed backbone called *vBNS*). It is a collaborative effort in several areas intended to support leading-edge applications not well supported by current internet technology. There are working groups in the areas of applications, middleware (covering standard approaches for authentication, authorization, directories, and security), advanced networks, and very high quality of service goals.

Internet Access Provider (business term)

An alternative term for *ISP* or Internet Service Provider. See *ISP* for more details.

Internet appliance (internet term)

Term used with not that much precision to describe a simple device that is connected to the internet; for example, a dedicated display terminal built to run a browser, rather than a full PC or workstation operating system.

Internet Architecture Board (organization)

See *IAB*.

Internet Assigned Numbers Authority (organization)

See *IANA*.

Internet Corporation for Assigned Names and Numbers (organization)

See *ICANN*.

Internet Explorer (product)

Microsoft's full-function web *browser* product which was introduced in October 1995, and has been integrated in the Windows 95 and Windows 98 operating systems. This integration was one of the focal points of the *Microsoft* anti-trust action in the USA.

Internet Protocol (technical term)

See *IP*.

Internet Relay Chat (technical term)
See *IRC*.

Internet Research Task Force (organization)
See *IRTF*.

Internet Service Provider (business term)
See *ISP*.

Internet Society (organization)
See *ISOC*.

Internet telephony (technical term)
Once upon a time phone lines carried voice, and data was added on top. Now the prime focus of telecoms companies is the transport of data. Internet telephony is an example of this, where voice messages are digitized and sent over the internet.

Internet time (slang)
The internet and e-commerce worlds have typically been very fast moving, and the term "internet time" has been used to reflect that pace, particularly when creating some kind of new startup. E-speed is a common equivalent.

Internetworking (internet term)
This section outlines some of the basic principles used for interconnecting multiple networks in an manner known as internetworking. Internetworking is one of the key structural concepts underpinning the internet.

To start, Figure 1 on page 156 shows a simple standalone office Local Area Network (*LAN*) where common resources such as printers, or servers for storing files are shared between PCs.

Now suppose that this network needs to be linked to another network in a different office, for instance to allow collaborative team working or wider access to a specialized computer hardware etc. (see Figure 2).

Could this be done by directly plugging the networks together to make one single network? The answer is generally no, for a variety of reasons:

➡ Networks vary, in terms of physical media, and software technology. Some users require very high-speed optical fiber. Others require more

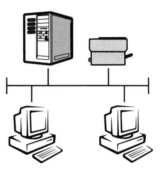

Internetworking 1: Standalone LAN

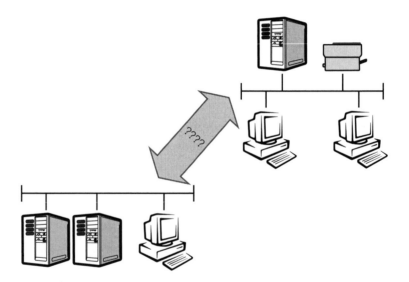

Internetworking 2: Linking networks

modest speeds but must operate over existing cabling. Others may need wireless operation over radio links.

➡ The design of most physical LAN technologies has been optimized for speed and cost by assuming that computers will be no more than a few tens of meters apart, and that the number of machines on the network will be sufficiently small to avoid the need for complex traffic management. This limits the scalability of a single LAN.

Internetworking provides a way of connecting heterogeneous networks by imposing a common format for the packets of information passing between the networks, through a "gateway" device.

One such common packet structure is defined by the Internet Protocol (usually referred to as *IP*) and the device that acts as the link between networks: in this case referred to as a *router* (although it has had a variety of more opaque names in the past ranging from Interface Message Processor or IMP to "fuzzball").

A router is a device dedicated to the purpose of shipping packets between networks using special routing tables. Other approaches have included the idea of *bridges*, which simply spray traffic across two networks, without the intelligence behind the routing concept (see Figure 3 below).

If the networks to be connected are geographically far apart then a single router will not help, and a router on each network needs to be linked by a point-to-point connection optimized for long distance. Fortunately the problem of moving data between two distant points is well understood by the

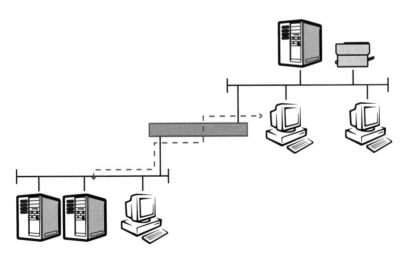

Internetworking 3: Using a router to connect two networks

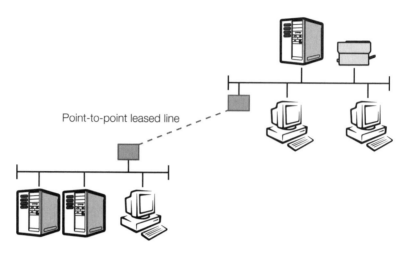

Internetworking 4: Linking routers using a point-to-point connection

Point-to-point leased line

telephone companies who can provide dedicated links running at a variety of speeds (for a variety of costs). This is shown in Figure 4.

This simple model can be extended by adding additional point-to-point links to routers on other networks. The schematics in Figure 5 shows our simple internet growing to include three and six networks.

Note that every network does not have a direct link to every other network, and it may be necessary for traffic from one machine to another to pass over multiple intermediate networks. Similarly there may be more than one route to a destination. This is actually desirable from a resilience point of view. If one of the point-to-point connections fails or is congested then there is an alternative path. The schematic in Figure 6 illustrates two possible routes between two interconnected networks.

An important principle is that routing is based on the destination network not the destination computer. This means that the structure of the individual networks is hidden from the outside world, allowing local changes to be made without impacting other networks. The "routing tables," which tell routers where to forward packets bound for destination networks, are the road map that make an internet work.

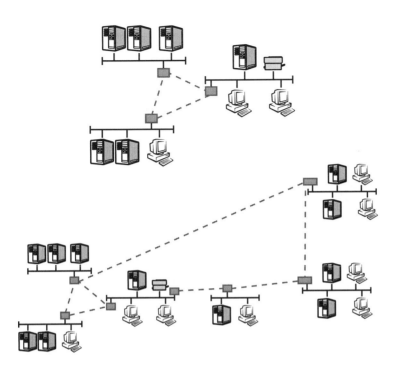

Internetworking 5: Adding point-to-point links

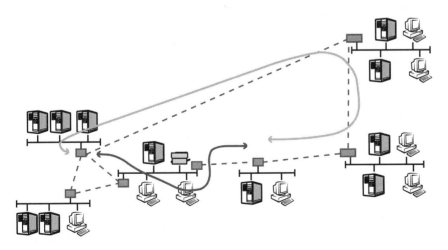

Internetworking 6: Alternative routes between two interconnected networks

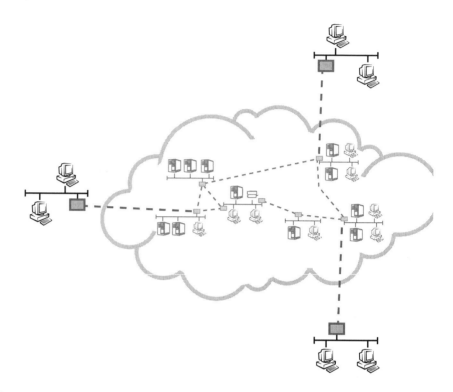

Internetworking 7: The internet as a single network

From the perspective of each network, an internet appears to be a single logical network, with all machines treated as peers (see Figure 7).

The main points of connection in the global internet have assumed special importance and are usually commercial Internet Service Providers or *ISPs*. However, the internet is nothing more (or less) than an interconnected series of networks held together by point-to-point links and routing tables, grown to a massive scale.

InterNIC (organization)

Used to be the US organization responsible for registering internet domain names (the NIC standing for Network Information Center). The registration process is now essentially privatized, and the *ICANN* organization has taken over regulation of the internet name space.

Interoperability (technical term)
A general IT term covering networks or machines that can work together – usually through a standard interface or network protocol – even if they have radically different architectures. The internet is, of course, a vehicle for supporting interoperability on the grand scale.

Interplanetary internet (technical term)
A marvellous initiative intended to allow spacecraft to be connected into a loose "network of internets" where networks are deployed in "low latency remote environments" (which means nodes are close to each other). Hubs (like Earth or Mars) are then connected via an interplanetary backbone that handles the high latency (or long delay) deep space environment. A serious scientific effort to connect the ever growing legion of spacecraft.

Interstitial (business term)
Literally, "in between." In the context of web advertising, a message, usually an advertisement, that pops up in a separate window during the transition from one web page to another. Most web users find it distracting and annoying.

In the zone (slang)
Slang term for the state of concentration involved in creating software.

Intranet (internet term)
A private network, internal to an organization, which uses internet technologies (such as the *TCP/IP* networking software) and world wide web technologies (such as common *browsers*) but is not visible to the public internet directly, although outgoing internet access through a *firewall* for security reasons might well be a feature offered to users. It is often implemented within a large organization to allow it to use increasingly standard web software to manage documents and data, provide corporate information in now-familiar website style, and so on.

Intrapreneur (business term)
An entrepreneur within a business – usually an employee – who is provided with support and financing to create an undertaking such as an e-commerce spin-off, often at least partially free of the bureaucracy that usually operates within large corporate environments.

IP (technical term)

IP stands for Internet Protocol, and is one of the major elements of the *TCP/IP* protocol suite, which is the fundamental network protocol engine of the internet.

The internet is formed from an interconnected series of tens of thousands of very different networks. IP forms the common language that hides the differences in these underlying networks. Every device connected to the internet (PCs, workstations, routers, servers etc.) must understand and generate IP.

The underlying job of IP is very simple. It transmits individual blocks of data, known as *packets* or *datagrams*, from one device to another. Data can be sent from a web server to a workstation that are separated by thousands of miles and many network links. IP does this without each packet needing to understand the different networks it must traverse.

IP is independent of physical media. IP datagrams can be transferred over lower-level *Ethernet* on *LANs*, or over *PPP* (Point-to-Point Protocol) for dial-up connections.

IP doesn't need to understand the data that it's carrying (which could be part of an e-mail, a web page, streamed video etc.) nor does it care about how one packet is related to any other. IP doesn't even guarantee that data will reach its destination; it simply tries to inform the sender if a problem is encountered and a packet has to be discarded. It is left to higher-level protocols such as *TCP* (Transmission Control Protocol) to add reliability, sequencing, and other details.

Every device that implements IP must have a unique *IP address* that identifies its logical position on a given network. This type of network address is analagous to a postal address or telephone number.

The current most common version of IP (version 4) was defined in a document called *RFC* 791 in 1981. Version 6, also known as *IPng* (IP – next generation) has been released but is not yet widely implemented.

IP address (technical term)

Every device attached to the internet is assigned a unique identifier known as an IP address, which allows *IP* – the Internet Protocol – to send it data, rather like a postal address allows mail to be delivered.

In the current most common version (version 4) of IP, an address is held in a 32-bit number (which is a number between 0 and 4,294,967,295). Such numbers are hard to read, so by convention each address is shown in a form called "dotted quad decimal." For example:

208.202.218.15

Each of the four numbers will lie in the range 0 to 255. The example above actually means the same as:

3502955023 (decimal)
11010000110010101101101000001111 (binary)

Even the quad form is hardly user friendly. The Domain Name System (**DNS**) means that in general we don't need to remember IP addresses, and more memorable domain names such as **www.amazon.com** can be used. These are translated into numeric IP addresses automatically by dedicated servers on the internet.

Every IP address is made up of two parts, the first representing the network that the device is attached to and the second uniquely defining the device on that network. It is the network part of the address that is used to route IP packets over the internet (see entry on *internetworking*). The relative size of the network part of the address compared to the device (or host port) originally varied depending on the *class* of IP address. The class concept allows networks of different sizes to be accommodated. The three main internet classes are defined below:

➡ Class A – supports 127 distinct networks, each with many millions of devices. The split between the network and host part of the address is illustrated in Figure 1 on page 164.

➡ Class B – supports 16,000 distinct networks, each with 65,000 devices (see Figure 2).

➡ Class C – supports 2 million networks but each network may only have 254 devices (see Figure 3).

However, the idea of IP address classes has become less and less relevant as competition for a finite pool of numbers has grown. Most allocated addresses

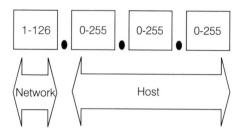

IP address: 1 – class A

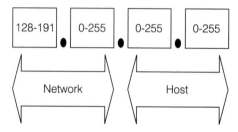

IP address: 2 – class B

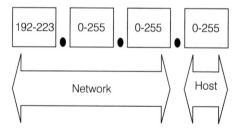

IP address: 3 – class C

now use a technique called **CIDR** which stands for Classless Inter-Domain Routing and provides much more parsimonious use of what is now something of a scarce resource.

As another tactical solution, techniques that allow IP addresses to be shared among users have been introduced (assuming that many devices are only occasionally connected). However, this is technically complex and will become of less use as "always on" connections (e.g. *ADSL, GPRS*) become more common, ensuring that more addresses are permanently in use and therefore cannot be shared.

The strategic solution is provided by IP version 6 which increases IP addresses to 128 bits (making the total number of addresses available approximately 3 with 38 zeros after it), which should provide plenty of room for growth. Implementing a new version of IP within the internet is the ultimate example of changing the engines when the plane is still in flight and is still being planned.

IP address class (technical term)

An IP address is a unique 32-bit number that identifies a computer attached to the internet. The range of IP addresses was originally subdivided into five classes (called A–E), although only classes A, B and C are commonly discussed, and allow networks of different sizes to be accommodated. Class E is reserved for experimental networks and class D is associated with multicasting, which is not yet widely supported (see entry on *multicast* and *MBone*).

So how would a user get a class A, B or C network address? The short answer is you can't anymore. IP addresses have now become so scarce that the allocating authorities no longer use the class terminology. Instead administrative organizations such as RIPE (Réseaux IP Européens) assign blocks of IP addresses using something called Classless Inter-Domain Routing (*CIDR*), which allows a more granular allocation of addresses. See entries on *IP address* and *CIDR*.

iPlanet (company)

An alliance between Sun and Netscape – two very well-known names in the e-c ommerce technology world – which supplies software development tools and services for building a variety of types of web and wireless solution on industry standard platforms (such as Java, XML, etc.).

IPng (technical term)

Stands for Internet Protocol – next generation and refers to version 6 of the protocol. The most significant improvement is the increase in the size of the IP address from 32 to 128 bits, which increases enormously the total number of IP addresses available. However, the internet faces an enormous transitionary challenge in adopting this standard.

IP number (technical term)

Means the same as *IP address*.

IPO (business term)

See *Initial Public Offering.*

IPSec (technical term)

Stands for Internet Protocol Security and is an extension of *IP* (the Internet Protocol) to add security features such as confidentiality and authentication. IPSec is intended to help standardize techniques for creating *Virtual Private Networks* (VPNs) which create secure "tunnels" through the internet, allowing what seem to be private networks to be run over the public internet.

IPv6 (technical term)

Denotes version 6 of *IP*. Also called *IPng.*

IRC (technical term)

Stands for Internet Relay Chat – a service that allows people to communicate online, in real time, by sharing typed text messages between users. Invented by Jarkko Oikarinen of Finland in 1988.

IRTF (organization)

Stands for Internet Research Task Force, a volunteer organization linked – like the *IETF* and similar bodies – to *ISOC* (the Internet Society). Its mission is "to promote research of importance to the evolution of the future internet by creating focussed, long-term and small research groups working on topics related to internet protocols, applications, architecture and technology." Current study topics include: authentication/authorization/accounting architecture, the interplanetary internet, and various activities around multicasting.

ISDN (technical term)

Stands for Integrated Services Digital Network, although only the abbreviation is in common use. ISDN is a standard for digital communications over phone networks which has been available for sometime. This does offer

some speed advantage over ordinary modem connections, but newer technologies such as *ADSL* offer much greater throughput.

ISM (technical term)

Stands for Industrial, Scientific and Medical and represents various bands of
the radio spectrum allocated (by international agreement) for non-communi-
cations uses (e.g. medical scanning, microwave ovens). Recently, part of the
ISM allocation in the 2.40–2.48 GHz band in the UHF (ultra high frequency)
range has been made available for Wireless Local Area Networks (*WLANs*) and
other *wireless* technologies such as *Bluetooth*. This part of the spectrum is unlicensed and can be used by anyone, in contrast to the spectrum bought at
auction by the *3G* mobile phone operators. To help limit (but not entirely
eliminate) the problem of interference between different users, devices may
only use relatively low power levels and are limited to short distances.

ISO (organization)

Stands for International Organization for Standardization. (ISO is not a mis-
typed abbreviation, the term "ISO" is ancient Greek for "equal" as in "isobar."
This is an important standards body involving 130 countries, and is the
sponsor behind many communication and information standards efforts. It is
not directly related to the internet, but you will come across it in contexts
such as the *MPEG* standards for video and audio.

ISOC (organization)

Stands for the Internet Society. Founded in 1992, the Internet Society is a
key group in terms of development of the internet and sits at the center of a
constellation of more specialist technical and professional groups. It has
more than 150 organizational and 6,000 individual members in many countries. Its bold mission statement is "To assure the open development, evolution
and use of the internet for the benefit of all people throughout the world."

The Internet Society is the ultimate sponsor of those groups responsible
for internet infrastructure standards, in particular the Internet Engineering
Task Force (*IETF*) and the Internet Architecture Board (*IAB*). It has also developed a pronounced social agenda and is making efforts to broaden its
membership as much as possible.

It's worth noting that development of the world wide web (which is just one of the services that sit on the base internet) is sponsored by the World Wide Web Consortium, otherwise known as *W3C*.

The main website for ISOC is **www.isoc.org**.

ISP (business term)

Stands for Internet Service Provider. A business that offers end-user internet connectivity and often other services to individuals and businesses. This is a multi-billion-dollar market and there are thousands of businesses globally that can be categorized as ISPs. However, the market is intensely competitive, with some types of service being offered free in some geographical areas. Many ISPs lose money, while others rely on value-added services being bought by customers over a multi-year period. The ISP business is tough and dynamic.

The types of service an ISP can offer include:

➡ Access for home-users over modems and Public Switched Telephone Networks (PSTNs) to the internet (which generally includes providing an e-mail account name).

➡ Management of routers and other networking devices that handle IP packets originating from the networks of small or large businesses.

➡ General consulting, training, and similar services around network design and network management.

➡ Web-hosting – basically running end-user websites on single or multiple servers.

➡ Managing a business customer's *Virtual Private Network*, which looks like a closed network, but is run securely across the public internet.

➡ Support for some forms of e-commerce (e.g. access to online credit card services).

Online Service Providers – AOL for example – are very similar in concept, but tend to offer more of their own content, rather than just access.

ISTF (organization)

Stands for Internet Social Task Force. A recent offshoot of *ISOC* (the Internet Society), this group is an international and open organization that aims "to identify ways in which the internet can be a positive force in social and eco-nomic dimensions." Interest areas include accessibility for the disabled and underprivileged, and dealing with social, economic, regulatory, and other barriers to internet use, privacy matters, education, regulation, and tax.

The main website is at **www.istf.org**.

ITU (organization)

Stands for International Telecommunication Union. Previously known as the *CCITT*, and controls important pre-internet networking standards such as *X.25*.

iTulip.com (website)

Stimulating and interesting website which has a somewhat cynical (it would say realistic) view of the dot-com world, and links it to past *bubbles*.

iTV (technical term)

See *interactive television*.

J2EE (technical term)
Stands for Java 2 Enterprise Edition. A definition of the *Java* platform for enterprise scale applications. See entry on *EJB* (Enterprise Java Beans).

J2ME (technical term)
Stands for Java 2 Micro-Edition and is a version of the *Java* platform designed for devices with limited processing capabilities. Potential applications for J2ME include intelligent mobile phones and *PDAs* and an important part of J2ME is the Mobile Information Device Profile which defines a common set of services which should allow Java programs to run on any device avoiding differences between manufacturers (such as user interface). Java applications developed for the Mobile Information Device Profile are known as MIDlets.

Jabber (product)
Jabber describes an initiative to produce an *open source* and *XML*-based *instant messaging* system with a more open and distributed architecture than other approaches (such as *ICQ* or *AOL* Instant Messenger). It supports a vibrant and active community of users.

Jargon file (slang)

A legendary list of hacker jargon terms started by Raphael Fintel at Stanford in 1975. Documented in the very amusing *The New Hacker's Dictionary* compiled by Eric S. Raymond.

Java (technical term)

Java took the world by storm in the late 1990s. It was originated, and very successfully marketed, by *Sun.* At its core is an elegant programming language, although this is surrounded by other standard components, and other proprietory development tools are readily available. For Sun, it is the center of a complex and wide range of products. It is also a Sun trademark. Here we just focus on the core language, and most basic services.

Java is important to e-commerce and the internet because for many it is the language of choice for developing the more complex aspects of websites – both on the *client* and *server* sides of the network. Modern *browsers* will run *Java applets* directly, allowing a high degree of customization of websites.

Java really covers a variety of things:

➡ The core Java programming language. Java programs, like programs in almost any serious programming language, need to be "compiled" in a form that can then be executed. However, unlike traditional languages that normally get translated in a form linked to a particular type of computer, Java is normally compiled into a standard intermediate form which can then be executed by the Java Virtual Machine (or, sometimes, JVM). Hardware can be built to run compiled Java programs directly, but more typically the JVM is usually implemented as another piece of software. This distinctive – although not unique – feature, is important because it allows *portability.* Compiled Java can be run on Windows-family PCs, Apple, UNIX, and other systems, reflecting the diverse nature of hardware on the internet.

➡ The term "Java platform" is sometimes used to refer to both the core language and surrounding essential components. Any Java system will be broken down in self-contained *classes* that define an integrated set of data, and functions, or methods which will act on that data. The Java platform provides predefined and standard classes for input/output, user-interface control, networking, and other key areas. Java 1.0 contained just 212 such classes. Java 1.2 increased this to 1,520 classes.

There is no doubt that Sun marketed Java effectively. At one point, there were more books on Java than the number of days the language had been officially released. Nevertheless, Java has become extremely popular, and part of this is very much down to the language's intrinsic merits. These include:

⇒ **An open, portable, standard**: summarized by Sun as "write once, run anywhere." Because of the Java Virtual Machine approach, Java programs should run on many of the computer platforms connected to the internet, including Windows-family PCs, UNIX, Apple computer and others. For those who don't want to be tied to more proprietory approaches – as offered by Microsoft, for example – this is very attractive. Sun is also expanding Java to support other types of device, aiming ultimately for "smartcard to super computer scalability."

⇒ **Familiarity**: Java looks like *C.* C is a more or less universal language which is widely used and understood by those who grew up with *UNIX-*based systems. Although Java is a more modern language, it is an easy conversion for those who know C, or *C++* – a version of C for object-orientated programming.

⇒ **Modernity***:* Java is a modern language. It allows cross-computer, network-center programming. It supports an *object-orientated* approach, highly suited to development of distributed solutions. It has been designed to address at least some security issues, and the JVM does not easily allow the creation of a conventional virus.

⇒ **Elegance***:* a word much loved by programmers. What does it mean? Essentially, Java is based on accepted techniques, is relatively simple and avoids the complexities and pitfalls found in languages such as C++.

⇒ **Security***:* Java applets downloaded across the internet run in a protected environment (a "sandbox" in early versions of Java) and can only do a limited range of things. This compares with the generally more permissive approach of Microsoft products.

Java example

Those who don't want to look at programming examples should look away now.

Traditionally, the first thing to do in any new language is to figure out how to display "Hello World" on the screen. So we make no exception here!

```
public class HelloWorld
{
    Public static void main(strings[] args)
    {
        system.out.println("Hello World");
    }
}
```

The text above (more accurately known as source code) would be saved in a file called HelloWorld.java and compiled to produce a file that is called HelloWorld.class.

To execute the program, the class file must be interpreted by a Java Virtual Machine, which looks for part of the program called "main" and in our trivial case simply prints "Hello World" to the screen.

Java development tools

The most basic Java program development environment is the Java Development Kit (JDK) distributed freely by Sun, which has a certain spartan attraction. However, for serious developers an Integrated Development Environment (IDE) is more likely to be required. An IDE allows code to be designed, written and debugged using a highly graphical environment.

Examples include:

➡ Inprise's JBuilder

➡ IBM's Visual Age

➡ SunSoft's Java Workshop

➡ WebGain's Visual Café

➡ Microsoft's Visual J++.

Java applet (technical term)
A Java program that can be run in, for example, a web *browser*. Java applets are used to add more complex features to websites. These could include dynamic calculations, multimedia effects, or support for games.

Java Bean (technical term)
The Java Beans architecture defines how independent software components should be written to allow other programmers to reuse them to assemble larger applications. One important feature of the Java Bean architecture is support for "introspection" so that third-party application builder tools can examine Java Beans (which may come from a variety of vendors) and figure out what they do and how they should be used. In theory this reduces the application development to simply hooking different Java Beans together in a graphical Integrated Development Environment (IDE). Unfortunately, the reality is not so simple, but nevertheless the Java Bean model is an important step towards achieving common, reusable software through componentization. To date the focus of Java Bean developers has largely been on graphical components such as charts.

Java chip (technical term)
A chip that can run Java directly, without the need for a *Java Virtual Machine* (JVM).

Java Development Kit (JDK) (technical term)
A set of tools developed and distributed free by Sun for helping with Java development. Includes a compiler, debugger, and other tools.

JavaScript (technical term)
Language intended to add interactivity and similar processing to web pages within a *browser*. A simple language with some Java-like syntax, but actually not really Java at all.

Java Server Pages (JSP) (technical term)
Java Server Pages allow Java code to be included in the definition of a web page. When the page is accessed, the code is executed on the webserver and the results sent to the browser as HTML. This allows information to be

inserted dynamically into web pages and is very similar in concept to Microsoft's *active server page* (ASP) technology.

JSPs were once known as Java HTML (JHTML) and the .jhtml file extension is still occasionally seen. Sun has transferred the reference implementation of JSPs to the *Open Source* community as part of a project called Tomcat (**jakarta.apache.org/tomcat**).

JavaSoft (company)
Discontinued name for the division of Sun that markets Java products.

Java Virtual Machine (JVM) (technical term)
The special program that runs a compiled form of Java application program. See *Java*.

JDK (technical term)
See *Java Development Kit*.

Jini (technical term)
Originated by Sun in January 1999, and linked firmly to Java, Jini is a software architecture for simple control of remote devices on a self-configuring network. Jini is designed to let Java-enabled devices (such as PCs, but also intelligent mobile phones, handheld computers, digital cameras, and printers) communicate simply, without complex installation procedures. The aim of Jini is to connect anything to anything at any time – Jini-enabled devices should be able to plug seamlessly into a network, find each other, and use one another's services. The core of Jini is its lookup service – a central registry of services available on the network, which is built up automatically. For example, if you plug in a Jini-compatible DVD player, it should automatically announce itself to every other device on the network and search for equipment with which it can talk. However, Java is not yet a common option for embedded devices, and take-up at the time of writing remains very limited.

Jobs, Steve
Very visible and charismatic co-founder of *Apple* Computer Inc., who was instrumental in introducing the Apple II (essentially the first usable personal computer), and Macintosh (the first commercial computer to offer a modern graphical user interface). Jobs left Apple in 1985 to work with NEXT and

Pixar Animation Studios, but returned to Apple where he then oversaw the introduction of the *iMAC*.

Joint Photographic Experts Group (technical term)
See *JPEG*.

JPEG (technical term)
JPEG stands for Joint Photographic Experts Group, but is normally used to refer to the standard file format from the group. This format allows images to be stored in computer files in a compressed form.

JSP (technical term)
See *Java Server Pages*.

Jump page (web term)
Also called a splash page. A page on a website that is the precursor to the main *home page*. Used to display a pre-site presentation, to force users to specify their preferred country or language, or to confirm the availability of certain software, e.g. *Flash*.

Just-in-time (JIT) compiler (technical term)
Java's portability comes at some cost to performance. To make Java programs run faster, a JIT compiler converts all of the bytecode into native machine code just as a Java program is run.

JVM (technical term)
See *Java Virtual Machine*.

K (technical term)
Symbol for "kilo" used in sizing quantities related to IT systems.

Kahn, Bob
Major figure in development of the internet (through the *ARPANET* project) and co-developer of the *TCP/IP* family of network protocols with *Vinton Cerf* in the early 1970s.

KB (technical term)
Stands for kilobyte.

Kbps (technical term)
Stands for kilobits per second – a measure of network speed. Most suitable for low- or medium-speed networks.

Kernighan, Brian
One of the pivotal figures in the development of the *C* language and the *UNIX* operating system, which were major base technologies in the development of the internet. Prolific and popular author of many fine technical books.

Key (security term)

A number or bit sequence used in encryption and decryption of information. Electronic encryption often relies on two keys – a *public key*, known to more than one person, and a *private key*, known only to one (typically the sender of information).

Keyword (web term)

A user enters a keyword, or a series of keywords, into a *search engine* to be rewarded by a series of links to relevant websites. Sometimes also used to describe reserved words within programming languages.

Kill (technical term)

Aggressive term for stopping a program running on a machine, particularly when it is misbehaving in some way (and possibly when the program is not reacting to normal commands, requiring the use of a special system command). Inspired by the *UNIX* "kill" command.

Killer app (business term)

An application software product or general type of application that is stunningly successful in its category (and sometimes invents its category). The first spreadsheet and wordprocessing applications were often describing as killer apps for the PC platform – although it is interesting to note that the first suppliers of these have been supplanted. The *browser* and *e-mail* are often seen as killer apps of the internet/web worlds.

Kill file (internet term)

End-user file used by some *Usenet* administrators to filter out messages on a particular subject, or from a particular user. Sometimes also called *bozo filter* for obvious reasons.

Kilo (technical term)

Prefix that multiplies an IT quantity by 2^{10} – which works out at 1,024. This parallels the use of kilo in the metric system, but reflects the fact that computers are based around *binary* arithmetic. Used in terms such as *kilobit* and *kilobyte*.

Kilobit (technical term)

2^{10} or 1,024 **bits** – a bit being the fundamental unit of computer storage, which takes the values zero or one. Kilobits per second (Kbps) is sometimes used as a measure of network speed for low- or medium-speed networks.

Kilobyte (technical term)

2^{10} or 1,024 **bytes** – a byte being 8 bits of storage, long enough to hold a numeric code for characters from the **ASCII** character set. Once used to size disk space and main computer memory, but now more or less redundant given the much increased capacity of computers, where prefixes like **mega** and **giga** are more useful. Sometimes used to size individual files.

Kiosk (technical term)

Describes a computer housed in a standalone unit for public use, and typically with an easy-to-use, multimedia-style interface. Examples could include a kiosk that supplements a display in a museum with facts relating to an exhibit, or a workstation at a major conference with delegate information. Some recent examples in the UK are intended to provide access to the internet for those who don't have PCs, and provide slots for reading credit cards for financial transactions.

Klienrock, Leonard

MIT researcher who devised in the early 1960s the concept of **packet-switching** – a key networking idea that underpins the internet.

Kludge (slang)

A technical fix to a technical problem which works, but is ugly to those with a professional interest in engineering excellence.

Knowledge management (technical term)

Covers management of knowledge and information as a professional discipline with the business aim of making knowledge "capital" more known and accessible by its potential users within an enterprise. Internet and web technologies are commonly used to support this type of activity across an organization's **intranet**.

LAN (technical term)

Acronym for Local Area Network – a network that consists of computers and devices distributed over a small physical area such as is typically found in a work environment. One of the key strengths of the internet (and its underlying network protocols and addressing schemes) is that it allows multiple LANs to be straightforwardly coupled together. At heart, the internet is a large collection of LANs (and home-users) connected by larger networks and *backbone* links.

Landgrab (slang)

Sometimes used to cover the rush for domain names in crowded business niches. Also used to cover an aggressive approach to building market share.

Last mile (technical term)

The final type of connection type between an end-user PC, or system, and the relevant service provider – such as an *ISP* (Internet Service Provider). For much home use, this is a telephone company's twisted-pair copper wiring, which generally gives slow network performance. Alternatives include coaxial cable TV as used by cable companies, or high-speed protocols for base copper – such as *ADSL*.

Lastminute.com (web site)

Lastminute is one of the most well-known European web businesses. It focusses on last-minute purchases of consumer products and services like travel and holidays. It received a large amount of media coverage during a high-profile flotation just before the decline in stock market valuations of *B2C* companies in early 2000. That said, it has built a very well-known UK and European brand.

Latency (technical term)

Latency refers to the time taken for a message to travel from one point to another over a network. In theory, signals pass over the network at near-light speed. However, *routers* and other network components need to process the information *en route* and slow things down considerably. Latency is as important as *bandwidth* when examining the performance of the internet, since applications that require lots of exchanges between the webserver and the browser will perform poorly on a high latency route, even if the messages exchanged are small and the bandwidth high. If so inclined, you can measure the latency between your machine and another machine on the net using the *ping* command.

Launch (technical term, business term)

Commonly used technically to cover the starting of an application from a system's user interface, it also covers the public start of an e-commerce service or business. In this latter context, a soft launch describes a situation where a service is turned on – usually for testing – without great fanfare. A hard launch is usually on a set date which is announced in a blaze of publicity. There have been several high-profile embarrassments (such as **boo.com** in Europe) where an advertising campaign has been followed not by a live service, but instead by a delay due to technical or performance issues.

Layer (technical term)

Complex systems are often designed as a series of conceptual "layers." For example:

➡ Computer network protocols are described using the *OSI* seven-layer model.

➡ Complex application architectures are often separated into (say) user interface, application and database layers.

In principle, good use of layering allows different parts of a system to be isolated and insulated from changes elsewhere in the system. The internet, where applications can be highly distributed across systems, means that layered architectures are very common.

LDAP (technical term)

Stands for Lightweight Directory Access Protocol. In this context a directory is anything that maintains a mapping used by an application or network component (e.g. an e-mail address book, or a domain name to network address translation). *X.500* was a standard for directory services defined in the early 1990s by the *CCITT*. LDAP was originally developed as a simple protocol for accessing data held in X.500 directories, but it has evolved to support different types of directory (since X.500 itself has not been widely implemented) and has become a popular way to access digital *certificates* used in *public key* security systems.

Leased line (technical term)

A communications link leased from a telecommunications supplier that permanently joins two locations, often used in corporate networks.

Legacy, Legacy system (technical term)

Legacy, or legacy systems, are terms that refer to older systems – often *mainframe*-style systems. The term "legacy" is typically used when new systems are being constructed to work alongside these older systems. With many types of new internet service for an existing company, developers have to spend significant time and effort connecting to major legacy systems through complex software interfaces. One good example is the insurance industry, where insurance policies are usually maintained on complex mainframe systems. In this case, an internet insurance sales system would need to connect to the back-end policy system, since duplicating the old functionality would be prohibitively expensive. A whole industry of *middleware* products has grown up to help this type of integration – often described under the heading of eAI for "e-Application Integration".

Legacy media (slang)

Slang term for either newspapers, radio, or television, or a disapproving stylistic description of website content written in a text-like manner.

LEO (technical term)

Stands for Low Earth Orbit. Satellites in Low Earth Orbit operate at around 500 miles above the ground and are one option being proposed for providing high-speed wireless internet access. Orbits are low in comparison with geostationary satellites which operate at approximately 22,000 miles above the Earth. This has the benefit that less power is needed for communications. The downside of the lower orbit is that many satellites are needed to ensure continuity of service, leading to greater infrastructure costs and technical complexity.

At the time of writing, the first LEO infrastructure (Iridium) has failed commercially and the constellation of satellites that support the system was in danger of being de-orbited, although it has been rescued at the last moment.

Letterbomb (slang)

Similar in meaning to *mailbomb*. Letterbomb denotes an e-mail message that is intended to inconvenience the target recipient, through sheer size, embedded viruses, and similar.

Lightweight Directory Access Protocol (technical term)
See *LDAP.*

Line-oriented (technical term)

Most users are familiar with GUI and mouse-based interfaces. Line-oriented interfaces have a longer history and allow a user to type commands in response to a simple prompt. Less friendly, but generally more powerful, this kind of interaction is favored by technically minded developers and system administrators.

Line-oriented browser (web term)

A web *browser* that displays text rather than the multimedia options provided by other types of browser. Not so interesting visually, but fast.

Link (web term)

Sometimes used as a shorthand for *hyperlink*.

Linkrot (slang)

Reflects the fact that *links* on the web, once created, have to be managed, or they become unusable as the referenced content is deleted or moved. The result of linkrot is a "404 not found" error message from the calling browser.

Linux (technical term)

Linux is an *operating system* that was first created for fun by a young student, named Linus Torvalds, at the University of Helsinki in Finland. Torvalds started with Minix, a small version of the famous *UNIX* operating system, which was intended as an educational aid. Linux has become much more sophisticated than Minix ever was. Version 0.02 of Linux was released in 1991 and Torvalds released a full version 1.0 in 1994. Linux is perhaps the best-known "product" produced by the *open source* movement, and its development involved many collaborators working with Torvalds over the internet. It now provides all the facilities associated with a full feature version of UNIX. Because of its origins, Linux has been in the past viewed with some suspicion by corporate users and hardware suppliers. However, Linux does have some strong features, including the following:

➡ It has the features of UNIX, always popular with many technicians.

➡ It comes with source code, again popular with a certain sort of technician.

➡ It is low-cost.

➡ It is stable and reliable. Linux servers are well known for staying up (i.e. not crashing) for hundreds of days. This is partly due to the collaborative process of development which has resulted in a fast, stable, and thoroughly debugged system.

➡ It is a good, cheap alternative to Windows, particularly on servers.

For these reasons, Linux has become a very popular choice for small internet sites running *webservers* (like *Apache*) or *FTP* for file sharing. A number of major manufacturers, such as *IBM*, *Compaq*, and others, now offer Linux as a system option.

Linux is distributed under the GNU *General Public License* – a standard way of doing things in the open source world. This means its source code (the human-readable code normally jealously guarded by commercial writers of software) is freely available to anyone. A copy of Linux can be charged for, but companies and developers must provide the source code and allow the user to distribute it as they wish. Companies that center themselves around Linux and Linux services include Caldera, Red Hat, and VA Linux Systems.

Linux is actually only the core operating system and typically comes surrounded by other software from the open source *GNU* project, which has led some people to refer to it as GNU/Linux.

Linux has an official mascot, a cutish kind of penguin, which was selected by Linus Torvalds himself. A good place to start to get more information is **www.linux.org**.

Linux Distribution (technical term)

Linux is a UNIX-like operating system which is freely available on the internet under the General Public License (GPL). A Linux distribution is a commercially packaged version of the software (typically on CD-ROM) intended to simplify the process of gathering and installing the freely available components. Although charging for software which is available for free may seem like a strange business model, companies such as RedHat have become big business. To differentiate their offrings, some distribution companies bundle other *open source* or proprietary software with the core GNU/ Linux software.

LINX (technical term)

Stands for the London Internet Exchange, an important part of the UK internet infrastructure. Linx is a network facility where UK Internet Service Providers (ISPs) can easily exchange traffic without having to go over the internet *backbone* networks.

Listserv (e-mail term)

A popular software tool for managing e-mail address lists.

Lit Fiber (technical term)

Lit fiber is the opposite of dark fiber, and covers optical fibers that are in use, and therefore "lit" by the light pulses passing through them.

Live3D (web term)
A *Netscape plug-in* that interprets Virtual Reality Modeling Language (*VRML*) – a language intended to offer 3-D interactive web graphics in a manner similar to games.

LMDS (technical term)
Stands for Local Multipoint Distribution System. This uses a Super High Frequency (SHF) radio link to transmit data. LMDS requires a dish antenna at both ends of the link and is not likely to be used by mobile users, but can provide an effective point-to-point replacement for cables between fixed locations.

Load (technical term)
A loose term that describes the processing demand on a *server*. In the case of a simple webserver this could mean the processing needed to return the pages of *HTML* requested. For a more complex application, it will include the computational effort needed to handle e-commerce transactions. Load will increase according to the number of users and complexity of the tasks they request. A key design issue for an e-commerce solution is understanding what load you should aim to build for. Some websites have collapsed on day one because the load was much higher than expected.

Load balancing (technical term)
For popular websites, a single computer is not enough to handle the number of users, and the *load* needs to be split across multiple machines. Load balancing makes sure that the effort is evenly distributed across all the machines available. Generally supported by *middleware* software products.

Local Area Network (technical term)
See *LAN*.

Localization (web term)
Localization means ensuring a web presence reflects the language, currency, and requirements of local markets and geographies. A big topic, which is often harder than people expect and ends up covering matters of law, tax, regulation, culture, and language.

Local loop (technical term)

Like the term *last mile*, describes the final connection medium between a subscriber and their telephone supplier. Usually, this is still traditional copper.

Look and feel (technical term, business term)

A phase used since the first Graphical User Interfaces (*GUIs*) were created. Describes how a system (including a website) appears ("look") and how its interaction works ("feel").

Loudcloud (company)

Provider of products and services to internet companies in the area of high-performance server back ends, with a particular focus on technical operations. Notable because one co-founder is *Marc Andreesen*, of *Mosaic* and *Netscape* fame.

Lurk, Lurker (internet term)

To lurk is to receive messages in a newsgroup without actively contributing. A lurker is someone who lurks.

Lycos (company)

Well-known general purpose *search engine* and *portal*.

Lynx (web term)

Lynx is a free, fast, text-based *browser* suitable for those with slow internet connections.

M (technical term)
Symbol for *mega*, used in sizing quantities related to IT systems.

Mac (technical term)
Common shorthand for a *Macintosh* computer, as produced by Apple.

Macintosh (product)
Introduced by Apple in 1984, the "Mac" was the first commercially significant personal computer to support a Graphical User Interface (*GUI*) and a
mouse. At the time, the Mac was a ground-breaking product, and was extremely popular with the publishing and graphics design communities. Microsoft
responded to the Macintosh by introducing the first generation of Microsoft
Windows, which resulted in a protracted legal battle between Microsoft and
Apple, although many of the concepts behind the Mac were themselves
derived from research conducted at *Xerox PARC*. The Macintosh brand has
found new life through the *iMac*.

Mac OS (product)
The operating system for Apple's *Macintosh* computers – a niche product
compared with Microsoft's range of software, but with a loyal following.

Macromedia (company)

Macromedia is a well-known supplier of creative content management and technical tools aimed at professional web developers who want to use animation, sound, graphics, and rich media in general within websites. Key products include *Flash*, which has become a very common feature of more dynamic websites, Shockwave for movie-like effects, and Dreamweaver, which has features suited to bigger enterprise applications.

MAE (internet term)

Stands for Metropolitan Area Exchange. MAEs are major points of interconnection between *ISPs* (internet Service Providers) and the various internet backbones. There are two principal MAEs in the US (MAE-East in Washington and MAE-West in San José, California); both are owned and operated by MCI-Worldcom. In the rest of the world there are regional equivalents such as the London Internet Exchange (*LINX*).

Mail (e-mail term)

E-mail is now so ubiquitous that the e- is often dropped in common usage.

Mailbomb (security term)

A large amount of *e-mail* data, sent as one or many messages, intended to disrupt the selected user or site – a primitive form of *denial of service* attack.

Mailbox (technical term)

A mailbox (or message store) is where *e-mails* are stored once delivered. However, e-mail transport protocols such as *SMTP* (Simple Mail Transport Protocol) or *X.400* expect the mailbox to be continuously available, otherwise there is a danger that the e-mail will be discarded, rather like the postman throwing your mail away if there was no one at home when they tried to deliver it! Therefore a user's personal mailbox is typically held on a continuously available server at an *ISP* or dedicated e-mail provider such as **hotmail.com**. When the user connects to the internet any new mail must be retrieved from their mailbox using a protocol such as *POP* (Post Office Protocol) or *IMAP* (Internet Message Access Protocol). Whether your mail remains in the server mailbox, or is copied and stored on your local PC, depends on the particular mail package being used.

Mail filter (e-mail term)

See *filter* and *e-mail filter*.

Mail header (e-mail term)

Structured text at the top of an e-mail message that contains details of sender, recipients, date and time of sending, the e-mail subject, and other information. Used by e-mail software for control and display purposes.

Mailing list (e-mail term)

A convenience feature offered by e-mail packages, which allows groups of *e-mail addresses* to be identified by a single name. Specialized software (such as Listserve or Majordomo) is available to manage such lists. Mailing lists are simple in concept but very valuable for distributing information within organizations, or across the wide internet. Many online businesses use mailing lists to keep customers informed of product updates and offers.

Mainframe (technical term)

A term that covers large, often expensive computers that can handle large *loads* and numbers of users. Very often used to describe IBM's range of mainframe computers which run the MVS operating system, the CICS transaction monitor system for online processing, the VSAM system for handling indexed files, and the DB2 relational database system. In terms of technical culture, this is a very different world from either the Microsoft technical community, or the community based around open platforms such as *UNIX*. Mainframe systems are often referred to under the heading of *legacy systems* and can often have a history stretching over decades. Nevertheless, many e-commerce solutions for major corporates will have a modern front end connected via *middleware* products – like IBM's own MQ-Series – to legacy processing on a mainframe.

Once mainframe hardware technology was quite different from the hardware used in smaller computer systems. These days, however, mainframes are more like other large server systems in terms of their hardware – the fundamental differences are really in the types of software used.

Majordomo (e-mail term)

A popular piece of software used to maintain *mailing lists*.

Mark-up language (technical term)

A mark-up language allows documents to contain text and instructions (usually called *tags*) on how to format and display that text. *HTML* – the main way of constructing *web pages* – is an example of a mark-up language.

Maximize (technical term)

In a Graphical User Interface (*GUI*), an option to allow a window to use all the displaying space on the PC or workstation screen.

MB (technical term)

Stands for *megabyte*.

MBone (technical term)

Stands for multicast backbone and is an experimental network supporting *multicast* routing of *IP* packets. Multicasting allows a single packet of data to be efficiently delivered to multiple machines and is intended for applications such as *webcasting.* However, the majority of *routers* within the internet currently only support point-to-point routing of IP packets and cannot support multicast. The MBone is formed from networks that can support IP multicast, linked together by "tunnels" through the rest of the non-multicast internet. These tunnels give the illusion that the MBone is a single multicast network within the internet. The MBone will eventually become obsolete when multicasting is a standard feature in internet routers.

Mbps (technical term)

Stands for *megabits* per second – a measure of network speed.

m-commerce (web term)

Short for mobile commerce. Although there is no rigorous definition, m-commerce is a general term often used for any electronic commerce activity that:

➡ uses mobile internet access (e.g. Wireless Application Protocol (*WAP*) or *iMode*);

➡ relies on mobile positioning technology;

➡ uses mobile phones for micropayment.

M-commerce was one of the big buzzwords of 2000, but the limitations of screens and keyboards on mobile devices, and the relatively slow data rates available over the current generation of mobile networks, have maybe dampened initial levels of enthusiasm, although there is little doubt that the next generation of devices and networks will remove some of these obstacles (see entries on *mobile computing* and *WAP* for further details).

Measurement (web term, business term)

Measurement of how much a site is used is seen a critical way of measuring the success of an online business, and media groups as such as Nielsen regularly publish website ratings in much the same way as they publish rankings for TV programs. Measurement is an important technique in the internet advertising industry. A variety of metrics can be used, with different strengths and weaknesses. The table summarizes some of the more common metrics.

Measure	Description	Limitations
Hit or gross exposure	Based on records of files sent to a web browser. Each element of the file – text, graphic, video – registers as a separate "hit." Of technical value to webmasters, who use this as one measure of the server's workload.	Over-counting – for example, if a page containing five graphics and two applets is sent by the webserver, it will be recorded as eight hits. This is computed by adding five graphics, two applets and one hit for the page itself.
Valid hits	A refinement on the concept of hits, which excludes any error messages, internal requests or computer-originated hits (e.g. a spider robot from a search engine).	Over-counting – as above.
Visit or visitor session	A visit is a series of requests from a single visitor to a website. The visitor session is normally said to have ended when no request has been made for a predefined period of time known as the "time-out" period. Attempts have been made to standardize this, with 30 minutes increasingly regarded as the norm. A subsequent request outside the "time-out" period from the same visitor would be treated as a new visit.	Poor identification – if the same individual makes a page request outside the original "time-out" period, it is regarded as a second visit. No industry standard – some advertising sales people reduce the "time-out" period to generate higher visitor-session figures for their site. Misleading analytics – some external measurement agencies use sample groups to estimate site visits, rather than analyzing

Measure	Description	Limitations
		actual site server logs, to which the site owners may not provide access. If the sample is unrepresentative, the resulting analytics will be equally unrepresentative of reality.
Page views or gross impressions	This is recorded when a complete HTML page, inclusive of all graphics, text, and interactive files, is delivered. This measure indicates the number of times a page was requested – and an advertisement potentially seen on the page. Works on the premise that if a page was requested, there is an intention to view the content. Only some pages of the site may qualify as advertisable page impressions – i.e. pages capable of hosting banner advertisements.	Each frame and frame parent document is counted as an individual page, so viewing a home page might actually be three or more page views. Over-counting – page views are counted irrespective of whether or not advertising was displayed on the page, so over-counting could still be present. Potential, not actual, viewing – the page might be viewed, but not the advertisement. Similar to a TV that is switched on, with the viewer channel-hopping during the advertisements. If users switch off graphics to increase browsing speed and read content, the number of page views – and potential advertising impressions – might rise, but it is even less likely the advertisements will be viewed. Changing the server's "refresh" frequency could instantly change the number of page views, as each refresh would register page views.
Advertising views or ad views	Number of times an advertising banner is served – and assumed to be seen – by the site visitor. Most web pages have more than one advertisement, so the number of ad views is greater than the equivalent page views. Payment is often on the basis of CPM – cost per mille or cost per thousand impressions. Example – a $20,000 banner campaign with a guaranteed 800,000 impressions would equate to a CPM of $25.	Under-counting – to speed surfing, a web browser can cache (store) recently visited pages on a user's hard disk. If the site is revisited, or the same ad appears on multiple pages simultaneously, the browser will display pages from disk, rather than the site's web server, thereby under-counting the number of ad views. To reduce this possibility, cache-busting software is deployed by servers pushing banner advertisements.

Measure	Description	Limitations
	Rates vary as to whether the ads are served run-of-site (i.e. anywhere) or if specific selections are required (e.g. geography, time of day, specific site location).	Other non-standard measures include counting a single impression on a co-branded banner as two impressions. Alternatively, an ad for software for kids could be counted twice – once in each category. Understanding the methodology used – and having access to ad server logs – is the only way to ensure an online advertising budget is being fairly spent.
Click-through or ad click	This occurs when a visitor physically clicks on an advertisement and is transported to another page or website, i.e. a tangible response to a banner advertisement. Click-through rate (CTR) is calculated as the number of clicks divided by the number of ad impressions multiplied by 100 and expressed as a percentage. Example – 15 clicks over 1,000 impressions would equate to a CTR of 1.5 percent.	Cost-per-click is another charging mechanism, i.e. $0.20 per click paid by the advertiser to the site owner. However, this can be abused by the advertiser, by placing an ad that does not call for action e.g. "click here now for …," as the ad will continue to enjoy ad views but no payment will be due to the site owner. The 'ad' may actually be a smaller-sized button, in which case location on the site is all-important if a high CTR is to be achieved. Buttons may be more responsive than banner advertisements, despite their size.
Keyword	This occurs when a keyword such as "flights" is purchased (e.g. by a travel agent) on a site, usually a search engine. Every time the search query includes the keyword, the banner ad provided by the travel agent will be served and charged at a predetermined rate per display.	Beware – a competitor could choose an organization's name as the keyword, ensuring that every time it was entered as part of a search query, the advertising banner served above the result (showing the organization's name) was that of the competitor.
Unique host	An attempt to identify site visitors by their IP address – i.e. the computer from which they arrived. A common advertising measure is unique hosts per month. It should track all unique hosts over a 30-day period to ensure each "unique" host is counted only once, irrespective	Under-counting in certain situations, e.g. in a cybercafé two separate individuals visiting the same site would share the same proxy server IP address and be treated as a single unique host, thereby under-counting the number of users. Over-counting – again, in a cybercafé

Measure	Description	Limitations
	of the numbner of visits during the 30-day period.	situation, a person visiting the same site twice with an interval between the two visits could be routed via two different proxy servers owned by the café. Although two unique hosts, it is still the same person. Some site owners compensate for the under-counting by multiplying their unique host numbers by an arbitrary number, say three, to arrive at a count for unique users. Unique hosts per month are often computed by adding together all the daily unique hosts over a 30-day period regardless of the fact that some of them might have visited on more than one day during that 30-day per-iod, thereby inflating the figures considerably.
Unique user	A distinct individual who visits a website or page within a specified "time-out" period. Identification is undertaken by user registration or other tracking devices such as cookies.	The same individual visiting the site outside the original "time-out" period will be counted as two unique users even though it is the same person. Cookies can be intentionally disabled by visi-tors or disallowed by corporate firewalls, making tracking impossible. If the user logs on via a different computer to the one on which the cookie was placed, e.g. a laptop, then a new cookie will be set and counted as a new unique user even though it is the same person.
Registered user	A distinct individual who visits a website, enters personal details and an identification password, and is granted access.	If the individual forgets or loses the password on an information (not transactional) site, they could re-register with a new password. Again, it the same person, but with two reg-istered user accounts.

Mega (technical term)

Prefix that multiplies an IT quantity by 2^{20} – a number close to one million. This parallels the use of mega in the metric system, but reflects the fact that computers are based around *binary* arithmetic. Used in terms such as *megabit* and *megabyte.*

Megabit (technical term)

2^{20} *bits* – a bit being the fundamental unit of computer storage and taking the values zero or one. Megabits per second (Mbps) is an often-used measure of network speed. For example, *T1* lines in the US – a standard leased-line offering for businesses – will offer speeds of around 1.5 Mbps.

Megabyte (technical term)

2^{20} *bytes* – a byte being 8 bits of storage, long enough to hold a numeric code for characters from the *ASCII* character set. Used to size large files, total amounts of disk space, and main computer memory.

Melissa (security term)

The name of a computer virus first spotted in March 1999. Melissa was the first well-known virus to exploit vulnerabilities in Microsoft's *Outlook* e-mail program and was written in Microsoft Word macro language (a variant of the powerful Visual Basic programming language). Melissa propagates from machine to machine by e-mailing itself as an attachment to the first 50 names in a user's Outlook address book. All an unwitting recipient has to do is open the attachment and Melissa will infect the machine and mail itself to another 50 people. Apart from increasing the *load* on the e-mail system, Melissa had no other apparent malicious effect. The technique of using visual basic commands to propagate via Outlook was copied by the more nasty "I love you" virus over a year later and close integration of programming languages and e-mail remains a significant area of vulnerability.

Melissa is classified as a virus rather than a *worm* since it cannot automatically forward itself, but requires the user to open the attachment for it to propagate.

Memex (technical term)

An unbuilt machine proposed by *Vannevar Bush* in 1945 – based on microfilm – which is seen by many to anticipate the PC and world wide web by four or five decades.

Menu (technical term)

Fundamental mechanism for user interaction, giving a list of options from which a user can select. Usually presented these days as a horizontal bar on the window in which an application is running.

Merchant services (business term)

An aspect of the *B2C* world in particular, merchant services cover outsourced payment processing, usually for credit and debit cards. Everyday manifestations are the point-of-sale terminals and electronic cash registers in shops and restaurants. For B2C sites, similar services are available over the internet.

Meta-tag (technical term)

Meta-tags are special forms of the tags used in mark-up language such as *HTML* (Hypertext Mark-up Language). The information held within meta-tags is not displayed on the page, nor do the tags affect how the page is displayed: they are literally information about the information.

HTML meta-tags have two general forms:

➡ `<META HTTP-EQUIV="name" CONTENT="information">`

➡ `<META NAME="name" CONTENT="information">`

The HTTP-EQUIV form is typically used to control a *browser* by emulating the instructions a webserver normally sends behind the scenes. Examples of this form of meta-tag are forcing the browser to refresh a page after a certain time or to redirect the browser if the location of the page has changed. For example:

```
<META HTTP-EQUIV="Refresh" CONTENT="5">
```

forces the browser to reload the page every five seconds;

```
<META HTTP-EQUIV="Refresh"
CONTENT="1;URL=http://www.newlocation.com/page.html">
```

forces the browser to load a www.newlocation.com/page.html after one second.

The table gives some examples of the NAME and CONTENT form of a meta-tag:

NAME	Typical usage	Example CONTENT
KEYWORDS	List of keywords used by some search engines	"glossary, internet, ecommerce, e-commerce, brilliant"
DESCRIPTION	Description of the page displayed by a search engine	"A truly fantastic glossary of internet and e-commerce terms"
AUTHOR	Details of who created the page	"A N Other"
GENERATOR	A tag added by some third-party authoring tools to record how the page was created.	"Mozilla/4.7 [en] (Win95; I) [Netscape]"
ROBOTS	Prevent a page being indexed by search engine robots or spiders	NOINDEX

In the future, meta-tags are likely to be superseded by the more standardized Resource Definition Framework (*RDF*).

Microbrowser (technical term)

A microbrowser is a lightweight version of a standard PC internet *browser*, often designed to be embedded into mobile devices such as *telephones*. Unfortunately, the two standards for mobile internet access, *iMode* and *WAP* (Wireless Application Protocol), provide incompatible definitions of the functions of a microbrowser. This is a market that the main PC browser vendors such as Microsoft have not (yet) dominated, leaving the field open to specialist companies such as *Openware.*

Micro competitors (business term)

Small businesses that offer niche products or services, made economic only by the internet, and chip away at the customer base of larger businesses in that sector.

Micropayment (business term)

An alternative to subscription-based use of credit cards, where a user has an electronic wallet containing a form of electronic money that can be spent in small amounts on websites, thus allowing the purchase of small pieces of content. Companies like Qpass offer the infrastructure to perform this kind of service, although it is not yet that common. See also *e-money*.

Microsoft (company)

Microsoft is now one of the world's most recognized brands of any kind, and through its PC operating system and applications touches the lives of hundreds of millions of people. It may therefore be hard to appreciate how unusual the Microsoft journey has been. Twenty years ago it would have been strange indeed to think a company based around software alone, and for a type of system then mostly favored by a small number of hobbyists, could grow to be one of the world's most powerful enterprises. Like all leaders, Microsoft can generate a variety of emotional responses, but there is no doubt that it represents one of the most significant commercial undertakings of the late 20th century.

History

In terms of history, the Microsoft story begins in 1975, when an article on a hobby-oriented kit computer – the MITS Altair 8800 – was published in *Popular Electronics*. The article inspired Paul Allen and *Bill Gates* – the co-founders of Microsoft – to develop a version of the simple BASIC language for the Altair. This was sold to MITS who became Microsoft's first customer. In 1976, "Microsoft" as a name was registered with the Office of the Secretary of the State of New Mexico. This was followed by a succession of products, including a flirtation with a derivative of *UNIX* called Xenix. Microsoft's major break came in 1981 when the *IBM PC* was launched, offering Microsoft's *MS-DOS* as one of the main operating system options. The first member of the *Windows* family of operating system software was announced in 1983 and released in 1985, although it wasn't destined to become the key driver of Microsoft's operating system business until the 1990s. (It was in 1992 that Microsoft shipped Windows 3.1 with over 1,000 enhancements. This was the version that created unprecedented user demand with over one million advance orders placed worldwide.) In parallel, Microsoft also worked with IBM on OS/2 – another PC operating system that gained some traction, but never the mass penetration of Windows.

Microsoft grew to dominate the PC software market, both in terms of operating system software and general applications (such as wordprocessors and spreadsheet software) during the 1980s and early 1990s. It wasn't unique in missing the growing importance of the internet and world wide web at first, but in the mid-1990s Bill Gates turned what was already a very large organization on its head to focus on internet technology. Its most successful offering in this area to date has been *Internet Explorer*, its own browser.

Products and services

The powerhouse of Microsoft's business is its platform software and business application software. However, its range of products and services is very broad, as the following much-edited list shows. Microsoft's offerings have been built up through a mix of its own internal developments, and acquisition of smaller companies with interesting products.

Operating system software

- **Business-users**: available options at the start of 2001 include:
  - Windows 2000 – built for reliability and able to support applications from personal business use up to very powerful servers. The Windows 2000 family marks a major attempt to capture more of the enterprise solution space (i.e. support large-scale, complex business systems). The one-millionth Windows 2000 server licence was announced in February 2001.
  - Windows-NT – although the NT stands for "New Technology", this predates the 2000 family, but is still used and sold for workstation and server applications. Previous versions of Windows (such as Windows 95 and Windows 98) are still in common use.
- **Home-users**: Main product at the time of writing is Windows Me, where the "Me" stands for Millennium Edition. Windows 95 and Windows 98 are still commonly found in the home environment.
- **Embedded devices**: a market where Microsoft dominates less than the PC world, Windows-CE is a cut-down operating system for embedded

systems and internet applicances. So you can find Windows-CE running on devices such as some types of *PDA*.

➡ **Internet platform software**: in particular, this covers the *Internet Explorer* browser.

Office products

Microsoft's Office suite contains tools that are used daily by a huge number of home and business users, such as Word (a wordprocessor), Excel (a spreadsheet), Outlook (an e-mail client program), and PowerPoint (for pre-sentations). Microsoft has become as dominant in the market for this type of personal, general application as it has in that for PC operating system soft-ware.

Server products

These include SQL*Server (a database engine), Exchange Server (for e-mail and information sharing), and Commerce Server (for building e-commerce solutions).

Developer tools

The most obvious example is the Visual Studio range which offers Visual Basic, Visual C++ and Visual J++ (for *Java*). These are tools familiar to many professional programmers,

Internet services

Such as **www.msn.com,** which is the entry point for the Microsoft Network (MSN), a full-function *portal* service.

Consumer products

These include the Encarta electronic encyclopaedia, games such as the famous Flight Simulator, toys, and the recently announced X-box games console.

Architecture initiatives

The world of IT and the internet revolves around a small number of major technology cultures. Microsoft products define one. There is also the base culture of the internet which revolves around more open standards, as opposed to the proprietary Microsoft product set. One result of this is the way different companies and organizations compete for the high ground in terms of architectural vision. The *Java* language and core surrounding concepts from *Sun* achieved stunning success in a short time. Microsoft also packages its own concepts. The *Active-X* framework for connecting technical components is one Microsoft example. More recent initiatives include the ambitious .NET which attempts to provide a way of building applications from a mixture of local and external web-based services.

Middleware (technical term)

Software that logically sits between application software that handles specific application logic and server software focussed on providing common services such as managing a database.

Middleware covers a wide range of software technologies and is often simply referred to as the "glue" or "plumbing" that holds a complex system together. Good examples of middleware include:

➡ software to support collaboration between distributed software components;

➡ software to guarantee the reliable processing of transactions;

➡ software to reliably route sort messages between different systems.

In some ways web technologies (such as *HTTP*) fulfill the role of middleware between the *browser* and the *webserver*. However, the main role of middleware on the web is to build complex server applications or to allow webservers to connect to *legacy systems*.

MIME (technical term)

Stands for Multipurpose Internet Mail Extensions. Originally e-mails sent over the internet were assumed to be text only; MIME redefines the format of messages to allow for:

➦ non-text messages (e.g. images or audio)

➦ international character sets (e.g. non-ASCII characters).

MIME defines a number of standard content types and also standard ways of encoding information for transmission by internet e-mail. For instance, a mail containing a *JPEG* image would have the following MIME header:

```
Content-Type: image/jpeg
Content-Transfer-Encoding: base64
```

MIME encoding is usually completely transparent to end-users, and is managed by the e-mail application (e.g. Microsoft Outlook). You will have been using it if you ever receive attachments via e-mail.

In addition to e-mail applications, web browsers also support various MIME types. This enables the browser to display or output files that are not in *HTML* format.

There is also a secure version of MIME called S/MIME.

Minimize (technical term)
In a Graphical User Interface (*GUI*), an option to hide a window without stopping the relevant program. In modern versions of *Windows* the name of the window appears on the *taskbar* at the bottom of the screen. Clicking on the name brings the window back to life.

Mirror site (technical term)
A file or webserver machine that contains a copy of the content of a popular server with the intention of spreading the *load* across multiple machines. Sometimes it is geographically dispersed to allow users to minimize the number of network links required to get at the desired content.

Mission critical (business term)
Used to describe a computer system that is fundamental to a business, rather than one providing discretionary functionality. So, for a major e-tailer, an example would be the online system that processes orders, which needs to be available as close to 24 hours a day, seven days a week as possible.

MME (mobile term)
Microsoft Mobile Explorer, which is a version of Internet Explorer aimed at

the mobile market and capable of displaying *WML* (Wireless Mark-up Language) as well as *HTML.*

Mobile, Mobile computing (business, technical, mobile terms)

Mobile computing – often just shortened to mobile – covers a range of technology and business developments that are often seen as the "Next Big Thing" in e-commerce. Some forms of mobile computing have been around for decades, but the big themes are the huge success of mobile telephony (which has seen Nokia become one of the world's most valuable brands, and mobile phones achieve higher levels of market penetration than personal computers) and new types of *broadband* wireless standard which offer potentially much higher data transmission rates than previous standards.

A new term, *m-commerce*, has been created to cover the types of business that can be run over mobile. As a sign of the seriousness with which this potential market is viewed, the UK auction in 2000 of frequencies for new model broadband services raised over $30 billion for the UK Treasury.

As usual, there is real opportunity, combined with over-exuberant hope and expectation – since physics will always limit what can be done from mobile devices. What mobile does offer is a major new channel for existing internet-based services – with some clear limitations on what can be done – and entirely new types of opportunity for point-of-need services. This is a competitive and energetic marketplace, with equipment manufacturers and service providers at times having very strong market valuations. There is also much ongoing consolidation among suppliers – some recent takeovers have valued individual mobile phone users at many thousands of dollars. However, the post-millenial gloom over technology stocks has impacted the telecommunications providers as much as anyone else. Valuations have fallen sharply, and there is concern over the amount companies have spent on acquiring broadband licenses, the cost of new infrastructure, and how fast take-up of new services will happen. Nevertheless, this remains an intriguing marketplace.

Mobile internet access (mobile term)

Mobile devices allow users to access the internet on the move, providing an extra channel for existing sites, or opportunities to build new types of site. A user needs two things to do this: a wireless data connection, and a portable device that supports a *browser*. People have been using PCs with modems connected to mobile phones for, say, e-mail for some time. Today the expectation is that the portable device may be a handheld *PDA* (Personal Digital Assistant) or an intelligent mobile phone rather than necessarily a PC.

To understand what's possible, and what's not, we will start with some lightweight physics.

The radio spectrum

The radio spectrum covers frequencies from around 3 kHz (Very Low Frequency or VLF) to 300 GHz (Extremely High Frequency or EHF). The extreme ends of the spectrum are only useful for specialist forms of communications. The table shows the ranges typically associated with everyday uses of radio frequencies.

Range	Frequency	Example use
VHF (Very High Frequency)	30–300 MHz	FM broadcast radio
UHF (Ultra High Frequency)	300 MHz–3 GHz	Mobile phones Terrestrial TV
SHF (Super High Frequency)	3 GHz–30 GHz	Satellite communications

Spectrum use

Unlike fixed connections, the radio spectrum is a globally shared resource (it is just the "airwaves" after all) and two people transmitting on the same frequency can interfere with each other. To control the potential for interference, the frequencies that may be used are regulated by the International Telecommunications Union (**www.itu.int**) and by national governments. Use of the higher frequencies has the advantage that these are much more likely to be virgin territory with no incumbent users. However, there are disadvantages. Higher frequencies are more easily absorbed by things (including people) that get in the way. VHF can penetrate normal buildings, but at SHF, even leafy trees and falling rain become significant obstacles to signals. Bypassing obstacles therefore requires greater transmission power, and that drains batteries more quickly. Even without battery constraints, there are limits to the amount of power that it is desirable to transmit. The energy of radio signals generates energy that can be turned into heat by the same process by which microwave ovens cook food. Since a common obstacle is the human body, there are safeguards about the amount of power that can be transmitted.

The explosion in demand for radio frequencies for "personal" voice or data communications has made the radio spectrum – bounded by the existing broadcast, civil, and military users at the lower end of UHF and absorption effects at higher SHF frequencies – a very valuable resource. In the UK and some other countries, radio spectrum has been turned into a source of income for the government, by selling licenses to use it to the highest bidder.

Spectrum auctions

The UK government sold a total of 140 MHz of spectrum for the next generation of mobile phones in May 2000. The lengthy auction process was designed by game theorists to maximize revenue.

Five 20-year licenses for different frequency ranges (the largest being 35 MHz) were sold. The winners were:

➡ License A: TIW UMTS (UK)
➡ License B: Vodafone
➡ License C: BT (British Telecom)
➡ License D: One2One
➡ License E: Orange

The sale raised £22.5 billion (or approximately £160 per Hz). This was a big windfall for the UK government, but has raised large concerns about the length of time required for the new owners to be able to make a profit.

Spectrum reuse

Since spectrum is so valuable, it is essential for a service provider to be able to reuse the frequencies they have been allocated. Fortunately, absorption effects cause transmissions to fade with distance, allowing different regional broadcast stations to use the same frequency without interference, providing they are sufficiently far apart. This principle has also been applied in traditional mobile telephony, where a "cellular" approach allows the same frequencies to be re-used by different locations. Cells are traditionally drawn as hexagons but are actually highly irregular shapes governed by the output of the transmitter and local buildings or terrain. The same frequencies can be reused in non-adjacent cells. If a user moves between cells during a call, the network automatically switches the phone to a channel in the new cell in a process called "hand-off."

Transmission mechanisms

Historically, the main use of cellular telephone networks has been for voice, but recent and forthcoming standards allow data to be transmitted over the same infrastructure. For example, the established *GSM* standard digitally encodes speech for transport and can also be used directly for transporting data (without the need for a *modem*). A single "timeslot" (the capacity required for one voice call) can support an effective data rate of 9.6 to 14.4 Kbps – the same as a slow fixed telephone link. Recent enhancements to GSM allow multiple timeslots to be combined, supporting data rates that are multiples of 9.6 or 14.4 Kbps. Many figures quoted for future mobile data rates assume that all the timeslots in a cell are combined. However, this is unlikely to be economically viable in the near future.

Data protocols

The mobile phone network provides a versatile and accessible means of moving "bits" to and from mobile devices. However, to access the internet a protocol stack is required on top of the raw data link, in the same way that *TCP/IP* operates over a modem link for fixed internet access. At the moment there are two common models for mobile internet access: TCP/IP and *WAP* (Wireless Application Protocol), which are described below.

Native TCP/IP

The same protocols that are used for fixed-line internet access can operate over a wireless link. The advantages of this approach are:

➡ Interconnectivity between the mobile network and the internet is simple (effectively just a network *router*).

➡ Only one set of protocols need be configured on devices that operate on both fixed and wireless connections (e.g. laptop PCs).

➡ The strengths (and weaknesses) of the protocols are well known.

This model is used by the Japanese *iMode* internet-enabled phone system.

WAP

The Wireless Application Protocol has been developed by the WAP Forum (**www.wapforum.org**), and defines a set of new protocols optimized to the specific characteristics of a wireless link. The advantages of the WAP protocols are that they:

➡ Minimize the number of messages needed to communicate between the WAP client and the internet (and hence reduce the need for expensive radio spectrum).

➡ Support suspension of a session when a radio connection is temporarily unavailable.

➡ Minimize the processing needed to implement the protocol on the mobile device.

Mobile devices

There are a bewildering array of portable devices already on the market (or about to be launched) that support wireless internet access. It's hard to categorize these, due to the diversity and creativity of the product developers. Among the most tangible physical characteristics of these devices are the sizes of the screen and the keyboard:

➡ Small screen, numeric keyboard: typically "smart" phones.

➡ Big screen, qwerty keyboard: typically radio-enhanced laptop/palmtop PCs.

➡ Somewhere in between: the hard-to-define world of PDAs, organizers and communicators.

The choice of device really depends on what you need to do on the move. Small-screen devices will not be useful for surfing, but will be adequate to check a bank balance, or send e-mails.

There is great competition for the operating system such devices will use. Microsoft have a number of versions of Windows targetted at mobile devices (e.g. Windows-CE, PocketPC). However, EPOC and PalmOS are two non-Microsoft contenders from the PDA world.

Mobile positioning (technical term)

One of the potential benefits of *m-commerce* is the tailoring of information to the location of the mobile device. For location-dependent services to work, there obviously needs to be some means of automatically locating the mobile internet device and therefore its user.

There are basically two types of solution:

➡ Terminal-based location, which relies on the mobile device being able to determine its location and then report it. One way of achieving this is to integrate a Global Positioning System (*GPS*) receiver into the device.

➡ Network-based location where the network infrastructure locates the device using its normal transmissions. An example of this is the "Cell of Origin" system (COO), which simply determines which cell the phone is active in. However, the resolution is limited to the (variable) size of the cell.

Once the technology is in place, we will be faced with the more difficult question of just how much we want third parties to know our exact location.

Modem (technical term)

Stands for modulator/demodulator. A pair of modems allow digital information (1s and 0s) to be exchanged between two systems over an analog connection, most typically the PSTN (Public Switched Telephone Network). A modem connection to an *ISP* is a very common way of connecting to the internet.

At the simplest level, one modem makes a telephone call to another in exactly the same way as you make a voice call. Your computer transfers digital data to the modem as a long string of 1s and 0s and each is translated into an audible tone (this is the modulation part). At the receiving end the tones are converted back into 1s and 0s by the other modem (this is the demodulation part).

Although modern modems use much more sophisticated modulation techniques, this simple explanation illustrates some of the limitations of modems, namely:

➡ Connections are point-to-point – a single modem cannot support simultaneous connections to multiple remote computers. This means that ISPs must support large "pools" of modems to prevent their subscribers getting a busy tone during peak times.

➡ The range of frequencies (or bandwidth) used must fall within that supported by the PSTN (typically below 3.5 kHz). The relationship between bandwidth, noise on the line, and the maximum data rate achievable is complex (see *Shannon's Theorem*). However modern techniques can squeeze 30–40 Kbits over a standard dial-up connection and sometimes data rates as high as 56 Kbits where parts of the telephone network are known to be digital.

High-speed services such as *ADSL* and *ISDN* present a digital interface directly to the user so there is no need for a modem, although the interface boxes are sometimes colloquially called modems.

Moderated newsgroup (internet term)

Usually people's postings to *Usenet newsgroups* are made available to all subscribers. However, some newsgroups are configured so that postings are first e-mailed to a moderator who first validates the appropriateness of the posting before making it available to other newsgroup subscribers. Moderated groups generally have less *spam* and *flames*, but are also open to criticism over censorship.

The name of moderated newsgroups generally (but not always) end with .moderated, e.g. comp.lang.c++.moderated.

Moore's Law (technical term)

Not a law in any real sense at all, but a well-known observation from Gordon Moore (a co-founder of Intel) that the capacity of silicon chips (capacity meaning the number of individual transistors on a chip) doubles roughly every 18 months. Although chip developers worry about the limits of physics, Moore's Law has remained remarkably valid since the 1970s. One consequence is the ability of PCs to run **GUIs** and complex **browser** software with multimedia **plug-ins**, a task way beyond the first commercial PCs.

Mosaic (technical term)

Mosaic was the first widely distributed graphical web **browser** and a direct conceptual ancestor of two of the most popular browsers in use today. Mosaic was developed by a team at the National Center for Supercomputing Applications (NCSA) at the University of Illinois, and first released in 1993. Some of the development team (including **Marc Andreesen**) then left NCSA to form Netscape Communications (originally called Mosaic Communications) and went on to develop the popular **Netscape Navigator** product.

The University of Illinois licensed Mosaic to Spyglass Inc., who in turn licensed Microsoft some parts of Mosaic for use in **Internet Explorer.** Spyglass merged with OpenTV (an Interactive TV vendor) in July 2000 and the Mosaic name lives on in the form of Spyglass Device Mosaic, a browser for use within set-top boxes and other internet appliances.

Mouse potato (slang)

An online version of a couch potato.

Mozilla (slang, technical term)

Name of the cute dinosaur mascot from early releases of Netscape's browser, drawn by Dave Titus (**www.davetitus.com**). Also the name of the open source browser project that has a symbiotic relationship with recent versions of Netscape (**www.mozilla.org**).

MP3 (technical term)

Derived from MPEG Audio Layer – 3. Used to hold music and audio in a highly compressed digital form. The file sizes required for MP3 are 10 per-cent or less of equivalent standards. As a result, MP3 has spawned a large sub-culture where members swap commercial music tracks illegally.

MPEG (technical term)

Stands for Motion Picture Experts Group, a group charged by **ISO** with the development of standards for coded and compressed representation of digi-tal audio and video. The main standards defined are:

→ **MPEG-1** – used for video encoding, but more famous for spawning the MP3 standard for audio compression (MP3 refers to layer 3 of the MPEG-1 standard).

→ **MPEG-2** – the standard for digital television in Europe and also for DVD video disks.

→ **MPEG-4** – still in development but aimed at providing high-quality video over low bandwidth connections and suitable for the internet

MS-DOS (technical term)

Stands for Microsoft Disk Operating System. DOS was developed by Microsoft and IBM to support the launch of the IBM PC in 1981 and became the de facto standard for PC operating systems during the 1980s. MS-DOS has now been superseded by the Windows product range, although Windows still supports an MS-DOS-style command line interface.

It is an interesting quirk of fate that Microsoft was selected by IBM to supply the operating systems for its secret PC project. At the time Digital Research's CP/M was popular on various (pre-IBM) PCs and Microsoft did not actually have an operating system compatible with the Intel 8086 processor. However, Bill Gates seized the opportunity and licensed a product from a Seattle developer called Tim Paterson. The rest is history ...

Multicast (technical term)

Logical interactions over the web are typically between two machines, e.g. a workstation running a *browser* and a *webserver* (although many other intermediary machines may process the messages en route). One machine talking to another in this way is sometimes known as unicasting.

However, newer applications such as *webcasting* often require the same information to be sent to many machines at the same time. Currently webcasting requires every workstation to establish a connection to a server and for the server to send the same information back over the network to each workstation. This creates a very large amount of traffic. Some underlying *LAN* technologies such as *Ethernet* already support broadcast delivery where the same message is delivered to every machine on the network. While reducing the *load* on the network, this is wasteful of computer resources if only a small number of users are actually interested and is clearly not practical for the

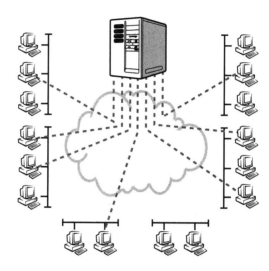

Multicast 1: Webcast using unicasting – the same information is duplicated to all machines

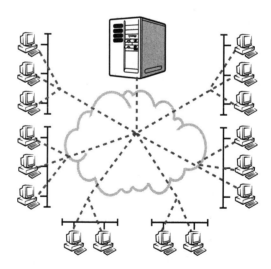

Multicast 2: Webcast using broadcasting – all machines get the webcast even if they aren't interested in it

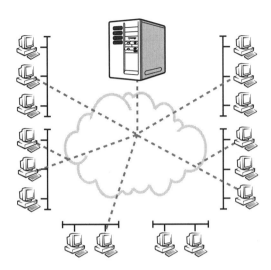

Multicast 3: Webcast using multicasting – duplication of information is minimized and only interested machines receive the data

entire internet. Multicasting is a "half-way house" between unicasting and broadcasting – it allows multiple end-user machines to subscribe to the same information as it passes over the network, but prevents the information being sent to machines that are not interested. The diagrams show how a webcast can be supported in a number of different ways.

The Internet Protocol (*IP*) supports the concept of multicast groups, which an arbitrary number of machines may be part of; each multicast group has a unique "class D" *IP address*. IP packets sent to multicast addresses are delivered to all the machines in the group. However, this requires the routers that make up the internet to support multicasting. At present this support is not widespread outside part of the internet called the *MBone* (multicast backbone).

Multi-channel (business term)

Channel is a term often used to cover the mechanisms by which businesses contact their customers: these can include the web and, for many businesses, will also include branches, call centers, conventional mail, and so on. With the advent of call centers, mobile telephony, and interactive television as new channels, some businesses are attempting to implement multi-channel technical and business architectures, which allow them to treat customers consistently, however they make contact.

Multimedia (technical term)

Describes content made up of mixed formats – including text, sound, images, video, and other forms of animation.

Multi-tasking (technical term)

This simply means the ability of an *operating system* to allow a computer to appear to be running multiple programs (or tasks) at the same time. Today this doesn't seem particularly thrilling, but in the days of *MS-DOS* or early releases of *Windows*, only one program could be executed at a time.

Multi-tier (technical term)

Multi-tier describes technology architectures that have multiple layers (see diagram opposite). In the early days of computers, systems centered on big, single boxes. The first generation of client server systems were often two-tier with PCs connected to servers. The modern computing world is focussed on much higher levels of distribution. A web service will typically run across several networks, and processing will be undertaken on the end-user's PC, and a variety of back-end servers.

My ... (web term)

Shorthand for a personalized version of a website. So if a website is called somesitename.com, it may have an option mysomesitename, which loads your particular configuration details.

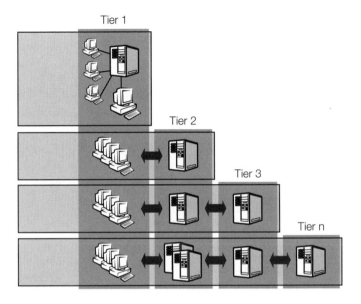

Multi-tier: technology architecture

Name.Space Inc. (company)

Name.Space Inc. (**www.name-space.com**) offers an alternative set of global *top-level domain names* including gems such as ".cool" and ".geek," by operating its own version of *DNS* (Domain Name System). It attempted to force *ICANN* to add these domains into the official DNS system, claiming that not to do so represented a violation of the First Amendment and an impediment to freedom of speech. This action failed, and unless users are configured to use the Name.Space name servers, these domains will not be recognized and are therefore of limited practical use.

Napster (company)

A controversial web application and company, which allows end-users to advertise files (typically containing music compressed using the *MP3* algorithm and of possibly dubious copyright status), and other users to locate and download these files for their own use. It is important to note that, while Napster maintains an inventory, the files themselves reside on the end-user's systems. Created in 1999 by 19-year-old Shawn Fanning, Napster has quickly become popular on college campuses, with MP3 file transfers becoming a major hog of available *bandwidth*. It is estimated that billions of file exchanges have taken place between Napster users.

The record industry has unsurprisingly become engaged in legal proceedings against Napster, claiming it is enabling illegal exchange of copyright material. However, at the time of writing, Napster has struck deals with some record companies to provide access to music on a subscription basis.

Nasdaq (organization)

Famous for being the trading home of many technology stocks, Nasdaq started on February 8, 1971 as the first electronic stock market, the abbreviation Nasdaq standing for National Association of Securities Dealers Automated Quotation. In recent years, Nasdaq has been the natural home for shares from many high-profile start-ups after their Initial Public Offering or *IPO*, and for technology companies in general. Its golden period for investors was in the late 1990s; 2000 brought much more nervousness and a halving of the value of the index.

Navigation (technical term)

Loosely used term observing how a user moves through an application program, which of course includes *browser* software, and websites themselves. Easy intuitive navigation is a key aspect of successful web design.

Navigator (product)

Short-hand form of *Netscape Navigator* – one of the two most popular browsers, the other being Microsoft *Internet Explorer*.

Nelson, Ted

Ted Nelson, a student of philosophy and sociology rather than computing, is the inventor of the term *hypertext*. He based his ideas on those of *Vannevar Bush* from the 1940s, and invented the concept of *Xanadu* in 1960. The main focus of Xanadu was a networked system that would store and index literature and other forms of information. Hypertext – with links between text being based on association rather than sequence – was the way Xanadu would be navigated. Xanadu also included a workstation concept very much like the modern PC, and had notions of information exchange over networks. These concepts are very much at the heart of the world wide web, although Xanadu itself has never been fully realized.

Net (slang)
Shorthand form of internet.

Netiquette (slang)
Covers standards of good behavior for *e-mail*, *Usenet*, or similar. Failure to comply can be punished with being *flamed* and being placed in a *bozo filter*. Things to avoid if you want to display netiquette include:

- personal insults
- posting large amounts of irrelevant material
- commercial activity with non-commercial discussion groups
- cross-posting the same material to many discussion groups.

Netizen (slang)
Someone who is a major user of the internet.

NetPC (technical term)
The NetPC initiative is based around a specification for a low-cost PC designed for network applications. A NetPC is intended to run *thin-client* applications and will lack disk drives and similar features that drive up cost. It is similar to the "network computer" initiative from *Sun* and *Oracle*. Although initiatives like these have yet to demonstrate real success, they do indicate how the industry is thinking about the future of the "normal" PC as the average user's standard computing platform.

Netratings (company)
Company based around techniques for measuring website usage. See also *Nielsen//Netratings*.

Netscape (company)
One of most well-known names to spring out of the early days of the web, Netscape was founded in April 1994 by *Jim Clark* (who founded Silicon Graphics prior to this) and *Marc Andreesen* (who as a student created the NCSA *Mosaic* browser, which was the first *browser* to display graphics and was built for ease of use). Netscape's business – although more diverse these days – has always centered on the *Netscape Navigator* core browser product,

which, until Microsoft's introduction of *Internet Explorer,* dominated this particular part of the technology marketplace.

Netscape held its initial public offering (*IPO*) in August 1995, only 16 months after its founding, and was valued at around $2 billion. In many ways, Netscape set the fashion for internet start-up IPOs. Described at its peak as "the fastest-growing software company in history," it entered a more troubled period when Microsoft entered the browser market and gave away the Internet Explorer product for free, or as a tool bundled with its operating system software.

These days Netscape offers a suite of downloadable software, still centered around its browser, and a comprehensive *portal* service with the usual focus on additional services such as e-mail and messaging.

Netscape Navigator (product)

The first *browser* to become a true commercial success, and a descendent in some sense of the *Mosaic* browser created by *Marc Andreesen,* who was a co-founder of Netscape. The Navigator product is a full-function, graphical browser which allows novice users to use the web and internet, and incorporates graphics, multimedia, and *plug-ins.* Though it was very successful initially, Microsoft's move into browsers – with *Internet Explorer* – changed the ground rules, since it was treated as a free add-on to the Windows operating system. This has proven contentious and led to the complex US anti-trust action against Microsoft. Netscap Navigator remains popular, but only with a fraction of the market share of Internet Explorer.

Netsourcing (business term)

Provision of application functionality, or business services over the internet or other network. This is a hot topic in business at the time of writing. See *ASP* and *BSP* for a slightly longer discussion.

Network (technical term)

A network is a group of computers and associated devices (such as printers) which are in some way connected to share information. A network can contain two computers, or millions, as in the case of the internet. Computer networks are now a fundamental feature of the technology landscape. However, until the 1990s, the most common form of technology solution

consisted either of a central system that supported multiple directly connected users, often performing radically different tasks, or PCs that might be
standalone or connected in a small Local Area Network (**LAN**).

Now networking is essentially ubiquitous (leading to slogans such as
Sun's "The network is the computer"). Most organizations have a collection
of connected LANs and the internet is used everywhere as a global resource.
Modern computer systems are more distributed, involving PCs and workstations, and multiple types of back-end server system. The growth of mobile
computing increases this level of distribution.

The term "network" usually covers:

➡ the physical network infrastructure (cabling, routers and other devices);

➡ the protocols that are used to exchange different forms of information
(examples include low-level **Ethernet** for LANs, the very common **TCP/IP**
family used on the internet, proprietary forms of network protocol such
as SNA from IBM, and older standards such as **X.25**);

➡ applications and services that are network intensive (e.g. file serving).

Network cloud (slang)
The traditional way to represent a high-level view of a network in systems-
design documents is a picture of a cloud. Data packets disappear into the
cloud and "automagically" appear at the right place.

Newbie (slang)
Can be an almost affectionate name for a newcomer to a particular service, or
a vaguely insulting term for a newcomer to a **Usenet** usergroup.

New Economy (business term)
Vogue term of the late 1990s used to describe the extraordinary period of
growth (and raw speculation) in technology businesses and the wider US
economy during that period. To economists it had a real meaning tied to the
apparent growth in underlying productivity due to use of computer technology – an effect at least some observers think was real. Also used much more
loosely to describe the interconnected world of venture capital, high-tech
start-ups and dot-com companies. Whatever the underlying economic facts,
it seems clear that the nature of past and future technological innovation

will continue to have significant impacts on the way we do business and other activities (see the entry on *ubiquitous computing* for example).

News (general term)

In a pure internet context, the term "news" covers e-mail-like postings made via the *Usenet* system of newsgroups. However, more recently news (typically financial, current affairs, or sport) has become an important form of content for *portals*. Dedicated news sites (e.g. **www.bbc.com**) have also proven very popular.

Newsgroup (internet term)

A discussion forum on the *Usenet* relating to a particular subject. News groups are organized into hierarchies and discussions within a newsgroup are organized into threads which contain postings made in response to a question or announcement. Threads can often grow to many hundreds of individual postings, especially if a *flame war* is raging.

Newsgroup hierarchy (internet term)

The *Usenet* contains thousands of individual newsgroups and the number is growing all the time. To put some kind of structure to this, groups are organized around a number of major hierarchies including:

➡ `alt.`   alternative

➡ `biz.`   business

➡ `comp.`   computers and IT

➡ `news.`   news about the Usenet

➡ `rec.`   recreation

➡ `sci.`   science.

Each of these are (sometimes) logically subdivided, for instance major parts of the `comp.` hierarchy include:

➡ `comp.dcom.` data communications

➡ `comp.lang.` different programming languages

➡ `comp.sys.` different vendors' computer systems.

Each of these is further subdivided as required, e.g.:

➡ `comp.sys.hp.hpux`

➡ `comp.sys.hp.mpe`

➡ `comp.sys.ibm.pc.games.flight.sim`

➡ `comp.sys.ibm.pc.hardware.video`

Not all hierarchies are of the same depth and there are many more top-level groups than those listed above, including country-specific hierarchies such as the `uk.` and organization-specific such as `microsoft.`

Newsreader (technical term)

Software to allow a user to browse, read and respond to items posted on the *Usenet.* Newsreader capabilities are typically integrated or bundled with web *browsers* (such as *Internet Explorer*). Newsreaders need to connect to a news server that holds a copy of the latest newsgroups and postings. Today, news servers are typically operated by *ISPs* such as Demon Internet in the UK. Alternatively, sites such as **www.deja.com** provide access to Usenet news directly via the web and provide extended search capabilities.

News server (technical term)

Software that manages a local copy of a set of *Usenet* newsgroups. News servers exchange news items with other servers using the Network News Transfer Protocol (*NNTP*). ISPs often operate news servers for access by their subscribers. In general, news server operators claim no responsibility for the contents of the newsgroups they carry. However, in a landmark UK legal case (Godfrey v. Demon Internet Ltd), Demon Internet was held responsible for the content of a posting to the `soc.culture.thai` newsgroup, even though this was a copy of information replicated throughout the Usenet.

Nielson, Jakob

A guru of web design and web site usability, and author of *Designing Web Usability*, who has a strong focus on simplicity.

Nielsen//Netratings (company)

Nielsen Media Research is a well-established company known for rankings of television programs. Nielsen//Netratings is a partnership with Netratings which publishes much-used metrics on website popularity. Sites often in the top ten include the major general *portals*, such as *AOL*, *Yahoo!*, MSN (see *Microsoft*), *Lycos* and *Excite. eBay* and *Amazon* are also usually there.

NNTP (technical term)

Stands for Network News Transfer Protocol, used to transport *Usenet*-style *news* messages over *TCP/IP* and a replacement for the original UUCP (Unix-to-Unix Copy Program) protocol used on the first versions of the Usenet news system.

Node (technical term)

Common way of referring to a point on a network where a device (such as a computer system) is found.

Nokia (company)

A global leader in mobile telecommunications, and owner of one of the most powerful brands to emerge from the telcomms space. That said, Nokia was actually founded in Finland in 1865, and started life as a paper company, later branching into chemicals and rubber, then electronics, before specializing in telecommunications in the early 1990s. Nokia's recent success has been in handsets for mobile telephony where an early focus on the *GSM* market paid off. It now manufactures one-third of the cell phones sold globally.

Nokia is currently repositioning itself as a mobile internet player, having developed the first web surfing mobile phone (the Nokia Communicator) in 1996 and is one of the main supporters of the Wireless Application Protocol (*WAP*).

Non-repudiation (security term)

Really means not being able to say you didn't send something you did. Enforced via use of secure *digital signatures*.

Not-com (slang)

Describes a traditional company – a play on *dot com*.

NSA (organization)

Stands for National Security Agency – a US government agency. Sets the agenda for what can be used in the US in terms of electronic encryption. For example, when the popular *DES* algorithm was introduced, NSA requested modifications, which were widely supposed to be to weaken the algorithm – in fact they were strengthening DES against a form of analysis that had not been discovered outside NSA.

NSF (organization)

Stands for the US National Science Foundation which was involved in the early development of the internet and at one time provided the internet's major backbone network (*NSFnet*). See also *ARPANET.*

NSFnet (technical term)

Until 1995, the major backbone network of the internet, an area now dominated by commercial organizations.

Nym (slang)

Stands for pseudonym. A nym is a name invented to hide a user's real identity, or construct a new one specifically for the internet. Allows someone to protect their privacy in a *Usenet* or web-based forum, take part in activities such as auctions anonymously, and so on.

Object (technical term)

Use of objects refers to a way of designing and writing software systems. An object consists of data and functions (sometimes called methods) that act on that data. Each time a program wants to handle data for, say, another customer, it dynamically creates another object in memory that encapsulates the data and primitive functions needed to represent that customer.

This approach contrasts from previous programming approaches which tended to end up with monolithic programs with less fine structure. A program written in an object-oriented way essentially consists of multiple self-contained objects that send and receive data to and from each other. This, of course, suits distributed systems in general, and the internet in particular. Many tools, including the *Java* language, are specifically designed to support object-oriented approaches.

The use of objects can have its downside. Object systems can have performance problems, and a serious application can involve many thousands of different types (or classes) of object. You may therefore come across the phrase "component development," which is a technique for grouping together objects into more manageable collections.

Object orientation (technical term)

Refers to using objects in designing and developing programs – a powerful technique suited to distributed environments such as the internet. See *object* for more explanation. Often abbreviated to just OO.

Off-line (technical term)

The opposite of online. Working on a PC or other device without a connection to the internet or other network.

Online (technical term)

A general computing term that covers systems with an interactive component that users can access with a PC or workstation. In the context of e-commerce, the term has a specific focus on *web*-based systems. So you will come across expressions such as online auctions, online share-trading, and so on.

Online Services Provider (business term)

A term that describes a company like *AOL* which offers users more than just internet access, including, for a subscription, additional content and services. A standard *ISP* (Internet Service Provider), on the other hand, offers plain access to the internet, although the distinction between an ISP, or Online Service Provider and many types of *portal* is not often that clear.

On the fly (slang)

Expression meaning in real time. A general technical term but commonly used when a web page is constructed automatically from underlying data at the moment it is requested by a user. Allows a site to include dynamic data, such as changing items in a product catalog, or share prices.

OO (technical term)

See *object orientation.*

Open (technical term)

Two main meanings. The first is trivial and covers the act of opening a file or similar resource for use. It has a more profound meaning when describing a computer component design or software specification that is in the public domain, allowing developers to utilize it freely. See also *open source* and *open system.*

Open source (technical term)

Denotes a major movement that sees software as something to be shared freely allowing users to modify and distribute it. Open source is software *source code* that is made freely available to all. The internet provides the perfect vehicle for distribution of open source and collaborative development between interested parties. It is culturally rooted in the *UNIX* world where source code was for many years given to non-commercial UNIX users for free.

At its best, an open source approach creates very good software, since software is developed, tested, and documented by a community of motivated individuals. *Linux* – a derivative of UNIX – is the most obvious example of this, where the work of a young student (*Linus Torvalds*) has become a major operating system and a global "brand." As a result, open source ideas are bubbling into the commercial world. For example, *Netscape* released the code for its *browser* into the open source world in 1998, and major corporates like Sun are experimenting with the approach. Companies like Red Hat, Caldera and VA Linux Systems have made real businesses out of serving the Linux community. Other examples include *BIND*, *Perl*, and *Apache*.

Open source software is generally supplied with a license (like the GNU *General Public License*) which may allow a distributor to make money, but enforces the rights of others to free copies of the same code.

Major figures in the open source movement include the famous Richard Stallman – the driving force behind the *Free Software Foundation* – and Eric Raymond. Raymond's book *The Cathedral and the Bazaar* is a good industry text, which uses his own experience of open source development of a mail system.

Open system (technical term)

A system built on public domain standards (which are controlled consortium-style through standard bodies, or evolve as de facto standards through popular use). A big theme of the 1980s and 1990s, the open system movement encompassed fundamental platform technologies such as *UNIX* or *TCP/IP*.

Openware (company)

Recent new name for *phone.com*.

Operating system (technical term)

Core software that drives the basic operation of a computer. Key features of an operating system usually include the following:

- Some kind of kernel that works invisibly to users and:
    - handles the running and scheduling of programs
    - handles the use of system memory
    - handles peripheral devices such as terminals, printers and scanners
    - provides fundamental facilities – called by application programs – to manipulate files, handle communications between programs, support networking to other computers, allocate and de-allocate memory segments, and so on.
- Fundamental facilities or commands to handle basic operations such as system start-up and shut-down, or moving and copying files between folders or directories.
- User interfaces, which may be text-oriented (where the user types a command in response to a prompt) or a *GUI* (Graphical User Interface) where the user drives the system using a mouse.
- Libraries or frameworks that package up operating system facilities for use within programs by application developers.

General purpose operating systems have a tendency to get bigger and add features over time (**Windows** has shown exactly this sort of evolution). Modern operating systems also support highly distributed environments (such as the internet, of course), where applications run across multiple machines.

Examples of operating systems include Windows-NT, Windows 2000 and Windows-CE (a small version of Windows for handheld PCs), *UNIX* and derivatives of UNIX like *Solaris* or *Linux*, *Mac OS* from Apple and MVS on *IBM* mainframes.

Optical (technical term)

An adjective used to describe the use of light rather than electronics in IT systems. Examples of current optical technology include optical storage (e.g. CD-ROMS) and optical fiber for high-speed networking. Optical storage tends to have much higher capacity than traditional magnetic tapes. Similarly, optical networks have much higher data rates than wire-based cabling. In the future, processing may also be performed using optical computers rather than semiconductors, which may prove to be faster and smaller than today's machines, although this is still mostly in the research stage. Some observers think that optical technology will be very big in business terms and there are many startups in the US and Europe with a focus on optics, particularly in the area of networking.

Opt-in e-mail (business term)
See *permission marketing.*

Oracle (company)
Led by the charismatic *Larry Ellison*, Oracle is a major supplier of software products and services based around database technology, with a turnover of over $10 billion in 2000.

The Oracle story begins in 1977 when Larry Ellison and others founded Software Development Laboratories in Santa Clara. The aim of their first project – called Oracle – was to build a "relational" *database management system.* Previous generations of database management system used indexed file schemes, hierarchical models of data, or more complex network models. These were often complicated to set up and use, and tended to hard-code links between data items. The relational model represents data logically as flat tables of information where relationships between tables can be treated more dynamically, allowing simpler ad hoc queries. The relational model is now more or less ubiquitous in serious database systems. Oracle was one of the first companies to commercialize the concept (other well-known relational database management systems include IBM's DB2, *Informix*, Sybase and Microsoft's SQL*Server).

In 1978 Software Development Laboratories changed its name to Relational Software Inc. (the name change to Oracle came in 1982) and moved to Menlo Park in Silicon Valley. Its first commercial system was shipped a year later. A distinctive feature of the Oracle database system, even in its early days, was its portability across PCs and open, *UNIX*-based systems. During the 1980s and 1990s, Oracle became the leading supplier of database systems outside the *mainframe* world, took its database system through several major updates with the increasing influence of distributed systems, built a strong global network, and surrounded its core products with application software and development tools.

At the time of writing, Oracle is one of the world's largest and most dominant software suppliers. Its product range includes:

➡ Various forms of its core database engine from lightweight configurations to enterprise-level systems; you will find this underpinning many well-known e-commerce websites.

➡ A family of development tools for developing internet solutions, portals, and more traditional applications.

➡ Internet application server products that allow the construction and operation of websites

➡ Integration products – essentially *middleware* – that allows connection with legacy and other types of system.

➡ A broad range of applications under the general heading of e-Business Suite that includes products that cover sales and marketing, procurement, manufacturing, financial management, human resources, and more. One of Oracle's recent marketing campaigns is based on its own internal cost-cutting initiative centered on the use of these tools.

Orphan brand (business term)
A *brand* that has fallen into disuse due to a lack of investment, changing customer tastes, or failure of the business that originally launched it.

OS (technical term)
Common abbreviation for *operating system.*

OSI (technical term)
Stands for Open Systems Interconnection. OSI was an *ISO* initiative in the mid-1980s to develop a set of standards for interconnecting computer systems. OSI was conceived when computer networking was dominated by proprietary systems such as IBM's System Network Architecture (SNA) and when use of the internet (and *TCP/IP*) was confined to academic and experimental networks.

The most enduring output from the OSI work is the seven-reference-layer model, which represents a way of thinking about network protocols as discrete layers. The OSI work developed (or adopted) standards for protocols at each of the seven layers, including File Transfer and Management (FTAM) for file transfer, a variety of lower-level "transport classes" for operation over public wide area networks, and a Connectionless Network Service for use on *LANs*. These OSI protocols are rarely seen today and the internet protocol suite (TCP/IP) has emerged as the globally accepted open standard for networking.

A complete description of all seven layers is beyond the scope of this book. However, a simple description and comparison to TCP/IP is given in the table below:

Layer	Name	Key functions	TCP/IP equivalent	OSI
1	Physical	Characteristics of the physical media, e.g. shape of the connectors, voltages used, etc.	Ethernet, ADSL	X.25, Ethernet
2	Data Link	Low-level representation of data moving over the network	PPP, Ethernet	X.25, Ethernet
3	Network	Hides the differences in networks that data may traverse and allows data to be routed via different networks to reach the same destination	IP	X.25, CLNS
4	Transport	The end–end layer, which establishes a "virtual connection" between two machines wishing to communicate	TCP	TC0-4
5	Session	Manages the order in which information is exchanged between communicating systems	N/A	ISO8327/X.225
6	Presentation	Manages the presentation of information between different types of computer	N/A	ASN1
7	Application	Protocol specific to certain applications (e.g. file transfer)	FTP, Telnet, SMTP	FTAM, VTP

OSP (business term)

See *Online Service Provider*.

Out of the garage (slang)

Slang description of a startup that's moved into its first genuine office – which reflects the fact many startups are formed in residential areas (rather than real garages).

P2P (technical term, business term)

As a technical term stands for **peer-to-peer** which is described below. Also used to stand for "path to profit" – which came into vogue after the 2000 collapse of dot-com shares, and indicated a much increased focus on underlying business performance and early profits from startups.

Packet (technical term)

In **packet-switched** networks, data messages are split into small chunks of data to which header information is added (such as the destination address). The resulting packets are then transmitted independently to the destination. Packets are also sometimes called **datagrams**.

Packet switching (technical term)

A way of transmitting data across a network, where messages are divided into small **packets** which are sent independently to their destination for reassembly, possibly along different routes through the network. Packet switching is a concept dating to the early 1960s and was introduced to make computer networks efficient, and resilient. The internet and its underlying **TCP/IP** protocols are based on packet switching.

Page (web term)
Short for **web page**, a web document usually made up of **HTML** (the core language of the web which mixes text and formatting instructions) and associated links and graphical objects.

Page impressions (web term)
Same as **page views**.

Page requests (web term)
Same as **page views**.

Page views (web term)
The number of times a web page is requested. A more precise measure of **site traffic** than **hits**, which cover calls to the individual graphical elements on a page. See also **measurement**.

PalmOS (technical term)
Operating system used on the popular **Palm Pilot** and available under license for other mobile devices.

Palm Pilot (product)
Very popular **PDA** (Personal Digital Assistant) developed by 3Com, and the first platform using the **PalmOS** operating system. Although not the first to do so, Palm popularized the idea of occasionally synchronizing information between a PDA and a PC through a simple docking station (or cradle). The Palm range has occasionally flirted with wireless connections but these are not yet widespread. The PalmOS is now available under license to other PDA developers.

Palo Alto
Center of the Silicon Valley area, in between San Francisco and San Jose, Palo Alto is a small city that has been at the heart of computer technology development for many years (the famous **Hewlett Packard** garage is located in this area). Close to Stanford University, Palo Alto is the home base of many technology startups and the home of the famous **Xerox Parc**.

Password (security term)
A string of characters entered when logging into a computer system, which

of course includes many types of website. Passwords will not be shown as they are being typed and for security should really consist of a random series of letters and numbers. When users first register on a website, they normally need to give a mnemonic user name (sometimes their e-mail name will do) and a password. Since there is no standard infrastructure for this, the internet is a graveyard of forgotten passwords.

Patent (business term)

Provides legal protection for a design or concept, allowing the holder of the patent to exploit it commercially. Since intellectual property is a hot topic in e-commerce, patents are often sought for software algorithms or even business processes. For example, *Amazon* somewhat controversially patented their one-click ordering system.

Payment Service Provider (business term)

An organization that simplifies the processing of credit card payments for e-commerce sites. Examples include Netbanx and Worldpay.

PC (technical term)

Stands for personal computer, and typically covers a single-person computer system which can work standalone or as part of a network. There were many early efforts in the 1970s and 1980s in this area, including developments at Xerox Parc, and kits such as the Altair and the Apple II computer. The dominant de facto standard was, however, created by the arrival of the *IBM PC* in 1981. The IBM PC architecture is sometimes referred to as "Wintel", because such machines usually run a version of the Microsoft *Windows* operating system, and usually contain an Intel microprocessor or clone as the *CPU*.

This is the type of system found in most home and office environments. Apple's distinctively different *Macintosh* range remains popular in some environments. The future of the PC undergoes periodic debate, now that networking is a dominant use of many PCs, supported by browser-based *thin-client* software architectures. There are also issues of convergence, as television, PDAs, and mobile phones are straying into the space occupied to date by the PC.

It is worth noting that the term "workstation" has often been used for more powerful single-person computers, running more complex software applications and with different hardware architectures. As PCs have grown in capacity, the distinction has become much less clear.

PDA (technical term)

Stands for Personal Digital Assistant, and covers lightweight, handheld computers which provide functions for personal organization, pen-based input, and communication with bigger PC systems (which allows e-mail to be handled, for example). Manufacturers include Palm, Psion, Compaq, Handspring, Vtech, and others. Unlike the PC world, there is less standardization of operating systems, and options include PalmOS and Windows-CE. The most recent devices (at the time of writing) are beginning to offer true *mobile internet access*, through wireless connections.

PDF (technical term)

Stands for *Adobe's* Portable Document Format. A format that allows documents suitable for high-quality printing to be electronically distributed.

Peering (internet term)

A relationship between two or more Internet Service Providers (*ISPs*) to route traffic between computers attached to their networks directly rather than via the internet backbone(s). In the UK, many ISPs interconnect via the London Internet Exchange (*LINX*).

The following output from the network utility *tracert* in the example below illustrates the route traffic takes between two UK ISPs – Demon Internet (**www.demon.net**) and RedNet (**www.red.net**):

```
Tracing route to www.rednet.com [195.74.130.4]
over a maximum of 30 hops:

1   157 ms   154 ms   152 ms   anchor-du-15.access.demon.net [195.173.57.15]
2   174 ms   165 ms   156 ms   anchor-core-1-fxp3.router.demon.net [195.173.57.251]
3   149 ms   153 ms   154 ms   tele-backbone-1-ge022.router.demon.net [158.152.0.181]
4   153 ms   153 ms   153 ms   tele-border-12-168.router.demon.net [194.159.36.212]
5   217 ms   203 ms   211 ms   linx-gw1.th.red.net [195.66.224.73]
6   172 ms   173 ms   175 ms   www.rednet.com [195.74.130.4]

Trace complete.
```

This shows that on hops 4 and 5, data goes directly from Demon to RedNet through a peering arrangement.

Peer-to-peer (technical term, business term)

Peer-to-peer (or P2P) is a model for distributed computing where workstations collaborate directly rather than accessing dedicated servers. In the past, the term has generally been applied to relatively small Local Area Networks (*LANs*). More recently the term has been applied to web applications (such as *Napster*) that allow a workstation to act as both a client (to initiate search requests) and a server (to respond to requests and transmit files). This allows communities to share files without any central co-ordination. The difficulty with P2P sharing is that, in general, the people doing the sharing may not be the owners of the copyrighted material being shared.

Perl (technical term)

Perl is a popular script programming language supported on a number of operating systems, and commonly used to develop simple interactive web applications in conjunction with the Common Gateway Interface (*CGI*). This allows programs to generate HTML content *on the fly*. Originally created by Larry Wall, Perl is a derivation from the popular *C* programming language and also incorporates features from some *UNIX* tools. It has a large (and passionate) user base.

Permission marketing (business term)

Permission marketing happens when a potential customer agrees to receive marketing information, such as e-mail that announces offers and new products (which also leads to the term "opt-in e-mail"). Many *B2C* websites have a check-box to gain permission for such e-mails during user registration. Avoids the emotional heat that goes with less targetted and frowned-upon *spamming*.

Personal computer (technical term)
See *PC* and *IBM PC*.

Personal Digital Assistant (technical term)
See *PDA*.

Personalize (business term)
To modify a website or similar service to the needs of a particular user (usually done by the users themselves using facilities provided by the website).

PGP (technical term)
Stands for Pretty Good Privacy. PGP is a utility to allow information to be encrypted and decrypted for secure transmission over the internet. PGP uses a combination of two encryption algorithms (called RSA and IDEA) to provide simple key distribution (via public keys) but also high performance when encrypting large files.

Phone.com (company)
Phone.com (recently renamed Openware) supplies UP.Browser, a "microbrowser" that can be embedded in a mobile device to support mobile internet access. UP.Browser is used in phones from many of the key mobile phone companies, with the notable current exceptions of Nokia and Ericsson.

PHP (technical term)
Stands for Personal Home Page and is similar to Microsoft's *active server pages* (ASP) and *Java Server Pages* (JSP). PHP allows the "dynamic" generation of HTML pages on a web server, allowing content to be based on the real-time output of a program. PHP is *open source* and is very popular in the *Linux* community.

Ping (technical term)
Ping is a common tool for checking basic connectivity between systems over the internet. Ping sends a series of "echo request" messages to the target machine. An example is shown below. It tells us that we can establish basic connectivity with a web server and that the average round trip time for a message is 326 milliseconds.

```
c:\> ping www.oracle.com
Pinging bigip-www.us.oracle.com [205.227.44.44] with 32 bytes
of data:
Reply from 205.227.44.44: bytes=32 time=310ms TTL=242
Reply from 205.227.44.44: bytes=32 time=308ms TTL=242
```

```
Reply from 205.227.44.44: bytes=32 time=344ms TTL=242
Reply from 205.227.44.44: bytes=32 time=342ms TTL=242
Ping statistics for 205.227.44.44:
    Packets: Sent = 4, Received = 4, Lost = 0 (0 percent loss),
Approximate round trip times in milli-seconds:
    Minimum = 308ms, Maximum = 344ms, Average = 326ms
```

PKI (security term)
See *Public Key Infrastructure*.

Platform (technical term)
A fairly imprecise term used to denote a fundamental piece of technology infrastructure. Can be used to refer to base hardware (PCs, workstations and servers), operating system software (Windows, UNIX, Linux), or other types of technical software such as database management systems and middleware.

Play (business term)
Used to refer to an e-commerce business or business concept, as in phrases like "another B2C play in travel is unlikely to succeed." The term "pure play" usually refers to a business or business concept that is wholly based on internet or similar technologies.

Plug-ins (web term)
A plug-in is a third-party piece of software that extends the capabilities of a *browser* to view information in a proprietary (e.g. non-*HTML)* format. Plug-ins were originally introduced by Netscape but are now supported by the majority of browsers (although Microsoft Internet Explorer refers to them as "multimedia components"). Among the more common plug-ins at the time of writing are:

➡ Macromedia Shockwave and Flash – supporting animation and interactivity

➡ Apple QuickTime video player

➡ RealPlayer for playing streamed audio and video

➡ Adobe Acrobat to view Portable Document Format (PDF) documents.

Plug-ins can either be dynamically downloaded over the web or (in the case of the more popular ones) may come pre-installed with the browser when you buy a PC. Plug-ins can introduce security vulnerabilities to a browser and should be treated with some caution.

POP (technical term)

Stands for Post Office Protocol, a popular protocol used to allow e-mail to be downloaded from mail boxes on servers to PCs. Also stands for Point of Presence, a networking term from the earlier days of the internet.

Pop.com (company)

Backed by Microsoft co-founder Paul Allen and film-maker Steven Spielberg, pop.com intended to produce and distribute movies straight to the net and fundamentally alter the Hollywood studio system. At the time of writing, the lack of widespread broadband infrastructure has lead to pop's plans being scaled back.

Portability (technical term)

The ability to run a program on different technical platforms (especially different hardware). The *C* language is a very portable language. *Java* aspires to go further, as shown by Sun's slogan of "Write once, run anywhere." *Java applets* should therefore run within any compatible browser on a variety of PCs, or other types of workstation.

Portable Document Format (technical term)

See *PDF*.

Portal (web term)

A website that provides access to content and other sites through same sort of hierarchical navigation structure. Big general-purpose portals include *AOL, Yahoo!*, msn, excite and Lycos. UK equivalents include local versions of AOL, Yahoo! with the suffix .co.uk, and UK-specific organizations like Freeserve or LineOne. For many users, these sites are primary ports of call for navigating the world wide web. Portal-like services tend to evolve naturally from online service providers like AOL, or search-engine software.

As competition is intense, portals tend to offer additional services such as news feeds, free e-mail, instant messaging, community services, and the like.

The main income streams for portals are advertising (a tough way of making money) and in the case of some services, such as AOL's, a subscription fee.

More specialized types of portal are seen as important in the future, leading to the concept of *vortal*, a vertical portal that focusses on a specific, vertical business community. Other focussed portals serve specific communities and interest groups, such as women, older or younger people, people living in or visiting a specific town or area, and so on.

Post (e-mail term)

To submit a message or article into a *newsgroup* or similar conversation mechanism.

Postel, Jon

Pioneer and one of the architects of the internet, the late Jon Postel was a founding member of the Internet Architecture Board, editor of many of the original internet standards, and had a significant influence on the way that internet domains and addresses were allocated. This latter responsibility was achieved through leading *IANA*, the original control point for internet domain names and IP addresses. This control role has passed to *ICANN*.

POTS (technical term)

Stands for Plain Old Telephone System. Used to contrast the traditional voice-orientated *PSTN* (Public Switched Telephone Network) with the newer digital services such as *ISDN* and *ADSL*.

Powered by … (business term)

A reference on some websites to an infrastructure service used to build the website, e.g. "This site powered by Acme web server software."

PPP (internet term)

Stands for Point-to-Point Protocol. PPP is the most common low-level protocol used to transfer *IP* (Internet Protocol) packets over a serial connection, such as a *modem* or *ISDN* connection, between a PC and an *ISP* (Internet Service Provider) connected by the phone network.

PPP encapsulates the IP packets being generated by applications (e.g. a *browser*) running on a PC and transfers them to the ISP where they are routed on to the main internet, and vice versa for traffic destined for a PC. PPP is defined in *RFC* 1661.

Prime real estate (web term)

For a serious website, every square inch of the starting home page is considered prime real estate, and decisions as to what should appear there – when, where, and in what format – are important parts of the overall site design.

Privacy policy (business term)

A statement on the collection, storage, and use of personal data – whether based on legislation (e.g. Europe) or self-regulation (e.g. USA). Usually listed online in serious websites.

Private IP addresses (technical term)

Every device that is directly connected to the internet needs to have a unique *IP address*. However, there are networks that use internet protocols such as *TCP/IP*, which are either completely independent of or only partially connected to the internet. There is no need for these networks to have globally unique IP addresses (although the addresses must be unique within the private network). Three blocks of IP addresses have been reserved for such private networks.

➡ 10.0.0.0 – 10.255.255.255

➡ 172.16.0.0 – 172.31.255.255

➡ 192.168.0.0 – 192.168.255.255

These address ranges can be used without having to apply for permission to a co-ordinating body, and also allow reuse of valuable IP addresses in different private networks.

Organizations may choose to use a private address space simply because it provides access to a larger range of addresses which makes network design and administration easier. However, there can be no direct connectivity to any host outside the private network without a mechanism to translate the internal private address to a globally unique address. Increased demand for internet connectivity from within previously standalone private networks can lead to complexity that outweighs the simplicity of using a private scheme. The pros and cons of private addressing are described more fully in *RFC* 1918.

Private key, private key encryption (security term)

Covers a class of encryption algorithms that depend on a single private key – a long number – which therefore needs to be known by the sender and recipient of e-mails or other messages. This needs a secure way of sending private keys, and this can be done with a more complex *public key* algorithm. Private keys are at the heart of the popular *SSL* standard which enables secure use of e-commerce websites.

Property (business term)

A specific URL or website. Many types of organization will now own several such "properties."

Protocol (technical term)

It is impossible to talk about computer networking (or internetworking) without hearing about "protocols." Put simply, a computer network trans-

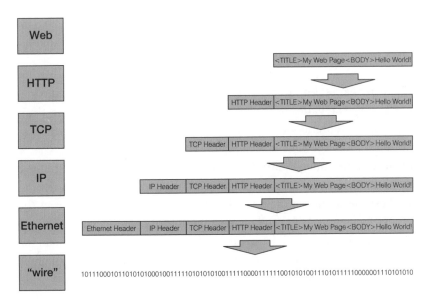

A "stack" of protocols

mits a series of 1s and 0s over a wire or fiber optic or radio connection. A protocol provides a common set of rules for what different parts of the stream of 1s and 0s mean and how devices should sequence a conversation, allowing devices from different vendors to work together.

Modern protocols are "layered," with the application data wrapped by a series of different protocols, each concerned with providing a different service. The illustration on page 254 shows the "stack" of protocols involved when transferring a web page over a Local Area Network (*LAN*).

The International Standards Organization (*ISO*) has defined a seven-layer model for describing network protocols (see *OSI*).

Proxy (technical term)

A piece of software that acts as an intermediary for users accessing internet-based services. For example, in the case of the world wide web, a *browser* connects to a web proxy which then connects to the required *webserver*, retrieves the information requested, and then resends this back to the browser.

Proxies are used for a number of reasons including:

➡ allowing access to the web to be monitored and controlled

➡ allowing popular pages to be "cached" on the proxy to reduce the load on the web.

PTA (slang)

Stands for personal technology assistant. This is a new fashion accessory to emerge from Silicon Valley – a personal technology assistant to the CEO. With engineer–entrepreneurs returning to their IT-based roots as chief technology officers, finance and marketing-biassed CEOs are again in vogue. Unfortunately, their understanding of technology may result in poor strategic and tactical decisions. Given technology's role at the heart of any modern e-business, these decisions could prove disastrous. Enter the PTA, who turns the operationally focussed CTO's thinking into the sort of commercial logic that a CEO needs to understand and act upon. Look for this position to become the norm over the next few years as blue chips increasingly come to recognize the impact of poor technology directives from their executive team.

Public key, public key encryption (security term)

Covers a class of *encryption* algorithms by which a message may be encrypted (coded) using one "key" – basically a long number – and decrypted using a different, but related, key. Only the combination of the two keys works. The message cannot be encrypted and then decrypted with just one of the keys. One key is kept secret (or private) and the other can be distributed freely (the public key). This has many benefits including:

➡ Allows a secure channel between two parties to be established, without having to have previously exchanged a key.

➡ Messages which can be decrypted using the public key must have been encrypted with the private key, and can be assumed to have originated from the personal owner of that key.

Public key infrastructure (PKI) (security term)

Public key cyptography is a useful tool when implementing security on the internet. However, it does bring some new complications:

➡ How are new public and private key combinations generated?

➡ How is the public key made available to the public?

➡ How is the format of the key agreed upon?

➡ How can we trust that the public key is the real public key?

➡ How can compromised keys be revoked?

A public key infrastructure aims to address these problems by defining important standards and roles within a community wishing to exchange public keys. Components of such an infrastructure will include the underlying security software and algorithms, and a nominated certification authority (like Versign) who is trusted to hold the public key information.

Pure play (business term)

A business or business concept that uses internet or similar technologies as its primary *channel* to consumers. *Amazon* is an example of a pure play. Barnes & Noble – which sell books via the internet and in its original shops – is not therefore a pure play.

Push (internet term)

Most internet applications use an approach where users request (or pull) information from servers. By contrast, some applications explicitly push information to specific internet-connected devices. Supporting push *protocols* is much more technically complex than pull, since it requires applications to be capable of handling new information that can arrive aynchronously at any time (rather than synchronously in response to a request). It can also result in significant network *load* (at least until technologies such as *multicast* are more widespread). To date, true "push" applications have tended only to be used for applications such as real-time financial markets information, although the term has also been used loosely to cover applications that appear to use push but in fact work by continuously requesting the latest information from a server (called polling).

The Java Messaging Service (JMS) is an emerging standard for the application programming interface (*API*) used to push services.

Quality of service (QoS) (technical term)

A general technical term that covers the time between request and delivery of a service to the end-customer. Applied to a network, it covers the guaranteed throughput or data transfer rate. This is an issue for real-time streaming of voice or video, since quality of service can be impacted by network congestion. One of the major goals of the Internet2 consortium is a focus on quality of service.

Quantum computing (very technical term)

We include this because quantum computing has attracted a degree of interest outside the science fiction and academic worlds, where it really belongs (at least for the time being). In theory the very strange behavior of the matter at subatomic scales offers interesting opportunities for computation and telecommunications. A theoretical quantum computer is made up of quantum bits, or *qubits* which can exist simultaneously as 0 and 1 (this is a principle from quantum mechanics called superposition). The power of a quantum computer would come from its ability to be in multiple states at once and to act on all these possible states simultaneously. Another prediction of quantum mechanics is "entanglement" where qubits that are separated by incredible distances can interact with each other instantaneously (a behavior so strange that Einstein referred to it as "spooky action at a distance"). Even though it remains highly theoretical, quantum computing has attracted a lot of speculation especially in its application to cryptography where it may be able to crack existing algorithms very simply but may also offer completely new ways of securing information, but don't hold your breath.

Query (technical term)

A command to a program to search for data. It is sometimes used to describe a search with a search engine, or a more technical query to a *database management system.*

Quicktime (product)

Macintosh/Apple software developed for multimedia content such as video, graphics, music, and other formats. Quicktime is embedded in the Macintosh generating system, and can be played on most PCs with the right software. It is often used with browsers with appropriate plug-in components. Quicktime has now been incorporated into the MPEG-4 specification as a standard format for transferring this type of content.

RAD (technical term)

Stands for Rapid Application Development. RAD is actually a specific collection of techniques introduced by James Martin which support a fast, user-centered design and software development process. It is often used imprecisely, however, for any attempt to build software quickly – and sometimes as a cover for unstructured development. Development speed has been an important driver for many types of e-commerce business that wants to provide a service before its competitors. RAD techniques are therefore often discussed and tried. The downside can be delayed launches (since development timescales were too compressed), or issues related to performance, scalability, and resilience were missed.

RAID (technical term)

Stands for Redundant Array of Independent Disks. The "I" used to stand for "inexpensive". It is a set of disks where data is mirrored across several different disks. This means multiple copies are made of any updates. This allows the system to cope with disk failures and also supports recovery processes if things go badly wrong. Behind any serious e-commerce solution, you will typically find data held on RAID technology.

Raster graphics (technical term)

Raster graphics are digital images captured as a series of pixels (essentially dots). Bitmaps, *GIF* and *JPEG* files are all forms of raster graphics. Compare with *vector graphics*.

Raymond, Eric S.

A commentator on hacker culture and the *open source* movement. Author of *The Cathedral and the Bazaar*, a major text on open source.

RC4, RC5, RC6 (security term)

Stand for Rivest Cipher #4, #5 and #6 respectively (named after their inventor Ron Rivest of *RSA algorithm* fame). These are *encryption* algorithms sometimes used on the web to make data secure.

RDF (technical term)

Stands for Resource Description Framework. RDF is an emerging W3C (World Wide Web Consortium) standard technically to describe a website and its content, in a more general manner than is possible with *meta-tags*. RDF will be a step towards what *Tim Berners-Lee* has described as "the semantic web," where relevant information is more easy to locate both for humans and their software agents (e.g. search engines). RDF is defined using eXtensible Mark-up Language (*XML*).

Readme (technical term)

A text file (usually plain *ASCII* text rather than a formatted document) that comes with many software distributions and software products. A Readme file will often contain notes on last-minute changes, or *bugs* that were detected late in the development and shipping process.

Real time (technical term)

Describes actions undertaken by a computer system as an immediate response to an event or imput. Can be used to describe safety-critical systems (like aircraft flight control software) or much more trivial computer interactions, such as real-time chat. Similar in meaning to *on the fly*.

Red Herring (magazine)

Popular and now international publication that focusses on e-commerce start-ups, venture capital and hot technologies.

Redundant navigation (web term)

This means allowing users to access parts of a site through several alternatives – text, icons, buttons, etc. Usually designed intentionally to allow long-standing users access via a familiar pathway, while also enticing new users through larger, more visually attractive, routes. (For example, *Yahoo!* e-mail can be accessed in three different ways from the top third of the Yahoo! home page.)

Registration (internet term, business term)

Registration has two general but very different meanings in the e-commerce world. It can cover either registration of a new *domain name*, or user registration on a site where a new user enters basic details about themselves.

Domain name registration

Organizations or individuals get rights over domain names (e.g. **www. amazon.com**) by registering them with an approved organization (sometimes called a registrar). So, a name based on one of the global top-level domains (the most famous being *.com*) may be registered with a relevant organization that is authorized by *ICANN* (Internet Corporation for Assigned Names and Numbers). A name related to a country top-level domains – such as .uk – can be registered with organizations authorized by the respective government. For example, Nominet (**www.nominet.net**) is responsible for the .uk domain.

The fees, length of ownership and conditions for being granted a name vary between registrars. Selected parts of the information provided during the registration process are made available in the registrar's *whois* database. The domain name "land grab" mentality has led to many organizations providing services to simplify the name registration process (e.g. **www. register.com**).

User registration

Most commercial sites need to know more about a user than their *IP address*, and therefore ask users to subscribe or register before allowing them to submit transactions (e.g. buy things from an online catalog). The registration process normally requires a new user to specify a user-id (sometimes an e-mail address will do) and password, and then provide additional details about themselves (e.g. real name, postal address, credit card details). The user-id is used to identify the user to the site when they return. Some infrastructure-style services allow the registration process to be done once and then shared across sites. However, the lack of any standards in this area have stifled acceptance of this type of approach and repeatedly guessing unique user-ids and typing in your postal address have become some of the more tedious aspects of *B2C* e-commerce.

Resilience (technical term)

Often used to describe how robust a computer system is. A highly resilient system is usually designed to recover automatically from some types of hardware or software failure. This is an important topic for serious e-commerce systems where users expect high levels of service and *24 x 7* availability. One common technique is to build redundancy into a system architecture – through multiple servers and disk mirroring, where data is duplicated across multiple disks.

Reverse auction (business term)

An auction of any type (including online auctions) where a buyer sets the target price which the sellers try to meet. Common in the *B2B* world. See also *auction* and *agora*.

RFC (internet term)

Stands for Request for Comments. RFC documents define the core internet protocols. For instance the Internet Protocol (*IP*) is defined by RFC 791. RFCs are issued by the Internet Engineering Taskforce (*IETF*) and are freely available on the internet (**www.ietf.org**). Although the surrounding processes can seem a little informal, they are very open and RFC documents are really the key determining standards documents for the internet.

RFCOMM (mobile term)

Part of the *Bluetooth* wireless system, this is a protocol designed to provide a wireless replacement for the venerable RS-232 serial interface standard used to connect PCs and peripherals such as modems and printers.

RIPE (organization)

Stands for Réseaux IP Européens (**www.ripe.net**). RIPE is responsible for the allocation of *IP address* ranges in the European region.

Roberts, Lenny

Led the creation of *ARPANET* from 1967.

Robot (web term)

See *crawler*.

Router (technical term)

Routers and their makers (principally *Cisco*) have achieved near-mythical status during the recent expansion of the internet. However, the basic job of a router is simply to interconnect two or more networks and to transfer *IP* (Internet Protocol) packets between machines attached to two of these networks without allowing traffic to "spill out" to the others. This apparently simple functionality allows an arbitrary number of networks to be internetworked (see *internetworking* for more details).

In the early days of the internet, routing was typically done by general-purpose computers running special routing software (in the very early days these had the bizarre name "fuzzball"). However, today a router is typically a dedicated network device from a vendor such as Cisco or 3Com.

Routers come in all shapes and sizes, from small devices connected to a *LAN* to very large and resilient machines for the internet *backbone* networks.

Routing (technical term)

The process of directing *IP* (Internet Protocol) packets to the appropriate network within an interconnected "network of networks" (e.g. the internet). This function is either carried out by a dedicated device (simply known as a *router*) or by a more general-purpose computer-running routing software. Routing is carried out based on the network component of an *IP address* and a set of *routing tables*.

Routing table (technical term)

Routing tables are the network roadmap to the internet. Held on routers, they contain the rules to tell every router how to move a data packet to the next stage on its journey, which will usually involve many routers. The complexity of these rules can vary dramatically, as follows:

➡ Routers on smaller networks simply need to know to forward all traffic to an *ISP* (Internet Service Provider).

➡ Routers within ISPs or nearer the internet *backbone* can need tens of thousands of routing rules; in fact the problem of routing table size in this situation was one of the motivations for the development of *CIDR* (Classless Inter-Domain Routing)

RSA-129 (security term)

Name given to a challenge issued by *Scientific American* magazine in 1977 to decrypt a message encrypted using the RSA (Rivest, Shamir and Adleman) algorithm. The *RSA algorithm* relies on the difficulty of finding the factors of a large number, in this case a 129-digit (425-bit) number, which proved to be strong enough until 1994 when the message was revealed to be "THE MAGIC WORDS ARE SQUEAMISH OSSIFRAGE." This feat was accomplished in eight months with the help of about 600 volunteers and 1,500 computers on the internet from more than 20 countries.

RSA algorithm (security term)

The most popular algorithm for *public key encryption* is based around a mathematically "hard" problem of factoring large numbers, and is named after its three inventors: Ron Rivest, Ali Shamir, and Leonard Adleman. Recently declassified information suggests a similar approach had been (secretly) developed at the UK's GCHQ by Ellis, Cocks, and Williamson prior to the more public development in the USA.

SAN (technical term)

Stands for storage array network. In its simplest form a SAN represents a collection of storage devices (typically disk drives) attached to a number of servers using a dedicated network. This arrangement provides greater flexibility in terms of sharing, expansion and management of storage than the more traditional approach of each server having its own dedicated disks.

Sandbox (security term, technical term)

The playfully named "sandbox" is a way of limiting what applications written in the *Java* language can do to the host system on which a program or *applet* runs. It offers protection when applets are downloaded over the internet. It places very strict limits on how an applet can manage files or other system features. The sandbox concept originated with the earliest versions of Java. As of Java 1.2 this changed, and privileges granted to Java applications can vary under user control.

Schneier, Bruce

Bruce Schneier is a highly influential computer security expert and is the author of *Applied Cryptography*, which introduced *encryption* to the general web community, and *Secrets and Lies: Digital Security in a Networked World*, which discusses cryptography in the context of other security considerations. He is also the creator of the Blowfish and TwoFish encryption algorithms and co-founder of Counterpane Internet Security (**www.counterpane.com**).

Scripting language, Script (technical term)

Scripting languages are (relatively) simple programming languages typically used to tie together smaller applications or operating system commands to perform a more complex task. Typical examples of scripting languages are *Perl*, UNIX Shellscript, and Microsoft Visual Basic script. Scripting languages are almost always interpreted, i.e. they are not compiled into native instructions for a particular computer but are analyzed and executed at runtime by a special program.

Scroll (technical term)

The act of moving down or across a page of information, usually by using a graphic "scroll-bar."

Search engines (web term)

Search engines index material on the web and allow users to find pages based on a set of keywords. The index is either built automatically using spiders (also known as robots or *crawlers*) or manually by content experts visiting sites and reviewing them (more accurately, the latter technique is used to build directories rather than search-engine indexes – however search engine as a term is often used generically).

A guide to how search engines work and the characteristics of individual search engines can be found at **www.searchenginewatch.com**.

Results

Given the size of the web, even a quite precise request can return many hundreds of matches. The exact mechanism used to rank results (which determines the order in which results are displayed) varies from engine to engine. In general it will be based on a combination of some of the following characteristics:

➡ The number of matches to search keywords the page has and where in the text these occur.

- The number of other sites to which the page links.
- Whether the keywords match the description in the title of the web page.
- Whether the keywords match the description in a *meta-tag*.
- Whether the site was selected from a previous search using similar keywords.
- Whether the site appears to be attempting to "fiddle" the rating by excessively repeating the same phrases. This can result in the entry being pushed further down the ranking.
- In the case of directories, whether the site has been reviewed.
- Whether the owner of the site has paid for a high ranking. This is the **goto.com** business model.

Meta-tags

Meta-tags are embedded descriptions within web pages that aren't displayed, but do contain useful information on the web page. Not all search engines use these, but some do. The following meta-tags are used by relevant search engines:

- `<META name="description" content="Visit this page / PLEASE!">`

  This is the description of the page that will be displayed by the search engine in its summary of results page.

- `<META name="keyword" content="armadillo,fajitas">`

  Some search engines will use a match between words in this tag and those entered by the user.

- `<META name="ROBOTS" content="NOINDEX">`

  By convention, this tag prevents the web page being indexed at all.

Checking your popularity

The only way to check how well your site ranks with the various search engines is to submit a query. There are services that will regularly check how well you rate, using a search based on certain keys. One example is **www.did-it.com**.

Examples

Popular search engines include:

- ➡ *google.com*, which presents a very simple interface, and is actually the technology that underpins Yahoo! search facilities.
- ➡ *Lycos*, *Excite*, which are popular search engines that have evolved into general *portals*.
- ➡ *Yahoo!*, which provides both a directory structure and search services. Again it has evolved into a general portal.
- ➡ deja.com, which includes functionality to search both the *web* and the *Usenet* news system, and has recently been acquired by google.

And many more …

Security (business term, technical term)

Electronic security is an extremely broad topic with much history, existing theory and folklore. The starting point for any coherent discussion of security is an understanding of "threat" from a security perspective and this short section focusses on some of the threats that are relevant to e-commerce applications, and some of the measures to deal with them.

Background

E-commerce and internet solutions have characteristics that are extremely important in a security context:

- ➡ **Scale:** the internet is a network several orders of magnitude larger than other kinds of network. The number of pages and interactions per day is in the billions. E-commerce volumes can be extremely large in monetary terms.
- ➡ **Openness:** the internet is, by intent, open. If you run a publically available site, then ultimately you have little knowledge of – or control over – its users. The internet, although technically varied, is largely based around well-understood standards and products. Some of these have well-understood security flaws.

➡ **Culture:** the web is based on a fusion of very different cultures. There are those who believe that software should be free, or see breaking into websites as a recreational activity.

Threats to the surfer

Fraud

The threat relating to suppliers reneging on deals or supplying defective or unwanted products is essentially the same in an e-commerce world as it is in the *bricks and mortar* world. However, the ability to judge the credibility of an organization online is greatly diminished, since the quality of the website is no guarantee of the quality of the organization behind it. This is a major reason why *brand* remains a key influence of consumer behavior on the web.

To counter this, a number of respected third-party organizations are now independently auditing sites to provide assurance that they operate to adequate levels of customer service. Examples include eTrust and Trust-UK.

Vandalism/denial of service/theft

Connecting a PC to the internet exposes it as a potential target for several forms of malicious attack (generally covered by the terms *hacking* or *cracking*). More specifically these types of attack can be classified as:

➡ Theft, where either materials are copied without the user's permission, or where a configuration is altered to act to the hacker's advantage, e.g. modify an automated transfer of money.

➡ Vandalism, where the motivation for the activity is simply to disrupt the normal operation of the PC; called more formally *denial of service.*

These forms of attack can be by:

➡ direct access (e.g. hackers logging in to your machine when you are connected to the internet, which is rare);

➡ malicious code hidden within an apparently benign application (a *Trojan horse*);

➡ malicious code which is copied from machine to machine by stealth (a *virus*).

Invasion of privacy

Surfing the internet is not an anonymous activity. Simplistically, you can avoid responding to questions on the site that ask for details of who you are. However, there are many things that your *browser* will reveal about you automatically (e.g. the name of your computer). Similarly, it is not only the site you have visited that could monitor such information. The network *packets* that carry information between you and a site must travel through many third-party systems (e.g. your *ISP*) as they traverse the net. Since they conform to a common standard, they are simple to interpret using techniques known as sniffing (where individual packets are examined).

Threats to the service provider

Vandalism

Service providers are usually a much more engaging target for vandals, since any disruption they cause will inconvenience many more people than attacking a single end-user. There have been many high-profile modifications of the content of web sites, including sites operated by the CIA and Number 10 Downing Street.

Denial of service

Similarly, mounting a denial of service attack on a server inconveniences far more people than attacking individual end-users. Typical forms of denial of service attacks either rely on a system weakness to destabilize the webserver platform (e.g. ping of death – where an appropriatedly formatted *ping* request could cause some types of system to crash) or utilizing a large percentage of a finite resource (e.g. *bandwidth* to the site), hence blocking access from other users.

Unauthorized usage

On sites that charge for access to content, unscrupulous end-users may exploit weaknesses in the design of the site or poor choice of common passwords, which allows them access without payment.

Theft of confidential information

Customer information, such as who is registered, their credit card details, etc., represent an inviting target for malicious third parties, who may try to steal this information. There have been a few cases of credit card details being obtained for many thousands of users by one hacker.

Mechanisms and counter-measures

There are tools and techniques that can help defend against some of the risks of engaging in e-commerce transactions. Many of these are based around cryptographic techniques using ciphers (codes). Of course, encryption is just part of the solution, in the same way that strong locks are only part of effective security for your home. The foundation of good security is a defined policy that identifies specific threats and the counter-measures (or sometimes security-enforcing functionality) that will be implemented to protect against these.

Halt! Who goes there?

Enforcing control over what external users can and can't do is an obvious defense. Access control – which controls who can do what – can be enforced by the network (e.g. through use of a *firewall*), the system software (e.g. the *webserver*, the *operating system* or the *database management system*), or by the application software itself.

To allow different users access to different parts of the system, they must be identified. Authentication can be accomplished by a number of mechanisms – the simplest is asking the user to identify themselves by a entering a user-id and a *password*. More complex mechanisms can require the user to:

⇒ have a special token (e.g. a secret key or a smart card);

⇒ be in a specific place (e.g. be on a specific workstation);

⇒ even subject themselves to a biometric scan (e.g. a fingerprint).

For most applications a user-id and either a password or a password and a secret key are adequate. This leads, of course, to the problem of users either entering a variety of different passwords they can't remember, or using just one password across multiple sites with the danger that an unscrupulous site may try and use the details you have provided to access popular *e-tailing* or similar sites.

Once a user is authenticated, the specific functions that they are authorized to do must be established – this is often referred to as an Access Control List. One source of an ACL is an electronic directory and hence *LDAP* – a very common directory standard – is often referred to as a security technology, although it would be more correct to think of it as a repository of information used by security-enforcing software.

Even when users are authorized to perform certain actions, you may still want to record that they have exercised this right. Audit trails provide this record, and writing appropriate information to these logs is an important security function.

Audit, authentication, and access control are the major features identified in the US Department of Defense's Orange Book (or C2) level of security which is intended to offer a basic degree of protection. Software that implements these functions is sometimes called a trusted computing base.

Securing the line

The most commonly perceived threat to e-commerce transactions is the theft or modification of information while in transit. Fortunately there are several defenses, which use encryption to provide confidentiality. The same techniques can also allow attempted modifications to messages to be spotted (integrity checking). Two widely known web/internet techniques are Secure Sockets Layer (*SSL*) and HTTP-Secure (*HTTPS*).

Who guards the guards?

So how can developers be sure that they have implemented a secure system? For commercial systems, managed penetration testing by "white-hat" hackers (or "tiger teams") is a good way to build confidence that the system offers adequate protection. Sites such as **www.shieldup.com** also allow simple (but informative) analysis of the strength of a site's protection.

Seed capital (business term)
A relatively small amount of investment money – possibly from an *angel* investor – which enables a start-up to get moving in preparation for larger funding. Usually in the tens or 100s of thousands of pounds, euros or dollars.

Semantic web (web term)
Tim Berners-Lee's vision for the future of the world wide web, where the *meaning* of information is available to allow more intelligent decisions to be made automatically using rules (which are called ontologies). Widespread adoption of *XML* (extensible mark-up language) is a first step towards this goal.

Server (technical term)
At the most general level, "server" can refer to any hardware or software component that responds to a request for a specific service, for instance:

➡ file servers respond to requests for specific files;

➡ webservers respond to requests for specific web pages;

➡ database servers respond to queries for records in a database.

"Server" is also used to describe the larger hardware systems offered by some vendors, although, to be pedantic, even a PC-class machine can act as a server e.g. in a *peer-to-peer* model, or where there are a small number of client machines.

Server farm (slang)
Covers a data center room filled with back-end server hardware for (typically) web-based systems. Often provided by specialized *hosting* companies. Means much the same as *web farm*.

SETI@Home (web term)
The Search for Extraterrestrial Intelligence (SETI) project has spent many years looking for radio signals from space that may indicate the existence of alien civilizations. To analyze all of the data in detail requires a very large amount of computer time. The SETI@Home project (**http://setiathome.ssl. berkeley.edu**) allows individuals to contribute spare *CPU* time from their own systems to the project using a special screensaver. To date, 342,000 years of

CPU time have been donated. The authors' own facility has proudly contributed more than 34 CPU years (but has yet to find any trace of ET).

Set-top box (technical term)

Refers to the device required to decode *digital television* (DTV) transmissions for display by normal TV sets. The name simply reflects the fact that the decoder box is (allegedly) normally placed on top of the TV set. The set-top box (STB) has a potentially important part to play in e-commerce as it is an alternative to the PC as a platform for user interaction.

Shannon's Theorem (technical term)

An important theorem linking the maximum data rate over a connection with the available *bandwidth* and the relative strength of a signal, which was first proposed by Claude Shannon in 1948. It says:

$C = B \log_2 (1+S/N)$ where:

C is the data rate in bits per second

B is the bandwidth in Hz

S/N is the ratio of signal to background noise (often quoted in decibels).

Don't worry, we won't test you on this.

Shannon's Theorem applies to any medium used to transmit information. It may be a pair of wires, a coaxial cable, a band of radio frequencies, a beam of light etc. For low noise links (such as high-quality phone lines) Shannon predicts a maximum data rate of around ten times the bandwidth available, based on a signal to noise ratio of 1,000/1 (or 30 decibels). For noisier environments, such as radio, a maximum data rate of three to four times bandwidth is more likely, based on a signal to noise of between 9 and 11 dB. Great engineering skill is still required to get real data rates anywhere near the maximum achievable.

Shockwave (product)

Shockwave – from Macromedia – is a common *plug-in* technology for multimedia playback of video and creation of infrastructure multimedia extravagances.

Shortcut (technical term)
In *Windows* a shortcut is a link to a local file or a location on the web, which allows fast access, and is represented by an icon on the desktop.

SIG (technical term)
Stands for Special Interest Group, an alternative name for an e-mail-based discussion group or forum (although on the *Usenet,* "newsgroup" is the more commonly accepted term).

Silicon Alley (slang)
A play on "Silicon Valley." This refers to the high-tech industry in New York. Other less common plays include Silicon Glen, a marketing term used in Scotland, or even Silicon Lane, for the Chancery Lane area in London, which houses a few high-tech businesses among the legal firms.

Silicon and carbon (business term)
Describes a business that depends on both electronic and human interaction. A term a bit like *clicks and mortar*.

Silicon Valley (slang)
Refers roughly to the Santa Clara Valley in California, and the area around *Palo Alto* in particular, where many high-tech and e-commerce companies have been founded. The original garage start-up in the area was the now venerable *Hewlett Packard*. The importance of Silicon Valley to the world economy is well known, and similar to the impact of parts of the UK during the Industrial Revolution.

Site (web term)
Commonly used truncation of *website*.

Site traffic (web term)
A description of the number of times a website is accessed. Various metrics are available (e.g. *hits*, *page views*), but measurement can be difficult because of caching, where commonly accessed pages are held in system memory for efficiency. See *measurement*.

Skins (technical term)

This refers to the ability to customize the physical appearance of a device or software application to a user's preference. New skins are simply "clipped on" to the original product, either physically (in the case of some mobile phones) or virtually (in the case of customized software).

Slash tilde (/~) (slang)

In UNIX the tilde character "~" represents a user's home directory (e.g. ~someuser). Many webservers follow this convention, so often *URLs* have the form:

www.somehost.com/~someuser/somepage.html

This is fine for a personal home page, but is considered poor form for a commercial site. It indicates that the company doesn't have enough faith in their business or technical competence to register their own *domain name.*

Small to medium-sized enterprise (business term)

See *SME.*

SMDS (technical term)

Stands for Switched Multimegabit Data Service. SMDS is a Wide Area Network (*WAN*) protocol designed to allow flexible connections between *routers* attached to Local Area Networks (*LANs*) in different locations. It supports data rates between 0.2Mbits and 25Mbits. SMDS is a public-switched service allowing any location (or organization) to exchange data with any other user of the SMDS service. SMDS is typically used to build internal corporate networks rather than support connection to an *ISP* for internet access.

SME (business term)

Stands for small to medium-sized enterprise. These organizations are a key target of some *B2B* services. The rationale is that SMEs won't be able to afford the technology infrastructures enjoyed by larger corporations. Delivering services over the web allows costs of set-up and operations to be shared. Conversely, the web allows SMEs themselves – who may excel in a niche area – to reach a global audience.

Smiley (e-mail term)
Also known as *emoticons*.

SMS (technical term)
Stands for Short Message Service. SMS allows mobile phone users to send and receive text messages of up to 160 alphanumeric characters. Messages are stored by the network until they can be forwarded to the recipient. By late 1999 an average of 2 billion SMS messages were being sent globally every month. See also *text*.

SMTP (technical term)
Stands for Simple Mail Transport Protocol. A network protocol used to transfer e-mail over a *TCP/IP* network (in particular, the internet). SMTP is implemented by e-mail servers such as Microsoft's Exchange server and is defined by *RFC* 821.

Smurfing (security term)
A *denial of service* attack where an attacker causes a number of machines on a network to all simultaneously send messages to a single target machine, leading to network congestion.

Snail mail (slang)
Ordinary, physical mail. Used as a contrast to *e-mail*.

Sneakernet (slang)
Common slang for moving data between computers using physical media – like disks – rather than through a proper network.

SOAP (technical term)
Stands for Simple Object Access Protocol. This is a technology backed by Microsoft to allow programs running on different computers to communicate directly using *HTTP* and *XML* (eXtensible Mark-up Language). It is comparable but incompatible with Java-Remote Method Invocation (JRMI) and standard Object Request Brokers (ORBs).

Soft launch (business term)
See *launch*.

Solaris (product)

An *operating system* used by *Sun* on their servers and workstations; a well-known derivative of *UNIX*.

Source code (technical term)

A generic term covering the form of a computer program that can be both written and read easily by human beings. A program in this form will consist of key words and names for variable quantities which will be laid out according to the syntax rules of the language.

Various things can happen to source code once it is written.

➡ It can be interpreted in its readable form by another software program, e.g. a *browser* reads *HTML* in this manner. This often gives slow performance.

➡ It can be "compiled" into machine instructions that can be directly run by the relevant computer system, which is what happens with languages like *C* or *C++*. This gives fast execution.

➡ It can be translated into an intermediate form that is close to the machine instructions of a computer, but is actually run by a program that mimics a computer – sometimes called a "virtual machine." This is what happens with *Java* and is designed to make Java portable across different systems.

Sourceforge (product), Sourceforge.net (website)

Sourceforge is an *open source*, web-based toolset to support collaborative software development. Sourceforge.net (**www.sourceforge.net**) is a hosted version of sourceforge, made freely available to encourage the development of open source projects. At the time of writing **Sourceforge.net** hosts thousands of development projects and is an importnt part of the *open source* landscape.

Spamming, Spam (e-mail term)

The sending of messages (almost always via *e-mail*) in an indiscriminate manner to a large mailing list, without reference to the needs or desires of the target audience, and usually with a view to selling them something. Named after the legendary Monty Python spam sketch, where spam came with everything. The financial cost of spamming is so small that even a minimal response rate results in a profit. Spam generates a great deal of negative emotion from many types of user and the response to spamming often takes the form of *flaming*.

Spider (web term)
See *crawler*.

Spin-off (business term)
A spin-off is a new company that is created out of an existing organization. This is an approach used by some existing companies to "get into" e-commerce. For example, Freeserve is a major UK *ISP* which was started out of the Dixon's retail chain. Sometimes such a spin-off is called a *dot corp* – where the "corp" comes from "corporate." Some *incubators* have specifically targetted the dot-corp market. Spin-offs were in many cases defensive moves against new start-up competition. However, in some ways, it is the existing major corporates and their spin-off initiatives that are really succeeding with e-commerce. As one example, the Tesco supermarket chain in the UK is the world's largest online grocer.

Splash page (web term)
See *jump page*.

SQUID (product)
A program that caches web pages and other internet content on a server closer to the user – in terms of network links and geography – than the main website. This is intended to increase access speed. It is an example of *open source* software.

SSL (internet term)
Stands for Secure Sockets Layer, a security protocol that provides communications privacy over the internet. Originally developed by *Netscape*, it has been widely accepted in the internet community (and is also sometimes given the slightly different name of Transport Level Security or TLS). It is implemented by most *browsers*. The actual cryptographic algorithms used can vary, but the most common configuration is the use of an RSA *public key* algorithm to exchange securely a numeric session key between the browser and the server, and then to use an algorithm called *RC4* for bulk encryption to protect information from being monitored in transit. In Microsoft's *Internet*

Sample digital certificate (SSL)

Explorer, an SSL connection is indicated by a padlock in the bottom right-hand corner of the window. Double clicking on the padlock displays details of the digital *certificate* on the server used to establish the link. This can be used to provide authentication that the site is really what it claims to be (an example for **amazon.com** is shown above).

Stallman, Richard

Richard Stallman is one of the most significant figures in the *free software* movement, both as a contributor of influential software (e.g. *EMACS*) and also as founder of the *Free Software Foundation* and the *GNU* (GNU's not UNIX) project.

Stickiness (slang)

A key aim of web designers. A "sticky" website will hold the attention of users, provide services and information they value, and attract repeat visits. For any *B2C* business, this is a fundamental part of building a business with a chance of success.

Streaming (technical term)

Historically, multimedia content such as music or video clips were small enough to be downloaded in their entirety and then played. However, for very large files or for "live" broadcasts this is undesirable. Streaming provides a way to overlap playback with file transfer, provided that the rate of download can keep up with the speed of playback. Conceptually streaming is like sending one frame of a movie at a time instead of downloading an entire reel. Streaming requires special software on the *browser* (in the form of a *plug-in*) and on the server. The major vendors in this area include RealNetworks and *Microsoft*.

Stunt marketing (business term)

Promotional activities designed to draw attention to an online presence by being loud, outrageous, and generally difficult to ignore. Results are often temporary and could turn off future potential customers if tasteless.

Style sheet (technical term)

See *cascading style sheet*.

Suit (slang)

Used by those working in the e-commerce world to describe those who work for traditional companies and dress in traditional attire. It's true to say that many traditional organizations have responded to the e-commerce revolution by introducing changes to their own internal culture, and informal dress codes. It is also true to say that with the sharp decline in the value of dot-com companies in 2000, many ex-dot-com people are joining these traditional corporates.

Sun (company)

Sun is one of the biggest names in both the world of the internet and e-commerce in general. With a small number of others, Sun's products are part of a "golden circle" of standard products used in many e-commerce systems.

Founded in 1982 with just four employees, Sun's first focus was high-end *UNIX*-based workstations. Over the next few years, Sun expanded rapidly into Europe, Asia, and elsewhere. It also began – in 1984 – a long history of introducing major innovations with NFS (Network File System), which allowed files to be used across networks in a simple, transparent way. In 1988, Sun reached $1 billion in revenue – an incredible rate of growth. In 1989, Sun introduced its SPARC station workstation, the first so-called "pizza box" system with a base unit measuring just 16 by 16 inches. This was engineered round Sun's own microprocessor architecture.

The year 1995 marked the introduction of *Java* – now an almost universally used language, and a key component of many serious internet applications. Extremely well marketed, the language has also become successful through its own intrinsic merits of portability, elegance, and simplicity. As a $10-billion-a-year corporation, Sun's main service and product lines currently include:

➡ **Hardware:**

— enterprise servers, used as back-end systems in many dot-com or e-commerce businesses

— network storage devices

— high-end workstations.

➡ **Java technology:** since Java is an extremely important part of the Sun offering, we discuss it in more detail below.

➡ **Solaris:** a derivative of UNIX with good networking, internet and Java support. Now its source code – in the spirit of the internet and the very original versions of UNIX – is also available.

➡ **Embedded technologies:** based around JavaOS (or Java-based *operating system*), Ultra Sparc microprocessors and other specialist areas.

Sun and Java

Java is a core part of Sun's corporate mission. Sun describes the Java platform, in very general terms, as a "stable, secure and features-complete" environment for the web, aimed at "smartcard to supercomputer" scalability.

Key aspects of Sun's Java offering include:

⇒ the base language, now very much an industry standard;

⇒ standard "class" libraries;

⇒ Java Software Development Kits (SDKs or *JDKs)*, and runtime environments for multiple platforms;

⇒ development tools such as *Forte* Fusion;

⇒ JavaOS, a lightweight *operating system* for a range of devices;

⇒ *Jini* – a connection technology to enable devices to connect easily with Java applications;

⇒ many other software products and extensions;

⇒ Java-based hardware offerings.

Sun has, as you might expect, a great deal of informational and marketing material on the web. Useful starting points are **www.sun.com** and **java.sun. com**.

Surf (slang)
You probably already know this, but we'll define it anyway. Slang for moving between websites, usually in a recreational sense.

Sybase (product, company)
Makers of a well-known *database management system* and surrounding tools.

Symbian (organization)
Symbian is a consortium of mobile phone manufacturers (once including *Nokia*, Motorola, and Ericsson) and the mobile computer manufacturer Psion. It promotes the EPOC Operating System for "Wireless Information Devices" such as SmartPhones and pocket computers. EPOC is a competitor to *Microsoft*'s Windows-CE and the Pocket PC operating systems.

T (technical term)
Symbol for *tera*, which is used in sizing very large quantities related to computer systems.

T1, T3 (technical term)
T1 and T3 are standards in the US for point-to-point digital communications that are typically used to link large organizations to an *ISP* (Internet Service Provider) or as part of the internet *backbone*. A T1 circuit operates at 1.544 Mbit/s and a T3 circuit at 44 Mbit/s. The European equivalent of T1 is known as E1 and operates at a higher data rate (2.048 Mbps).

Tag (technical term)
Mark-up languages are largely concerned with the formatting of text. *HTML*, which is used to layout *web pages* is an example of such a language. A "tag" is a keyword that gives an instruction to the viewing program (such as a *browser*). By convention, tags are written between angle brackets (< >) to distinguish them from ordinary text. Tags aren't explicitly seen by the end-user, but tell the viewing program to change font, center a line, start a new paragraph, and so on. The section on *HTML* contains examples of common HTML tags.

Taskbar (technical term)

A feature of modern versions of *Windows*. Allows active applications to be "minimized" and represented only by a button on the bottom of the screen. Clicking on the button opens up the application again.

TB (technical term)

See *terabyte*.

TCP (technical term)

Stands for Transmission Control Protocol, which fits into the *TCP/IP* protocol suite logically just above the Internet Protocol (*IP*). IP is concerned with the transfer of data across the interconnected networks that make up the internet. TCP provides reliable end-to-end communication between pairs of computers. So TCP compensates for the fact that IP may discard information in transit due to errors, or that data may arrive "out of sequence," by taking different routes across the internet. The aim of TCP is to reassemble complete messages from IP packets.

TCP allows higher-level protocols (such as the web's *HTTP*) to use the concept of a *virtual circuit* to simplify connecting to a remote machine. A virtual circuit will look to the calling program like a direct connection.

TCP is defined in *RFC* 793, an internet standard document.

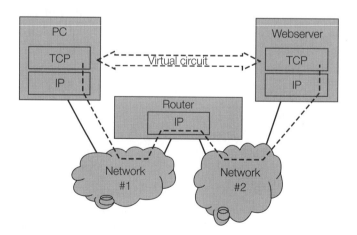

The role of TCP in connections

TCP/IP (technical term)

Stands for Transmission Control Protocol/Internet Protocol and is the generic term used for the suite of network *protocols* used on the internet. Named after two of the most important members of the family (*TCP* and *IP*); others include:

➡ *FTP* (File Transfer Protocol)

➡ *SMTP* (Simple Mail Transfer Protocol)

➡ *Telnet* (remote terminal access).

See also *IP* and *TCP*.

Telco (business term)

Shorthand for telecommunications company. These are important players in the e-commerce space, since they provide the physical fixed or wireless communication links for much of the internet and other types of network.

Telnet (technical term)

A network *protocol* used to obtain remote terminal access to a computer over a *TCP/IP* network (e.g. the internet). This allows a user to log-on to a distant machine. Telnet is implemented on most operating systems and also in many network devices (e.g. *routers*) to allow remote access and configuration. Providing this type of remote access is obviously a great opportunity for malicious hackers to gain access, so careful consideration is needed of who is allowed to log-in remotely, and how they must identify themselves. Today, unless you are a systems developer or administrator, you're pretty unlikely to come across telnet. Telnet is defined in *RFC* 854, an internet standard document.

Tera (technical term)

Prefix that multiplies an IT quantity by 2^{40} – a very large number indeed, which is close to one trillion or one million million. Used mainly in the term *terabyte*. If you need to go higher, the prefix peta- stands for 2^{50} which is close to a round quadrillion.

Terabyte (technical term)

2^{40} *bytes* – a byte being 8 bits of storage, long enough to hold a numeric code for characters from the *ASCII* character set. Used to size very large amounts of disk space. Terabyte databases used to be at the absolute leading edge of technology. However, they are increasingly common in global or national-level systems.

Text (slang)

Covers the text messages sent by mobile phone users to each other, typically using **SMS** (Short Message Service) which allows up to 160 alphanumeric characters. Can also be used as a verb (as in "text me").

SMS text messages were originally almost a technical afterthought to the voice services offered by mobile telephony. They have of course created a business world and culture of their own. There are commercial services based on text messages, and text is used for business communication, but its most obvious application is personal communication, particularly among teenagers and 20-somethings – hence the phrase *generation text*. One story we have heard (which we hope is true) is that the most lucrative value-added service provided by one Nordic telecommunications provider was "Insult of the Day" – accessed via SMS by kids who copied it to their friends in bulk. The rise of text as a social medium parallels the early days of the **ARPANET** and internet (where e-mail accounted for the bulk of traffic and personal websites became popular very early on). As a result, billions of text messages are now sent across the world's mobile networks each month.

Given the hard limit of 160 characters, text has encouraged an even more aggressive form of abbreviation than e-mail (although e-mail abbreviations are also much used). Examples include:

Abbreviation	Meaning
2	to
4	for
cya	see ya (i.e. bye)
k	okay
l8	late
m8	mate (i.e. friend)
nrn	no reply necessary
soz	sorry
sup	derived from "wassup" which is derived from "what's up" (i.e. how are you)
txt	text

Thin client (technical term)
A type of *client-server* system where the *client* software on a PC is relatively small and the most significant processing is done on the *server* side. Because of the nature of *browsers*, the world wide web lends itself most naturally to a thin-client approach, and most serious websites do the vast majority of processing on the server end of the system.

Thumbnail (web term)
Describes a small, compact version of an image that is displayed on a web page.

Tier 1 ISP, Tier 2 ISP (internet term)
Tier 1 refers to an *ISP* (internet Service Provider) that also provides some of the internet *backbone* infrastructure, thereby allowing users "direct" access to the main internet without going through a third party. Tier 2 ISPs need to route their traffic to a Tier 1 ISP for it to reach the internet backbone. However, inter-ISP peering arrangements and regional exchanges (e.g. *LINX*) now make the picture much more complex, and the service an end-user receives is unlikely to be influenced by which tier their ISP falls into.

TLD (internet term)
See *top-level domain*.

Tomlinson, Ray
Inventor in 1971/72 of *e-mail* between systems, working for BBN as part of the legendary *ARPANET* project. He was also the man who selected the "@" symbol in e-mail addresses.

Top-level domain (internet term)
Domain names such as **www.amazon.com** are a way of providing human-friendly identities for sites on the internet. They are hierarchical (when read from right to left). Top-level domains are the first division of the internet name space, and the main seven general-purpose domain names are .com, .gov, .org, .edu, .mil, .net and .int. There are also two letter top-level domain names which stand for countries (examples being .us and .uk). See the entries on *//*, *.com*, *domain name*, and *DNS* for more information.

Torvalds, Linus

Born in Helskinki, Finland. Creator and inspiration behind *Linux*, a freely available *open source* version of the *UNIX* operating system. Torvalds posted the original version of the Linux source code on the internet, and co-ordinated e-mail from many programmers all over the world who suggested changes and improvements. Linux is now a serious server-side operating system, used in many e-commerce companies. It is supported by a host of software companies, hardware makers, and application developers, and is the best example of the power of the open source movement.

TPM (technical term)

Stands for Transaction Processing Monitor. See description under *transaction*.

Tracert (technical term)

Short for trace route, this is a common tool for tracking the route taken by information passing over the internet and a way of exploring how the internet is built from a series of interconnected networks. There are a variety of implementations of tracert, including several graphical versions (e.g. neo-trace from **www.neoworx.com**). The output of the text version of tracert supplied with MS Windows is shown below – it traces the route of traffic between a user of Demon Internet (**www.demon.net**) and Sun Microsystems (**www.sun.com**). Note the total of 17 intermediary systems (probably routers) that process the information en route.

```
C:\> tracert www.sun.com

Tracing route to www.sun.com [192.18.97.241]
over a maximum of 30 hops:

  1  159 ms  152 ms  153 ms  anchor-du-15.access.demon.net [195.173.57.15]

  2  153 ms  152 ms  154 ms  anchor-core-1-fxp3.router.demon.net [195.173.57.251]

  3  190 ms  152 ms  153 ms  anchor-access-1-11.router.demon.net [195.173.57.245]

  4  156 ms  151 ms  155 ms  tele-core-1-fxp3.router.demon.net [194.159.254.100]

  5  164 ms  152 ms  154 ms  tele-backbone-1-ge020.router.demon.net [194.159.252.54]

  6  235 ms  235 ms  229 ms  ny2-backbone-1-ge020.router.demon.net [195.173.173.9]

  7  231 ms  236 ms  230 ms  ny1-border-1-211.router.demon.net [195.173.173.122]

  8  234 ms  231 ms  237 ms  sl-gw9-nyc-0-2.sprintlink.net [144.232.173.9]
```

```
 9   234 ms   232 ms   229 ms   sl-bb20-nyc-3-0.sprintlink.net [144.232.7.93]

10   251 ms   251 ms   253 ms   sl-bb22-chi-12-0.sprintlink.net [144.232.18.53]

11   253 ms   253 ms   249 ms   sl-bb23-chi-15-0.sprintlink.net [144.232.26.50]

12   249 ms   252 ms   250 ms   sl-bb21-chi-14-0.sprintlink.net [144.232.26.57]

13   259 ms   265 ms   264 ms   sl-bb21-che-9-0.sprintlink.net [144.232.18.5]

14   *        265 ms   265 ms   sl-fb1-che-9-0.sprintlink.net [144.232.9.2]

15   *        272 ms   273 ms   208.30.200.10

16   267 ms   273 ms   268 ms   border3.ge2-0-bbnet.den.pnap.net [216.52.40.7]

17   269 ms   273 ms   269 ms   sun-1.border3.den.pnap.net [216.52.42.42]

18   280 ms   279 ms   279 ms   www.sun.com [192.18.97.241]
```

Trace complete.

Transaction (technical term)

In business terms, this describes a sequence of steps that usually involve the exchange of money. With an e-commerce solution, the business process will be translated into a series of database updates, possibly calls to credit card validation software, creation of electronic instructions to a warehouse, and the like. There is complexity here. If part of a transaction fails, it is important that all prior steps are "rolled back" so no work is left half done. Transactions these days often involve the synchronization of data across different systems. As a result, most solutions will use the transaction control features of a *database management system* like Oracle, or a specific type of *middleware* called a Transaction Processing Monitor or *TPM*.

Trojan horses (security term)

A program or site that does rather more than expected. For instance a site that appears simply to display a cartoon could be modifying files in the background or scanning your disk for interesting data. To put it simply, a Trojan horse is a program that breaks security by appearing to do something else. Specific techniques available include those shown in the table on page 298.

Trusted (security term)

A term given to software or to a system that is relied on to implement some form of security functionality. For instance, to prevent users having to log-on multiple times in a distributed environment, some servers have "trust"

Trojan horses

Mechanism	Potential for hidden behavior
HTML/JavaScript	In theory low, since these are instructions that are interpreted within the browser. However, HTML/JavaScript pages can access details such as the history of sites visited, and the operating system installed.
Java	Variable. Java code executes with a "sandbox" which limits what it can do. However, the exact configuration of these limits is end-user defined. If the limits are too lax then the potential for problems is high.
ActiveX	Variable. The code within an ActiveX can access all of the facilities of the PC. Users must rely on no-one formally "signing" a malicious component.
Executables (i.e. .exe files)	High. As with ActiveX there is no bound to what the application can do and there is no signing mechanism to ensure that code is not malicious. Many famous viruses have been .exe attachments to e-mails.
Plug-ins	Variable. Some plug-ins allow third-party programming languages to be executed in collaboration with the browser. The plug-in *could* provide access to all the capabilities of the PC, and therefore provide a possible platform for attack.

relationships with other machines, e.g. "if machine X says this request comes from user Y then that's good enough for me!"

Tux (penguin)

Tux is the penguin mascot for the *Linux* operating system. Tux was originally drawn by Larry Ewing and introduced with version 2.0 of the Linux kernel, it was chosen simply because *Linus Torvalds* (creator of Linux) apparently likes penguins.

Tuxedo (software product)

Tuxedo is the name of a well-known Transaction Processing Monitor (*TPM*), used in complex, distributed data processing systems. It ensures that all of the actions associated with a business transaction, say a transfer of money across multiple machines, are successful. If a failure occurs, all elements of the transaction will be rolled back to ensure the various databases are in a consistent state. Tuxedo also deals with messaging, load-balancing, distributed database updates, and the like. Tuxedo was originally developed alongside *UNIX* by AT&T, but is now part of BEA Systems' WebLogic product range. See also *transaction*.

Ubiquitous computing (technical term)

As with many fundamental ideas, the notion of ubiquitous computing arose from work at *Xerox Parc* (the actual term was coined by Mark Wieser, in 1988). It is based on the notion of a world where computing power is so pervasive and part of the everyday fabric of life, it becomes essentially invisible with simple point-of-use interfaces, rather than the complex interfaces of PCs or even PDAs. Initial experiments focussed on devices such as tabs (like intelligent Post-it notes), pads (equivalent to notepads) and automated whiteboard-like structures.

Like much of what has been envisioned at Xerox Parc, it is taking the world a while to catch up. Nevertheless, even today the vast majority of microprocessors made do not end up in computers. Some of the devices where they do end up seem obvious (phones). Other destinations are less so (kettles). Computing devices are now available which cost a few cents and require no power supply – they are lit up, read and written to by radio signals. Wireless standards enable connectivity between devices at short range or long distances, and provide connectivity to the wider internet. It therefore becomes possible to build intelligence into items like product or package labels, and coding schemes exist which would allow every individual arti-fact ever made by man to be uniquely coded. Although the technology is developing, and in some cases may be challenging to use, its potential impact is thought by many to be profound, and we are heading for a world where even mundane objects are intelligent and connected.

UMTS (mobile term)

Stands for Universal Mobile Telecommunications System and is the European standard for the next generation of mobile communications designed to offer higher mobile data rates and integrated internet access. Data rates of 2 *Mbps* have been discussed. However, this is only likely to be achievable within a networked building; speeds of 384 *Kbps* are more realis-tic in metropolitan areas and 144 Kbps elsewhere.

Uniform Resource Identifier (web term)

See *URI*.

Uniform Resource Locator (web term)

See *URL*.

UNIX (technical term)

Very common, open and standard *operating system*. UNIX started off life in the late 1960s, become popular with academics and researchers in the 1970s, and then become a serious commercial platform in the 1980s. Well-known for its flexible toolset, and much favored in technical development, UNIX has been the server platform around which much of the internet was devel-oped. *Linux* is a descendent of UNIX.

Unmetered (business term)

A term applied to *ISPs* that provide access to the internet for a fixed charge rather than charging based on the time connected.

Upload (technical term)

Opposite of *download*, and refers to the copying of files from a PC or worksta-tion to a central system (such as an *FTP* server). Often this is done so that the files can be shared by others. *Peer-to-peer* services, like *Napster*, allow sharing to be done between PCs directly.

URI (web term)

A more general term than the much more common **URL** – a name used to identify a resource (such as a file) on the web. Stands for Uniform Resource Identifier.

URL (web term)

Stands for Uniform Resource Locator. A text string that gives the location of a resource (such as a website) in a human-friendly way. It will consist of a prefix identifying the relevant protocol used to transmit information (such as *http:* for a website), a *domain name,* and optionally a file name. The entries under *//,* and *domain name* give more detail. People will now ask for a URL as casually as they ask for a phone number.

Usenet (pre-internet term)

Usenet is a shorthand term for the UNIX User Network, which started life in around 1979 as a network and set of software tools for the exchange of news and views for *UNIX* users. The Usenet has a rich but different history from the mainstream internet, and predates the web by nearly a decade. Today "Usenet" is used interchangeably with "internet news" or just "news" and provides thousands of discussion groups on a wide variety of topics. It is no longer tied to the UNIX platform.

The Usenet was created at the end of 1979 as a link between servers at two universities in Carolina (the University of North Carolina and Duke University). Data was exchanged using dial-up connections and UNIX-UNIX-Copy Program (*UUCP*), a primitive tool for exchanging data. By 1983 a backbone of sites was distributing Usenet news, although costs of international phone links and relatively slow speed of modems at the time restricted the growth of the backbone outside the US. In the late 1980s the Network News Transport Protocol (*NNTP*) replaced UUCP and allowed the Usenet to migrate off its own backbone network and use the growing infrastructure of the internet to replicate news between servers. This greatly increased the number of sites holding Usenet data. NNTP also allowed access to Usenet servers from machines using client news reader software, such as PCs.

In the beginning, Usenet had two top-level hierarchies, mod.* for *moderated newsgroups* and net.* for unmoderated. This was later expanded by the addition of fa.* (standing for "from *ARPANET*"). Some additional domains were of "local" interest and not replicated between servers. During the "great renaming" of 1986/87 newsgroups were reallocated into seven main hierarchies: comp.* (computers), misc.* (miscellaneous), news.*, rec.* (recreation), sci.* (science), soc.* (society), and talk.* and the original groups disappeared. Following a disagreement about the creation of rec.drugs and the location of a recipe news group, the alt.* hierarchy was created as an alternative to the "official" seven hierarchies.

Occasionally newsgroup postings hark back to a more glorious past, when there were fewer general postings and the Usenet represented a groundbreaking use of technology for global collaboration. However, the Usenet still remains a great place to find information even if it often requires quite a lot of sifting to find the gold within the silt.

UUCP (technical term)

Stands for UNIX-UNIX-Copy Program. A old-fashioned suite of programs for file transfer between *UNIX* machines, which predates the much higher levels of connectivity provided by the internet. Doesn't provide true networking, but merely the ability to copy files over serial lines, usually phone lines. Of interest because it was the basis for the original form of *Usenet.*

Uuencoding (technical term)

A technique to allow binary data (e.g. images or programs) to be transferred over networks designed only for plain *ASCII* text (e.g. *Usenet* news groups). The file to be transferred is transformed into a series of alphanumeric characters (resulting in a much bigger message) and (potentially) fragmented into multiple parts for posting. Today this is generally done automatically by modern mail and news readers.

VAD (business term)
See *Viewer Attention Deficit*.

Valley (slang)
Short for *Silicon Valley*.

Vanity site (web term)
An internet presence established for reasons that cannot be justified by cold commercial logic, or a site that focusses on the personalities of the founders or executives rather than the needs of the users.

VB (product, technical term)
See *Visual Basic*.

vBNS (internet term)
Stands for very high speed Backbone Network Service. A network linked to the Internet2 initiative and used by researchers looking at potential next-generation features of the internet.

VBScript (technical term)
Stands for Visual Basic Scripting Language, which is a cut-down version of

the full *Visual Basic* programming language. Proprietary to *Microsoft*, it is an alternative to *JavaScript* for automating web pages, but it is only supported by Microsoft's *Internet Explorer* browser.

Vector graphics (technical term)

Images stored as mathematical-style descriptions of lines (direction, length, starting position). Can be significantly more compact than bitmap-style graphics and often used in web animation tools. See also *raster* graphics.

Venture capital (business term)

Capital (that is, money) that is invested into high-risk undertakings, but with potentially very high returns. A long-standing feature of the economic landscape, with a long history in technology, this type of investment was a conspicuous feature of the dot-com boom (or bubble) of the late 1990s. Used early in the life of a company, venture capital is given in exchange for a share of the ownership of an enterprise. The equity gained is not liquid (since the company's shares won't yet be publicly traded) and almost certainly not secured against any assets. The investor is essentially taking an option on the future – hoping that the company will grow, move into profit, and eventually "float" through a mechanism like an *IPO*, when the investor can sell its stock to the general public.

To cope with high levels of risk, a good venture capitalist will invest in a portfolio of different companies, with an expectation that only a tiny fraction of their investments will generate large returns. The dot-com boom period allowed some venture capitalists to make very large sums indeed out of companies that often had small turnovers and were loss making. From mid-2000 onwards, when the value of such companies fell sharply, new venture capital funding became much harder to get. It does remain available to business ideas that make economic sense, show a clear "path to profit," and have the right kind of leadership.

Venture capital funding is typically parcelled out in stages. Typical funding points are:

➡ **Seed funding:** supports development of idea, product, and business plan.

➡ **Startup funding or first stage:** supports completion of product development major funding round to begin real business operations.

➡ **Second stage**: further round, needed when the business plan shows a loss for a longish period.

➡ **Third stage or mezzanine**: supports expansion where the company has started to move into profit.

➡ **Bridge**: covers period just before the company goes public.

Venture capitalist (business term)

Organization (or individual) that manages the investment of *venture capital* funds into startup companies

Vertical portal (web term)

See *vortal.*

Viewer (web term)

General term for a *plug-in* to a *browser* that allows special file formats to be read by the end-user. The term "player" is also used for plug-ins that allow sound or video to be played.

Viewer Attention Deficit (business term)

The phenomenon that results in visitors to a website remaining for only a few seconds before moving on, unless the site effectively answers the question "what's in it for me?"

Vignette (company)

Well-known supplier of tools to help developers build web-based systems. Vignette offers products for *content management, B2C* web shopfronts, *B2B* systems, *portals* and e-marketplaces.

Viral marketing (business term)

Viral marketing is, broadly speaking, any technique that induces a website or user to carry a marketing message to another website or user, creating potentially exponential growth in the visibility and effect of the message.

There are at least three categories of marketing "virus" that can be used to carry a particular message to all corners of the globe.

Passive

This does not require any action from the original user, and is essentially dormant. Upon arrival, however, it can be activated by the recipient.

For example, a leading web-based e-mail service (e.g. Hotmail) attaches a one-line message to every outbound e-mail it sends on behalf of its customers. Customers have to do nothing – and are unable to object as they use the service free of charge. The recipient may click the hyperlink in the Hotmail message, visit the site, and open a free web-based e-mail account.

Participative

This requires the recipient to participate in a more active manner. The sender requires the recipient to take some action in order to conclude the transaction or obtain a benefit.

For example, X decides to use the services of a web-based greeting card company (e.g. Blue Mountain Arts). After designing the card, X decides not to e-mail it directly to Y, as the size of the graphics may require Y to spend considerable time downloading the file. Instead X uses a form on the site to e-mail Y advising of the availability of the card. Y has to go the site, using the hyperlink provided in the e-mail, to retrieve the card and enjoy the message. X has now forced Y to visit the site. What's more, the next time Y needs the services of an electronic greeting card site, Y is likely to return to the site introduced by X.

Evangelical

This is the most virulent type of viral marketing and involves X becoming an evangelist for the site in order to convince Y to use it. Of course, the key point here is that X really has to *like* the site in question.

For example, X wishes to use a particular chat program to communicate with Y (for example, ICQ). Unfortunately, Y is not particularly technologically literate, and finds the prospect of downloading and installing the software a daunting one. X will have to go to considerable lengths, such as visiting Y's home, logging on to the site, installing the program, and educating Y in its operation. Once they become regular users, both X and Y are likely to become evangelists for the site as they attempt to extend its usage to their friends.

Virtual circuit (internet term)

A virtual circuit is a way of simplifying application development by making a **packet-switched** link (e.g. one based on **IP** or the Internet Protocol) appear to be a circuit-switched connection. This mimics a direct connection between the systems. Once established, it allows applications simply to send (or read) a stream of data. Virtual circuits remove the need for the application to know that the data stream will be chopped into packets, which may arrive out of order (if they arrive at all). In the *TCP/IP* network protocol suite, the *TCP* (Transmission Control Protocol) layer implements virtual circuits for end applications.

Virtual Private Network (security term)

A technique for connecting two networks securely via the internet to create a bigger network that can be used privately and isn't visible to other internet users. This allows organizations to take advantage of the infrastructure made available by the internet, but ensures the confidentiality of data in transit.

Virtual Reality Modeling Language (web term)

See *VRML.*

Virus (security term)

Malicious software that infects a program or data file and is copied on to any machine that shares that program or file (either by external media or over a network link). Viruses can vary from the simply annoying (e.g. those that display a rude message on a particular day) to the malicious that vandalize a machine (e.g. by deleting or corrupting files). *MS-DOS* and early versions of Microsoft *Windows* were vulnerable to viruses that infected the computer's memory or the startup routines of the operating system. These vulnerabilities have been removed in more recent versions of Windows. However, more recent viruses use the scripting capabilities of the Microsoft Office application suite, and copy themselves as "macros" attached to office documents. The only way to avoid viruses (assuming that you will at some point exchange files with another user) is to install virus-detection software that can scan files for contents that match the fingerprint of a known virus. To date, virus writers have tended to target the PC user. However, in the future it is almost certain that destructive individuals will create viruses that effects PDAs, internet-enabled mobile phones, and other new forms of internet appliance on a global basis.

Visit (web term)

Used in networking usage of websites – and often in web advertising. A visit is the act of a visitor making page requests from a specific site in a single session (say, within 30 minutes). See also *measurement.*

Visitor (web term)

A term for a user who accesses a website – commonly used in web advertising.

VISP (technical term)

Stands for Virtual Internet Service Provider and describes an *ISP* whose technical infrastructure is provided by a third party and focusses purely on sales and marketing. Tesco.net and Virgin.net are two high-profile examples in the UK.

Visual Basic (product, technical term)

A trademark of *Microsoft*. Refers to a much-enhanced version of the ancient BASIC language intended for building modern distributed, graphical applications. It is Microsoft's own flagship development language, which is also found in simpler form within Microsoft application products (such as Word and Excel). A scripting language derived from Visual Basic is also available for programming websites. Visual Basic is often referred to as just VB.

Visual-Studio (product)

Reference to a family of *Microsoft* products for software developers that allow common programming languages to be used within a PC-based, graphical environment. Common examples include *Visual Basic*, Visual C++, and Visual J++ for *Java*.

Vortal (web term)

Stands for vertical portal. This refers to a *portal* that is focussed on a specific industry or area of specialism or interest. Often used as an attempt to create some kinding of trading community.

VRML (web term)

Stands for Virtual Reality Modeling Language – a tool for building 3-dimensional graphics for display on the web. Needs a specialized *browser* or *plug-in* for display.

Vulture capitalist (slang)

A predatory venture capitalist looking to profit from investing in e-commerce, who offers overly aggressive terms to the unwary.

W3 (web term)

Stands for www or *world wide web*

W3C (web term)

Stands for World Wide Web Consortium. The W3C was created in October 1994 at the Massachusetts Institute of Technology (MIT) to take over the responsibilities from *CERN* for stewardship of the web. On their website (**www.w3c.org**) the W3C state their goals for the web to be:

1. **"Universal Access:** To make the web accessible to all by promoting technologies that take into account the vast differences in culture, education, ability, material resources, and physical limitations of users on all continents;
2. **Semantic Web:** To develop a software environment that permits each user to make the best use of the resources available on the web;
3. **Web of Trust:** To guide the web's development with careful consideration for the novel legal, commercial, and social issues raised by this technology.

Tim Berners-Lee, who created the underlying architecture for the web, remains actively involved.

Walled garden (web term)

The web represents all of human life, including activities at the fringe of social acceptability, or beyond. In addition, the number of active web pages is in the billions. A walled garden is provided by some access providers to give controlled access to a limited range of destination websites. The aims of a walled garden can be:

➡ keeping children away from the more sexual or otherwise controversial content that is available on the internet as a whole;

➡ directing users towards links that have a commercial relationship with the site hosting the walled garden.

WAN (technical term)

Stands for Wide Area Network. Historically a WAN was the "long haul" component of a computer network. However, the trend towards *internetworking* of Local Area Networks (*LANs*) has often reduced the reality of the WAN component to being simply the leased line between *routers* or to an *ISP* (Internet Service Provider).

WAP (technical term)

The Wireless Application Protocol (WAP) is designed to be an open, standards-based architecture to support internet access from wireless devices. It has been developed by the WAP Forum (**www.wapforum.org**), which is an industry association comprising more than 200 members, including the major players in the wireless industry.

Although it draws on many of the protocols already proven on the internet, WAP is not *HTTP* over a wireless connection. Instead, it specifies a network protocol "stack" and a browser-based application environment highly optimized for a wireless environment. This means that a WAP phone cannot directly access traditional websites. The key components of WAP are described below.

The Wireless Application Environment (WAE)

The WAP end-user device is not assumed to be a PC, and will typically be a mobile device such as a mobile phone with:

- a screen capable of displaying only a few lines of 8–12 characters
- limited input devices (e.g. no mouse)
- a low-power CPU and a small amount of memory.

The WAE offers a simple mark-up language called, with complete obviousness, Wireless Mark-up Language or **WML**, which is designed to be displayed using a simple "microbrowser" and which can run on a low-power device.

The WAP programming model

The WAP model introduces a **WAP gateway** between the mobile network and the internet. The gateway allows some functionality to be offloaded from the browser (such as resolving the internet address for a website) and translates WAP protocols into those used on the web (**HTTP** and **TCP**). The gateway will also encode WML into a compressed form for transport over the wireless network (see figure below).

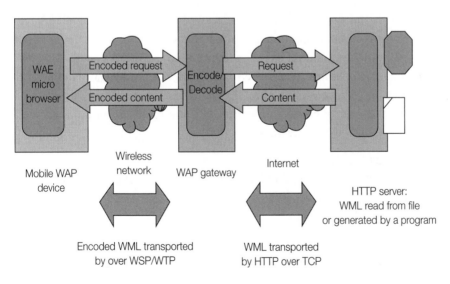

The WAP programming model

The WAP protocol stack

WAP defines the following protocols to replace HTTP and TCP for the wireless segment of the connection (between the mobile device and the gateway):

➡ Wireless Session Protocol (WSP), which allows a session to be suspended when the wireless link is interrupted, e.g. when a user passes through a tunnel.

➡ Wireless Transaction Protocol (WTP), the equivalent of TCP but optimized to reduce the processing capacity on the mobile device and to minimize the number of messages that must pass over the mobile network.

➡ Wireless Transport Layer Security (WTLS), an equivalent of the security protocol *SSL* optimized for wireless.

The WAP protocol stack is designed to be independent of the underlying wireless data network, and therefore should be portable across current and future wireless networks (e.g. *GSM*, *UMTS*).

WAP security translation

The WAP gateway plays a key role in security. The wireless device communicates with the WAP gateway over the wireless network using WTLS. The WAP gateway then communicates with the webserver over the internet, using SSL. This means that data is vulnerable to monitoring on the gateway, which must be operated by a trusted organization. These issues are due to be addressed in a future version of WTLS. In the meantime, if you do not wish to trust a third-party gateway operator then the only option is to bring the gateway on to your own network.

WAP gateway (technical term)

A device that connects a *WAP* (Wireless Application Protocol) mobile network to the internet. The gateway translates between the WAP protocols and those used on the internet.

WAP server (technical term)

A normal webserver configured to support content in *WML* (Wireless Markup Language).

Warez (slang)
Produced "wares." Denotes illegal copies of commercial computer software distributed anonymously via *FTP* servers and similar channels.

WASP (technical term)
Stands for Wireless Application Service Provider, a form of Application Service Provider (ASP) focussed on centrally running applications targetted at mobile internet users. At the time of writing this is a market very much in its infancy.

WAV (technical term)
A windows file format (identified by a .wav suffix on file names) that stores audio.

WBMP (technical term)
Stands for Wireless Bit Map and is an image format defined as part of *WAP* (Wireless Application Protocol). It is intended to allow simple images to be displayed on low-resolution mobile devices such as mobile phones.

Web (web term)
Mostly commonly used shorthand for *world wide web*, although www and w3 are also used. Can be used in conjunction with other terms to link a concept to the world wide web, as in *web page*, or *website*.

Web Accessibility Initiative (web term)
An initiative from the World Wide Web Consortium (*W3C*) offering people with disabilities a greater degree of web usability. If made mandatory in the USA, it will require a considerable reworking of most of today's websites.

Web browser (web term)
See *browser*.

Webcam (technical term)
A digital camera – often remarkably cheap – built to attach to the web and used to update a picture on a website. The subject matter varies dramatically from views of offices to mountain ranges.

Webcasting (technical term)

Short for web broadcasting, a webcast delivers audio or video transmission to multiple users simultaneously via the web. This is typically used for events that would not get global TV or radio coverage (e.g. corporate presentations or live concerts). The quality of webcasts is still limited by *bandwidth* and lack of *multicast* support within the internet. In addition, the broadcast rights for many events (UK Premiership football, Formula 1 racing etc.) are tightly controlled and are usually sold to TV companies on a region-by-region basis. Webcasting is inherently global, and therefore even if a company has the right to provide TV coverage of an event in a region, it is not permitted to webcast the same material. For example, the International Olympic Committee has stated that it will not be selling online rights to the Olympic Games until at least 2009. However, for niche-interest events, such as launches of the space shuttle, webcasting allows interested parties to have a (somewhat grainy) live view of the action (in this case at **www.nasa.gov/ntv/ntvweb.html**).

Web crawler (web term)

Software that recursively follows links on one website to another and builds up a "map" of the web, typically either to locate and report links to sites that no longer exist, or to index pages for *search engines*. Web crawlers are also known as robots or spiders.

Web design (web term)

Covers the design process involved in building a web presence. At one level this centers on technical tools, such as various flavors of *HTML*, animation and graphic tools like *Flash*, and the use of *plug-ins* for multimedia, or programming languages like *Java* for special effects. At another, it covers the appearance and, behavior of the site from a graphic designer's perspective, and how the site links in to concepts such as a *brand*. And at yet another it should cover the usability of a website focussing on ease of use and navigation to both novice and experienced users.

This area has created its own industry, with various web agencies and web integrators coming into existence (many of which struggled after the general decline in dot-com fever in 2000). Some teams have been built around roles (e.g. producer) taken from the film world rather than software development.

Common design failings can include:

➡ Too much focus on glitz and initial impact, rather then long-term use (see *designing for awards*).

➡ Insufficient attention to usability. This is one area where a number of common metaphors — like "shopping trolleys" — now provide a rough level of consistency.

➡ Forgetting the technical basics. There is plenty of folklore about websites that offer poor performance through modem connections (since they were tested on high-speed connections), websites that can't support large numbers of users and grind to a halt on day one, and websites that can't support one of the two most common browsers (*Netscape Navigator* or Microsoft *Internet Explorer*).

Much web design best practice settles around recognizing the web is its own medium (it's not text, and it's not TV), and the fine art of simplicity.

Web farm (slang)
Covers a data center room filled with back-end server hardware for (typically) web-based systems. Often provided by specialized *hosting* companies. Means much the same as *server farm*.

Webify (slang)
To convert something for use on the web. This can be the simple conversion of a file format (such as Microsoft Word, *ASCII* text or Adobe *PDF*) to *HTML,* the standard display language of the web. Or, much more loosely, it could cover adding a web interface to an existing system — a much more major undertaking.

Web master (web term)
The person (or team) who looks after the technical maintenance of a website. Some sites often give options to e-mail the web master directly if you encounter technical problems.

Web page (web term)
The building block of the web. A web page is a document on file that contains *HTML* (a mix of text, formatting, and other instructions) with links to

graphics, special programs or *applets*, and other web pages. A web page will be contained in a specific file in a specific directory on a specific server, and so will be identified by its own *URL*. Often abbreviated as a term to just *page*.

Web ring (web term)
A linked ring of websites where you can click through a sequence of sites that are about a given topic, eventually coming back to your starting point. A simple technique often used by small-scale, specialist sites.

Web-safe colors (web term)
A core 216 of the 256 colors that can be handled by most display systems (monitors) in use around the world today, and formed from certain combinations of red, green, and blue.

Webserver (web term)
Webservers implement the *HTTP* (Hypertext Transport Protocol) and are responsible for responding to requests for information originating from user's web *browsers*. For most users, a webserver is what sits at the other end of an internet network connection. The processing needed to be able to respond to the user (and hence the complexity of the webserver software) can vary dramatically. Some sites simply require the webserver to read the web page requested from a file. Others can require interaction with application servers or complex back-end systems to access and format the results. Popular software used by developers in building webserver systems include:

➡ Microsoft's internet Information Server (IIS)

➡ *Apache*.

Web services (web term)
Term recently introduced to describe an *API* (application programming interface) to an application defined used *XML* (extensible Markup Language) and accessed over the web using *SOAP* (Simple Object Access Protocol). The idea is that this will allow computers to interact directly over the web as easily as human users can browse websites. While still in its infancy the idea of web services is the cornerstone of some important iniatives such as *Microsoft*'s *.NET* architecture.

Website (web term)

A connected series of *web pages*, almost always accessed though a starting *home page*, which is reached via the site's *domain name*. A site can range from a small number of static web pages, to a very complex array of content and processing features – as with a major *B2C* business.

For an internet-based business, the website is the prime channel to customers, and a large amount of time will be spent on its graphic design, ease of use, attractiveness, and conformance with the *branding* intended for the business. A equally large amount of time is spent on measuring how many people visit the site, and how they use it. See also *measurement*.

Websphere (product)

Websphere is the name for *IBM's* suite of web development, *webserver* and application server tools.

WebTV (product)

WebTV is a service operated by *Microsoft* that allows access to the internet via a television and a set-top box rather than a computer. It also aims to provide some of the aspects of *interactive TV*, but is not itself a TV broadcast network.

WECA (organization)

Stands for Wireless Ethernet Compatibility Alliance (**www.wirelessethernet. org**), an industry group created to promote interoperability between different vendors' implementations of Wireless Local Area Networks (*WLANs)* based on the IEEE *802*.11 standard. The WECA has created the *Wi-Fi* "seal of approval" for compatible components.

We-commerce (slang)

An e-commerce venture entered into by more than one person.

Welcome page (web term)

Alternative term for *home page*.

White hat or white-hat hacker (slang)

Someone who is paid to attempt to breach the security of a computer system to check its integrity.

Whois (technical term)

Whois (which you won't be surprised to learn is taken from "who is") is a network utility that allows you to find out if a domain name has been registered and, if so, discover some limited details about who owns it. To do this, whois needs to know which registration database to query. Country top-level domains (e.g. .uk, .fr) are managed by different national authorities, and to further complicate matters, under the *ICANN's* shared registration system, the details of who has registered global top-level domains (such as .com) no longer resides with a single authority.

Fortunately, many online versions of whois make a guess at which registration database to check (e.g. nic.uk for .uk domains) and there is also **www.betterwhois.com** which uses the basic information held centrally on global top-level domains to locate the correct registrar's database to query.

Wi-Fi (technical term)

Pronounced like "hi-fi" and stands for Wireless Fidelity. Wi-Fi is a "seal of approval" created by the Wireless Ethernet Compability Alliance (*WECA*) to increase interoperability between different implementations of the IEEE *802*.11b standard for wireless local area networks (*WLANs*).

Windows (product)

Refers to a family of operating systems from *Microsoft*. Windows dates back to the 1980s, but it was Windows 3.1 that captured a large slice of the PC market in the 1990s. It has become the dominant *operating system* for PCs, and variants exist for home and business use, running servers and embedded or handheld devices. Very much the engine of the Microsoft business, particularly in the early to mid-1990s. Windows provides a *GUI* or graphical user interface (hence its name!) and the system-level tools you expect of an operating system. With Windows 2000, Microsoft have focussed on a reliable platform to gain more share of the market for big, enterprise-level servers. The Windows family is described in more detail in the *Microsoft* section.

Winsock (technical term)

Stands for Windows Sockets Interface, an application programming interface (API) that allows applications to access the *TCP/IP* protocol stack built into

Microsoft *Windows* in a standard way, therefore allowing third parties to develop internet-enabled applications that will run on the Windows platform.

Wired (publication)

Popular, and well-established, magazine with a general focus on the fashionable end of web technology and e-business, and advanced application technology in general. Through Wire Digital, it is also linked to a number of websites aimed at the cognescenti and the more savvy members of the general public. Specific websites under this banner include *hotBot.com* and *hotwired.com*.

Wireless (technical term)

Unsurprisingly this is shorthand for communications without wires, although the term is used with different and more precise meanings can cover a variety of different contexts, including:

➡ Communications between computers in offices (see entry on *WLAN*).

➡ Access to the internet from mobile devices, e.g. mobile phones (see entry on *mobile*).

➡ Connection between various devices without cables (see entry on *Bluetooth*).

➡ Highspeed communications between fixed locations (see entry on *fixed wireless* and *LMDS*).

➡ Voice communications via mobile phones (see entries on *GSM* and *3G*).

WISP (technical term)

Stands for Wireless Internet Service Provider – an organization that provides internet connectivity to mobile networks.

WLAN (technical term)

Stands for Wireless Local Area Network and represents a variety of technologies for connecting workstations and servers to form a Local Area Network (*LAN*) using wireless (radio) transmissions rather than the cables. Various standards for wireless LANs have been developed by working group *802*.11 of the Institute of Electrical and Electronics Engineers with a variant called 802.11b emerging as the most widely implemented (IEEE 802.11b is also the basis for the *Wi-Fi* interoperability initiative).

802.11b WLANs operate in an unlicensed part of the UHF radio spectrum (see entry on *ISM*) and may achieve speeds of up to 20 Mbps although much lower speeds are typical due to interference etc. *Bluetooth* and *HomeRF* are other wireless technologies which may prove effective in building smaller networks, but are unlikely to challenge 802.11b for the larger corporate networks. A recent innovation involves operating WLANS with highspeed connections to the internet in public places such as airport departure lounges, hotels and coffee houses.

WML (technical term)

Stands for Wireless Mark-up Language, a component of the *WAP* (Wireless Application Protocol) recommendations. WML is based on *XML*, so it looks very similar to *HTML*. There are major differences, however: you cannot display WML documents in a HTML browser, nor can HTML documents be viewed using a WML microbrowser.

To view WML you will either need to buy a WAP device, or use an emulator such as the Nokia Toolkit or use a web-based translator such as **www.gelon.net.**

An introduction to WML

As in HTML, text is marked up using formatting commands called *tags*, and links to other resources can be made using *URLs*. WML "documents" are delimited by the <WML></WML> tags and are structured as a number of "cards." A collection of cards is called a "deck." Therefore a WML document will have the following structure:

```
<WML>
    <CARD>
        ... contents of card
    </CARD>
    <CARD>
        ... contents of card
    </CARD>
</WML>
```

The following simple example illustrates the results of a browser receiving the following string (strictly speaking the browser will receive the compressed form of the WML, but here we use the human readable form):

```
<wml><card id="MainCard" title="My first WAP Page">Hello
World!</card></wml>
```

should produce something like:

All the cards in a deck are dwnloaded in one go, so navigation between cards in the same deck does not require communications over the network. There are device-dependent limits to the size of decks that can be downloaded (e.g. 1.4 KB for the Nokia 7710), although WAP does not define a standard limit. Only one card can be displayed at a time, and navigation between cards is via a hyperlink. The syntax for this is very similar to HTML and uses the <A></A> tag pair and an attribute (HREF) to tell the browser where to go.

```
<wml><card id="FirstCard" title="My first WAP Page">Hello
World !<br/><a href="#SecondCard"> Next</a></card><card
id="SecondCard" title="Fonts">This is the second card in the
pack</card></wml>
```

should produce something like:

And selecting the link should display the second card:

As in HTML, a link can be to a card from a different site as well as one in the same deck, which lets users navigate seamlessly.

Unlike a PC-based interface, the options for changing the format of the text displayed on a WAP device are very limited. WML text size can be changed using the intuitively named <big></big> and <small></small> tags. So:

```
<wml><card id="SizeCard" title="Size Matters">
<br/>This is normal<br/><big>This is BIG</big>
<br/><small>and this is small</small>
<br/></card></wml>
```

produces the following on one WML browser:

However, on another we see the following:

What's going on? An important difference between HTML and WML is that WML doesn't define how something should be displayed, so the `<big>` tag is really a request to display a larger font *if it is able to*. A difference in appearance across different WAP devices is therefore inevitable.

In addition, WML browsers do not support the same range of image formats as their HTML cousins. Images to be displayed must be in the Wireless Bit Map format (**WBMP**). Fortunately there are utilities such as **http://www. teraflops.com/wbmp** that allow *JEPG* and *GIF* formats to be converted. WBMP is designed to support compact encoding but with low computational costs in the client.

WML card (technical term)
The Wireless Mark-up Language (**WML**) equivalent of a "page." A card is the block of WML to be displayed at one time and should to be kept very simple, to allow for the limited display sizes of typical mobile devices.

WML deck (technical term)
A collection of **WML cards** which are downloaded together. Typically a deck represents all the steps need to complete a single business transaction. There are device-specific constraints for the size of a WML deck (e.g. 1.4 KB for the Nokia 7710).

WML script (technical term)
A simple scripting language for **WAP** (Wireless Application Protocol) mobile phones.

World Wide Web (technical term)
The world wide web (www), often just known as "the web," is for many users indistinguishable from the internet, although technically the web is an

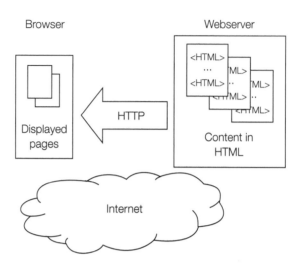

Simple view of the www

application running over the internet. It was the creation of the web and easy-to-use *browsers* that turned the internet from an important network for technology-literate users into a global phenomenon and a platform for many types of e-commerce.

Technical overview

The original structure of the web is straightforward. Web browsers connect to *webservers* and information formatted in *HTML* (Hypertext Mark-up Language) is transferred using *HTTP* (Hypertext Transport Protocol) which runs over the internet. The result is web pages displayed with a user's browser program. This is summed up in the diagram above.

However, this doesn't capture the spirit of the web and the reasons why it has become so popular. One critical feature is the ease with which the web allows any user to publish their thoughts in a form that can immediately be accessed by millions of people wordwide. No broadcast medium ever invented has been so powerful. Much of this power comes from its simplicity and its reuse of existing infrastructure. Other aspects include:

- HTML is a very simple, open, language. Anyone who can create a text file can create a simple HTML web page. Even extensions like *XML* retain this simplicity.

- The underlying model of individual pages with links between them is easy to understand.

- The keyword indexing provided by *search engines* is good enough for most queries.

- There is only one web, and any browser can connect to any server (security permitting). There is no need to manage multiple network connections or service providers.

- Operating over the internet allows the web to "stand on the shoulders of giants" and make use of an already mature and relatively stable global network.

- The web has become a multimedia platform, increasing its attractiveness to ordinary users.

The architecture of the web is now going through a process of evolution towards what Tim Berners-Lee has described as the semantic web, which the meaning of information can be captured and used. Increased power comes at some cost in complexity. Major developments include:

- *XML* (eXtensible Mark-Up Language) an HTML-like language which can be extended by the programmer and allows more information about the meaning and structure of text to be captured. This has become a favoured vehicle in – for example – integrating *B2B* systems. *XHTML* is a follow-on that supports the features of base HTML in XML syntax.

- Cascading Style Sheets (*CSS*) which offer a palette of features for styling and formating web pages and allows data (in XML) to be treated and generated independently of its presentation.

- *DOM* or Document Object Model which allows web pages to be treated as collections of objects rather than flat streams of text and data.

- *RDF* or Resource Description Framework which is an important step towards the semantic web, and gives a standard way of encapsulating *metadata* – that is data about data – which is much more powerful than the ***Metatag*** syntax within HTML.

Brief history of the world wide web

1989

➡ ***Tim Berners-Lee*** makes original proposal for a global ***hypertext*** system (originally called the "Information Mesh") while working at ***CERN*** (the European Organization for Particle Research).

1990

➡ First implementations of a browser (on a NeXT computer).

➡ "Information Mesh" renamed the "world wide web."

1991

➡ The world wide web project is announced on the internet via a posting to a number of newsgroups. Illustrative browser and server code is made available via ***FTP***.

1992

➡ The web consists of about 26 servers at mostly academic locations, including the National Center for Supercomputing Applications (NCSA).

➡ The term "surfing the internet" is first coined by Jean Armour Polly.

1993

➡ The web consists of several hundred servers.

➡ Very early version of ***Mosaic*** released by NCSA – the first browser to support images.

➡ CERN agrees to put web technology into the public domain and make it freely available to anyone.

1994

➡ Web consists of approximately 3,000 servers.

➡ A company called Mosaic (soon to be called ***Netscape***) is founded.

➡ CERN withdraws from web development to concentrate on physics.

- The World Wide Web Consortium (**W3C**) formed to lead web development (main site at **www.w3.org**).
- The *Yahoo!* search engine is launched.

1995

- Web grows to approximately 25,000 servers.
- HTTP – the engine of the web – becomes the largest form of traffic on the internet.
- *Amazon.com* launched.

1996

- Web grows to approximately 300,000 sites.
- Microsoft wakes up to the web and launches the *Internet Explorer* browser.

1997

- The number of websites grows to several million.
- The web becomes synonymous with the internet for most users.
- Focus of the web starts to move from information-sharing to commercial transactions.

1998

- *XML* (eXtensible Mark-up Language) is proposed by W3C as the architectural foundation for future web development.

2000

- The number of indexable web pages exceeds 1 billion.

Challenges

Despite (and sometimes because of) the web's incredible history, there are some major challenges that the web faces in the near future:

- The content space of the web is big, and finding relevant information is increasingly difficult (even with search engines that implement complex scoring algorithms).
- Web content is not always well maintained, leading to out-of-date infor-

mation and also to "broken" links, where the site referenced by another page or a search engine is no longer in existence.

➡ The ease with which information can be published and accessed via the web is one of its great strengths, but it also leads to increasingly complex issues regarding controlling access to pornographic, xenophobic, and otherwise unsavory material without jeopardizing freedom of expression.

➡ The privacy of online users is of increasing concern as cases of covert monitoring of activity and accidental disclosure of personal details become more common.

➡ Replication of data through *caching* increases the scalability of the web, but can also cause problems where information is updated frequently, leading to users receiving "stale" information from the cache rather than the more up-to-date site.

➡ Technical sophistication has led to incompatibility between older browsers and more modern sites. Also the proliferation of browser *plug-ins* increases the risk that a website may not work properly without downloading additional software.

Worm (security term)

A worm is a malicious piece of software similar to a *virus*, but which is capable of copying itself from machine to machine over a network without user intervention. The most infamous example is the Morris Internet Worm (1988), which crashed over 10 percent of the machines attached to the internet at that time. It would probably have done more damage if the worm didn't contain a bug that limited its life.

Wozniak, Steve

Co-founder – with the more visible *Steve Jobs* – of *Apple* Computer Inc.

WSDL (web term)

Stands for Web Service Description Language and is used to define the way in which applications (i.e. software programs) should make requests to *web services*.

X.25 (technical term)

One of a series of standards from the *ITU* (previously *CCITT*). This family of standards has been somewhat swamped by the standardization imposed by the popularity of internet protocols. X.25 itself is a series of equipment and network specifications that support an early form of packet-switched network. Somewhat archaic, but X.25 networks are common in the kind of e-commerce networks that pre-date e-commerce as a term, and the internet as a serious network. Example applications are found in financial settlement and clearing systems, and the like.

X.400 (technical term)

X.400 is a standard for exchanging e-mail between different systems that was developed by the *CCITT* during the 1980s. X.400 has largely been eclipsed by the popularity of internet e-mail (based around the older Simple Mail Transfer Protocol (*SMTP*)). However, X.400-style addresses are often used within common e-mail products such as Microsoft Outlook.

X.500 (technical term)

Related to *X.400*, a standard for e-mail directories for the primary purpose of looking up users' e-mail addresses.

X.509 (security term)

Popular standard for the presentation of *public key* certificates.

Xanadu (technical term)

The unrealized Xanadu project of *Ted Nelson* focussed on linking together information in ways that clearly anticipated the web and the PC. Although never fully realized, Xanadu was the source of the term *hypertext*.

Xerox Parc (organization)

Derived from Xerox Palo Alto Research Center, this name covers a legendary facility which in the 1970s and 1980s developed some of the fundamental technologies in use today. In terms of sheer volume of ideas, the contribution of this facility is staggering. Major contributions include:

➡ the first practical realization of the PC

➡ Windows-based user interfaces

➡ Local Area Networks and Ethernet

➡ laser printers.

Xerox is famous for not exploiting these technologies. This is close to the truth, but a little harsh since Xerox actually made billions of dollars from the laser printer.

XML (web term)

Stands for eXtensible Mark-up Language. Its forerunner *HTML* (Hypertext Mark-up Language) has proven to be one of the most popular languages for formatting information for human readers ever invented and is one of the cornerstones of the success of the world wide web. But HTML does not attempt to describe the data on a page, which makes it difficult for it to be interpreted and processed by a computer rather than a user. As computing legend *Brian Kernighan* observed, "what you see is all you've got."

Consider the following example of football (i.e. soccer) results in HTML:

```
<B>Final scores: 10 February 2000:</B><BR>
Arsenal 1-0 Ipswich <BR>
Aston Villa 1-1 Middlesbrough <BR>
```

```
Chelsea 1-1 Man Utd <BR>
Everton 2-1 Leicester<BR>
Leeds 0-0 Derby <BR>
Man City 0-1 Tottenham <BR>
Southampton 2-0 Bradford<BR>
Sunderland 1-1 Liverpool<BR>
<P>
```

This would be perfectly intelligible when displayed in a **browser**, but suppose you wanted to build an application to processes this information. It would need to rely on some fragile "parsing" rules to know that each match is on a separate line with the score appearing between the names of the two clubs. Any change in the format of the page would probably break the program. Now imagine that the **tags** used on the page could actually describe the data and explicitly mark the beginning and the end of each fixture, the name of the team, the score, etc. This is what XML allows us to do. In the simple example below we have invented a new set of tags that describe the data in more detail.

```
<Football>
<Date>10022000</Date>
<Premiership>
<Match>
<Club>Arsenal</Club><Score>1</Score>
<Club>Ipswich Town</Club><Score>0</Score>
</Match>

<Match>
<Club>Aston Villa</Club><Score>1</Score>
<Club>Middlesbrough</Club><Score>1</Score>
</Match>

<Match>
<Club>Chelsea</Club><Score>1</Score>
<Club>Man Utd</Club><Score>1</Score>
</Match>
```

```
<Match>
<Club>Everton</Club><Score>2</Score>
<Club>Leicester</Club><Score>1</Score>
</Match>
...
</Premiership>
</Football>
```

In this imaginary example we have invented a new sub-language based on XML which we could call Football Results Mark-up Language (FRML). For our completely hypothetical FRML to be useful, other developers must know that we have chosen <Match> as one of our tags rather than <Game> or <Fixture>, and <Club> rather than <Side> or <Team>. We also need a way of providing a definition of what represents a valid FRML document, e.g. ensuring that each match must include exactly two clubs. This specification comes in the form of a Document Type Definition (DTD), which defines the tags the mark-up language has, the order in which they may be combined, the attributes of tags may have etc. FRML is fictitious, but there are a growing number of XML-derived mark-up languages and accompanying DTDs for different kinds of information. Some real examples are:

- MathML – Mathematical Mark-up Language
- FixML – Financial Information eXchange Mark-up Language
- CML – Chemical Mark-up Language.

Obviously, we still want the data to be attractive and intelligible to a human user when displayed in a browser. This is where eXtensible Style Language (*XSL*) comes in. XSL describes how the data should be displayed, e.g. that the two clubs in each match should be on the same line with the scores between them.

The separation of meaning and appearance also has the advantage that the same information can be formatted in a manner appropriate for different kinds of end-user. For instance, in the example above the same data could be converted into *HTML* for display on a PC, or *WML* (Wireless Mark-up Language) for display on a mobile device.

Unfortunately XML isn't quite the magic bullet that some industry hype may suggest:

- The vast majority of information on the web is in HTML, and to convert it all to XML would be a Herculean task.

- Agreement is needed on the names and meaning of tags (something that the IT industry is notoriously bad at).

- Data marked up in XML can become very large and therefore slower to transfer (compare the size of the HTML and XML simple examples above).

- Writing good, modular XML is much harder than writing HTML; the above example could be improved by specifying the home side, including half-time results, etc.

- XML isn't a programming language and can't describe how to process the data (e.g. how to calculate the league points each team would receive).

Nevertheless XML is an important step towards the creation of what *Tim Berners-Lee* has described as the "semantic web."

XSL (web term)

Anagram of eXtensible Style Language and a relative of *XML*. Used to build style sheets in a much more sophisticated way than that offered by the more conventional *cascading style sheets* (CCS). See *XML* above.

Yahoo! (company)

In terms of business on the web, Yahoo! is an important, influential, and successful organization. It started small, when David Filo and Jerry Yang – Ph.D. candidates in electrical engineering at Stanford University – started a guide in April 1994 to keep track of their personal interests on the internet. During 1994 Yahoo! became a more generalized facility for the then relatively small internet community. Through a process of evolution, which at one stage involved migrating from academic systems to larger servers at *Netscape*, Yahoo! became a very broadly based *portal* supporting many types of community and interest, and providing a broad range of services. It is also one of the few sites to generate a real income from advertising. This is a truly popular site, dominant in internet ratings, and generating tens of millions of visits per month. Its primary focus remains providing a directory of web content.

Yang, Jerry

Co-founder of *Yahoo!*

Yellow Pages

Has several meaning inspired by yellow telephone directories:

→ Once the name of a *UNIX* utility originated by *Sun* (and now called NIS for Network Information Service) which mapped names to the location of servers and resources on a network.

→ A general term used by a variety of internet business directories, often together with a set of "white pages" covering details of people.

Yettie (slang)

Stands (roughly) for Young Entrepreneurial Technically-Orientated Twenty-Something.

YMMV (slang)

Text chat or e-mail abbreviation for "your mileage may vary," which arises from a standard disclaimer by American car manufacturers. When tacked on to advice, it generally means "but who knows what will happen." The full term is found as a warning in some *freeware*.

ZDNet (company)
Runs a popular website at **www.zdnet.com** that aims to provide "a premier full service destination for people looking to buy, use, and learn more about technology." A subsidiary of *CNET*.

Zimmermann, Phil
Phil Zimmermann is the creator of the Pretty Good Privacy (*PGP*) encryption program that allows users to exchange files and e-mails securely. PGP was widely distributed as freeware over the internet, which led to a three-year criminal investigation into Zimmermann by the US government for allegedly breaking US export restrictions on cryptographic materials (which at the time were classed as munitions). Charges against Zimmermann were subsequently dropped and the US export rules rationalized, making him something of a folk hero on the net.

Zine (slang)
Shortened form of *e-zine*, which describes an electronic publication or magazine.

Zip (slang)

Commonly used term for the act of compressing a file or set of files using a utility such as pkzip. Useful for massive files that consume *bandwith* such as e-mail attachments.

Zombie (slang)

To a *venture capitalist*, this means an investment that is in a sleeping state, neither heading for bankruptcy or success. To a *UNIX* programmer, it refers to a system process that has died but hasn't been removed from the system. To a *netizen*, it can refer to a site that has not had its content updated for some time.